TIME CAPSULE/1943

TIME CAPSULE/1943

A HISTORY OF THE YEAR CONDENSED FROM THE PAGES OF TIME

TIME-LIFE BOOKS, NEW YORK

TIME / **1943**

EDITORS *Henry R. Luce, Manfred Gottfried*
MANAGING EDITOR *T. S. Matthews*
SENIOR EDITORS *Patricia Divver, Sidney Olson,*
Dana Tasker, Charles Wertenbaker
ASSOCIATE EDITORS *Roy Alexander, Robert W. Boyd Jr.,*
Fillmore Calhoun, Robert Cantwell, Whittaker Chambers,
John Davenport, Robert Fitzgerald, Calvin Fixx,
Ernest C. Havemann, John Hersey, Wilder Hobson,
John Osborne, Content Peckham, Robert Sherrod, Leon Svirsky

EDITOR *Maitland A. Edey*
EXECUTIVE EDITOR *Jerry Korn*
TEXT DIRECTOR *Martin Mann*
ART DIRECTOR *Sheldon Cotler*
CHIEF OF RESEARCH *Beatrice T. Dobie*

SERIES EDITOR *John Dille*
ASSISTANT EDITOR *Carl Solberg*
RESEARCHER *Louise Samuels*
DESIGNER *Arnold Holeywell*
ASSISTANT DESIGNER *John Woods*
COPYREADER *Rosemarie Conefrey*

PUBLISHER *Rhett Austell*

COVER ILLUSTRATION *Lou Lomonaco*

EVENTS OF THE YEAR

Roosevelt and Churchill meet Stalin at Teheran
21
23 die in a Detroit race riot
53
Montgomery defeats Rommel in Africa
55
The Allied invasion of Italy
67
U.S. Marines capture Tarawa
88
A mysterious murder in the Bahamas
112
The Germans rescue Mussolini
125
"Oklahoma!" starts its Broadway run
140
General George Patton slaps a U.S. soldier
160
Amos 'n' Andy go off the air
167

Editors' Note

Much of the memorable news of 1943 revolves around the war. American troops, who had landed in North Africa the previous November, took a beating from the Germans at Kasserine Pass in Tunisia in their first major engagement, but the Allies prevailed in the end and succeeded by late spring in clearing all Axis troops out of Africa. In July, British and American troops commanded by General Eisenhower invaded Sicily, and a couple of months later landed in Italy to engage the enemy at last on the continent of Europe. In the Pacific, meanwhile, U.S. Marines seized the atoll of Tarawa from the Japanese in one of the bloodiest battles of the war. By the end of the year, the Allies were doing so well on the fighting fronts that President Roosevelt, Prime Minister Churchill and Premier Stalin took time to meet at Teheran in order to coordinate the final plans for victory.

In this volume, some of these events are first referred to in the U.S. at War section, starting on page 9. More complete details of the fighting are contained in the World Battlefronts section, beginning on page 55. Further references to the war crop up throughout the book; it even invaded the worlds of Sport, Business, Theater, Religion and other normally peaceful pursuits.

■

TIME CAPSULE/1943 is one of a series of volumes, each adapted and condensed from a year's contents of TIME, the Weekly Newsmagazine. The words, except for a few connecting passages, are those of the magazine itself, and therefore reflect the flavor, the attitudes and the state of knowledge of the day—sometimes innocent, sometimes opinionated, sometimes prescient. The book is divided, like the magazine, into departments, and is organized so that each department forms a chronological chapter for the entire year. The dates in the margin are the issue dates of the magazine.

U.S. AT WAR

The Presidency

Though the decisive battles of World War II were still a year or more away, 1943 was a turning point in the preparation for victory. The "arsenal of democracy" was at last in full production, and tanks, planes and ships were coming off the U.S. assembly lines in constantly increasing numbers. With Germany's defeat at Stalingrad and in Tunisia, the Axis tide that had been running for three years appeared to be finally slowing. Now, taking up his role as one of the grand architects of global strategy, President Franklin Roosevelt attended a series of fateful meetings with other wartime leaders—at Casablanca, Quebec, Cairo and Teheran.

JAN. 18 **STATE OF THE UNION:** The President of the United States labored up the long ramp to the Speaker's dais, leaning on the arm of his military aide Major General Edwin M. ("Pa") Watson. He grasped the edge of the reading stand with one big hand, discarded his thick mahogany cane, slapped down his old black notebook. For two minutes his audience applauded for this stouthearted man who cannot walk, yet does.

No man knew better than Franklin Roosevelt, who had endured the day-by-day shocks, despairs, glimmers, disappointments and hopes, what crucial days the U.S. had just survived. No man was more grateful than he, nor showed it more clearly. Now he could once more speak with the honest ring of triumph, with the assurance of a man who has felt out his enemy and is confident that he can withstand the blows to come.

Said Franklin Roosevelt: "The Axis powers knew that they must win the war in 1942—or eventually lose everything. I do not need to tell you that our enemies did *not* win this war in 1942. We know that as each day goes by, Japanese strength in ships and planes is going down and down, and American strength in ships and planes is going up and up. The eventual outcome can be put on a mathematical basis.

"I can report to you with genuine pride on what has been accomplished in 1942. We produced 48,000 military planes—more than the airplane production of Germany, Italy and Japan put together. We produced 56,000 combat vehicles. We produced 670,000 machine guns. I think the arsenal of democracy is making good."

The applause was terrific. It was applause now for a nation, not for one man.

ALL WE CAN SPEND: Franklin Roosevelt this week presented his second war budget. The figures ran right off the edge of the paper, the fiscal thinking soared right out of this world. In the fiscal year 1944 Franklin Roosevelt figured that the U.S. could spend $108,903,047,923. This was a staggering sum: 1) more than the combined income of all U.S. citizens in any year except 1942; 2) more than the budget of any other nation in any year in all history, past and perhaps future. [By the mid Sixties, the U.S. budget was running at an annual average of $106 billion and was still rising.]

APPOINTMENT IN CASABLANCA: Franklin Roosevelt, with his FEB. 1 great sense of historical drama, had again created history with a dramatist's breath-taking stroke. No President of the U.S. since Abraham Lincoln had ever visited a battle theater. No President had ever left the U.S. in wartime. None had ever been to Africa. None had ever traveled in an airplane. Now came Franklin Roosevelt, 32nd President of the U.S., to shatter all four precedents at once.

The trip, through air in which Axis planes roamed, over waters infested with Axis submarines, was veiled in secrecy and censorship; its story was presented to the world this week as a dazzling *fait accompli*. Even then many of the details were kept secret.

Winston Churchill was the first to arrive at Casablanca; the President landed a few hours later. Their discussions began at once: the first started at 7 p.m., lasted until 3 o'clock the next morning. For ten days, in the enclosure of a Casablanca hotel surrounded by barbed wire and bristling guards, they conferred, discussed, mulled over their problems. They were in close touch with Russia's Joseph Stalin, who was too busy with war on his own soil to join them, with China's Generalissimo Chiang Kai-shek. They brought together, for the first time, the two leading figures in the tangled French political situation: Fighting French General Charles de Gaulle and General Henri Honoré Giraud, High Commissioner of French Africa.

On the tenth day, U.S. correspondents were flown secretly to Casablanca for a press conference—the first any American President had ever held beneath a protective umbrella of fighter planes. In the desert heat, beneath the roaring planes, Generals de Gaulle and Giraud shook hands while photographers' flash bulbs popped. The President said this was a momentous moment.

The war leaders lived up to the moment. They explained that they had reached "complete agreement" on 1943 war plans, that the goal was "unconditional surrender" of the Axis nations. The President had some good morale-building words for American combat troops: "I have seen the bulk of several divisions. I have eaten lunch in the field, and it was a darn good lunch, too. Our soldiers are eager to carry on the fight and I want you to tell the folks back home that I am proud of them."

MARCH 1 **"AMONG FRIENDS":** Madame Chiang Kai-shek sat expectantly on the edge of the President's huge swivel chair, like a young girl at her first matinee. Only when she leaned forward did the tips of her tiny, open-toed pumps touch the floor. Franklin Roosevelt, master of almost a thousand press conferences, had the air of an indulgent uncle introducing a beautiful niece. Madame Chiang, he said, was a "special envoy very different from most"; he asked newsmen to confine their questions to the "non-catch type."

Madame Chiang said she had never been afraid on visits to the front in China; she was not so sure now as she saw the pencils flashing across the notebooks. "But I see flashes of smiles coming from your faces, so I feel I am among friends." The correspondents applauded. She was now in their hands.

Madame Chiang rose to answer each question, sat down

again when she had given her answer. Question: Is there any truth in reports that China is not using her manpower to the fullest?

Madame Chiang showed a touch of anger. China, she said, is using her manpower to the extent that she has munitions. China has trained pilots, but she has not enough planes or gasoline.

How is she going to get them? Madame Chiang turned deferentially to Franklin Roosevelt. He had solved so many important questions and come through so many crises, she could safely, she felt, leave that question to him.

Newsmen smiled to see how she had neatly tossed the ball to Franklin Roosevelt. Undeterred, the President picked it up and ran. There are immense difficulties in getting planes and supplies to China, he said, but the U.S. is working hard to get them there. If he were a member of the Chinese Government, he would certainly ask: But when and why not a little more? As a member of the American Government, however, he would have to reply: As fast as the Lord will let us.

Next question for Madame Chiang: Did she have any suggestions on how U.S. aid to China could be stepped up? She rose, stared straight ahead, then turned to the President. He had just said as soon as the Lord will let us. But, she remembered, the Lord helps those who help themselves.

A non-catch question had been beautifully caught. Said Columnist Raymond Clapper, frankly dazed by the show: "Some day they may put Helen Hayes in the part, but she'll never do it any better than Madame Chiang acted it in real life."

SPOTLIGHT: Of the many roles played last week by Franklin MARCH 22 Roosevelt, none was more admirably played than his performance as host at a White House party for the 119 new members of Congress.

The stage was the brilliantly lit, richly appointed state dining room. Tuxedoed Secret Service men stood on guard, waiters came & went, a homely beer barrel was cunningly concealed in a feathery bank of fern. Cheese & crackers went with the beer.

At the room's south entrance the President sat in a big

red leather chair, the famed ivory cigaret holder tilted audaciously, the famed charm sparkling and bubbling like champagne. So seductively supercharged was the Roosevelt manner that it shocked one of his guests to a state of real alarm. Said Nebraska's dapper freshman Senator Kenneth S. Wherry: "No man who has that persuasive power, such personal charm, should serve more than two terms. We've got to safeguard the American people."

JUNE 7   **HOMEFRONT CABINET:** Each time the President has set up a big new agency, most of the citizenry has sighed a whoosh of relief and gone off about their business. But by last week, when the Office of War Mobilization was created, the people had no breath left. They were all whooshed out.

But this time there were good reasons for believing the new reorganization might work:

¶ Jimmy Byrnes, who as chief of OWM is now really the czar of all Washington czars, is one of the country's ablest politicians, in the better sense of the word. He is trusted by Congress and the President—and Mr. Roosevelt is expected to back Byrnes' decisions to the limit. This was never true with former top administrators.

¶ OWM is closely geared to the military through the inclusion in its ranks of Secretary of the Navy Frank Knox and Secretary of War Henry L. Stimson.

¶ In placing Judge Fred Moore Vinson in charge of the Office of Economic Stabilization, the President seemed to have chosen wisely & well. Bulky, sad-eyed, drawling Judge Vinson, 53, is a first-rate authority on the U.S. tax laws, which he can quote, provision by provision, with all the "hereinafters" properly included, in a dazzling display of mnemonics. His special technique is to arm himself with such a mastery of the facts at issue that he can gently but thoroughly demolish the opposition.

The overall problem of the new overall board is to convince the U.S. public finally that gun production really means not just less butter but less real civilian income. The further task is to make the Government strong enough to exact the necessary sacrifices equitably. Said Czar Vinson, as he faced the problem: "I am smiling for the last time today."

One matter that plagued Roosevelt during the year was a se-
ries of coal strikes called by the always intransigent John L.
Lewis on behalf of his United Mine Workers.

WHO WON?: The year's third coal strike ended. The miners   JULY 5
straggled back to work. Now it was time for Franklin Roosevelt, for John L. Lewis and for every U.S. citizen to ask
himself who had won. One thing was certain. The U.S. people had not. They could reckon their losses in simple
arithmetic:

¶ 20,000,000 tons of coal.

¶ 75-100,000 tons of steel—a loss that would cause incal-
culable delays in war production.

This loss was irretrievable. The coal, the steel, the time,
had gone. Coal Boss Harold Ickes warned that coal might
have to be rationed by year's end.

Franklin Roosevelt had won nothing. His Administration
had relied on labor's no-strike pledge and on a wishful
hunch that the United Mine Workers rank & file would not
follow Lewis. It had let the coal strike grow into such an
issue that neither side could back down. Fortnight ago,
when the strike began—in defiance of a War Labor Board
order—the President had no ammunition left. Only coal miners can mine coal. Then, suddenly, John Lewis, standing
before crossed American flags, imperiously ordered his miners back to work. He set his own conditions: that the
Government operate the mines; that the deadline for a new
wage agreement be Oct. 31. The President was left with little to say or do.

In defeat, the President had been goaded into an awkward
gesture: he proposed a law making all men up to 65 eligible
for the draft, so that strikers could be put into uniform.
This suggestion shocked the press, from liberal to labor-hat-
ing. Congress took a hand: by passing the Smith-Connally
anti-strike bill over the President's veto, Congress in effect
voted no-confidence in Franklin Roosevelt's unsure handling
of the coal problem. [The bill authorized the President to
seize and operate any facility engaged in war production
that was threatened by a strike, and also required the
unions to furnish 30 days' notice of such strikes.]

The historic animosity of General Charles de Gaulle toward the United States began in World War II and was aggravated when the U.S. chose another French general, Henri Giraud, as senior military and political commander of French Africa and invited him to visit Washington.

JULY 19 **ATTACKING DE GAULLE:** When General Henri Honoré Giraud, his white uniform crinkled, stepped out of the giant C-54 transport at Washington's Bolling Field last week, generals and admirals were there in profusion to greet him on his arrival from North Africa—but nary a striped pants diplomat. Thus did the White House heavily underscore its attempt to strip the visit of all political significance. At the same time, the U.S. press blossomed with inspired stories (quoting "high officials," "unimpeachable sources") attacking the motives and personality of General de Gaulle. Pet reporters of the State Department and the White House were called in and given confidential tips. The drive became so hot that Columnist Walter Lippmann cried: It is time "to stop the official propaganda campaign for Giraud and against De Gaulle." Examples:

¶ Wrote Harold Callender of the New York *Times:* "In the opinion of high American officials General de Gaulle is less interested in helping to win the war than in advancing his personal political fortunes."

¶ The 100% New Deal Chicago *Sun* revived a six months' old anecdote, retold it as a choice bit of gossip: When President Roosevelt was in Casablanca, General de Gaulle remarked that the French people regarded him as the spirit of Joan of Arc. Later, he let drop the comment that the French people thought of him as the reincarnation of Napoleon. To which Franklin Roosevelt reportedly jabbed: "General, I think you should make up your mind."

From sources as unimpeachable as those which fostered the anti-De Gaulle stories had come many definite reports that Franklin Roosevelt even had won over Churchill to the sacking of General de Gaulle. Twice, it was said on high authority, Franklin Roosevelt had cabled Winston Churchill, actually suggesting the arrest of De Gaulle. Churchill refused.

People sought a reason. Why is the President so set

against De Gaulle? Why all the inspired anti-De Gaulle stories? No matter how unlovable a personality, De Gaulle is still, to most living Frenchmen, the symbol of French resistance. What is the President's case against him?

The President's case against De Gaulle appears to be this: he is convinced that the solution of European problems will be much easier if its basic lines are established by the three big powers—the United States, Great Britain and Russia. The President wants to assure all European powers, great & small, full independence and freedom. But he believes that they need not all be consulted; their voices would complicate a solution or even make it impossible. For that reason Mr. Roosevelt would prefer to have France absent when those solutions are worked out—in short, not only no De Gaulle, but no Giraud.

CAMPAIGN AT HOME: Franklin Roosevelt, fighting a rearguard action against inflation, last week ordered his aides to think up some new tactics. For the pressure was on. A.F. of L.'s William Green and C.I.O.'s Phil Murray, who have held labor in line with the Little Steel formula [which set a ceiling on wages at 15% of the levels prevailing on January 1, 1941], marched to the White House to threaten mutiny unless prices went down. The fall season for important wage negotiations begins on Aug. 5 with General Motors Corp. Soon afterward the Little Steel formula must stand or fall. AUG. 2

Last week the War Labor Board once more stood by the formula in a memorable opinion written by Public Member Wayne L. Morse. Brainy Wayne Morse, dean of the University of Oregon Law School, was an ace labor arbitrator on the West Coast, has moved impartially between labor's and industry's side. Last week, denying a wage increase to Los Angeles traction employes, he wrote:

"Workers are entitled to a standard of living of health and decency that will permit maximum war production, but beyond that workers should not expect wage increases in the midst of war. There is something almost sacrilegious about insisting upon improving the economic conditions of our civilians at home while at the same time so many of our young men are suffering and dying."

AUG. 9   **THE BIDDING BEGINS:** By next year's Presidential election, the U.S. will have an estimated 9,000,000 men & women of voting age in uniform. And for the first time in history, soldiers & sailors will find it easy, under a law passed by Congress in 1942, to vote in the election. For the first time in history, the Army & Navy form a large and potent voting force, and, conceivably, the candidate with the greatest appeal to soldiers & sailors will be the next President.

¶ Franklin Roosevelt had already stolen a march on other 1944 candidates. For nearly five minutes of his 30-minute fireside chat Franklin Roosevelt laid down an official Administration program to take care of returning soldiers at the end of the war, thus warming the firesides in Sicily and chilling the hearts of Republicans. Franklin Roosevelt, firing a shot heard round the world by short wave, now stood out as the No. 1 champion of largesse to World War II's veterans. The bidding had begun.

AUG. 16   **THE OLD FISHERMAN:** He fished from a launch in Lake Huron, in the clear blue icy waters around Canada's famed Manitoulin district. First trip out the Old Fisherman took five small-mouth black bass, one medium-sized musky. His tackle: a light trout rod, a pearl spoon.

He took along sandwiches: egg & pickle, cheese, and ham. The Old Fisherman liked the ham sandwiches best. Khaki windbreaker buttoned crookedly, white cloth hat drooped around his ears, the Old Fisherman was all grins as he rode back to his special train in an Army Jeep. He spread out his palms in the classic fisherman's gesture, shortened the distance between them, leaned back his head and laughed.

Said the Old Fisherman, back home this week at 1600 Pennsylvania Ave., Washington, D.C.: "This is the first tan I've had this summer."

AUG. 30   **RAINBOW AT QUEBEC:** Just before Franklin Roosevelt arrived in Quebec last week, a summer rain stopped, the sun came out, and a rainbow appeared in the southern sky. To some who waited at the railway siding, this was an omen. But whatever Roosevelt or Winston Churchill said—or did not say— the real story of their meeting in Quebec's Citadel would be acted out step by step, in the answers by action to these questions:

¶ How soon will the "second front" be established in Western Europe?

¶ How soon will the Allies get decisive help to China for the war against Japan?

¶ Will the U.S., Britain, China and Russia learn to live together as great powers must—now and after World War II ends?

At the Château Frontenac, the Canadian Government had taken over at the cost of $10,000 a day, had evicted all the 800 guests but one: 90-year-old Miss Alice Caron, who has lived there for a quarter-century and refuses to move for anybody. Mounties accompanied bellhops on their business in the halls. Every arriving package, even if just an Admiral's laundry, met a suspicious inspection. Rumor said that colonels were sleeping two to a room.

Brown-haired Subaltern Mary Churchill, the Prime Minister's daughter who had come along as his aide-de-camp, had a busy, flattering vacation. She went shopping, headed straight for the underwear counter, confided to the clerk: "the ones I've got on, I made out of the skirt of an old evening dress."

She held a press conference, described her father as "awfully nice to work for and not a bit difficult."

And newsmen learned that Roosevelt, who likes to work mornings, and Churchill, who likes to work over a Scotch & soda at night, had reached a compromise. They worked late, but got up for an 8:30 breakfast and began working again. Otherwise the conference was shrouded in secrecy.

FIRST FRUIT: Transplanted to Washington, the talks contin- SEPT. 6 ued. Franklin Roosevelt and Winston Churchill were now making their sixth war conference their longest. Was it also their most fruitful? No one, except the tight-lipped principals, could yet say. But last week came the first evidence of accomplishment.

¶ The first result of Quebec was limited recognition by the U.S. and Britain of the French Committee of Liberation [presided over at the time by Generals de Gaulle and Giraud]. This action did not fully satisfy the French patriots in

Algiers. It was, nevertheless, a forward step—and perhaps the strongest commitment that could now be made by two nations which must some day invade Germany through France. ¶ The second result was the appointment of Lord Louis Mountbatten as Allied Commander in East Asia. This step proved that the British were now 1) willing to undertake a major campaign against the Japs, 2) glad to assume responsibility for the campaign, 3) committed, by the choice of a young and vigorous commander, to push the campaign as forcefully as possible.

SEPT. 13 **MY DAY IN THE SOUTH PACIFIC:** Until last week Australians and New Zealanders could truthfully say that they had a good idea of what the U.S. citizen was like: they had met him in all his types—from General Douglas MacArthur to the G.I.s in the bars. But last week they met another U.S. citizen as different and astonishing to them as the koala, platypus, kiwi, wombat and dingo had been to their forbears.

Eleanor Roosevelt, leaving New Zealand breathless and charmed by her energetic gusto, flew on to Samoa, Australia and further conquests. If Franklin Roosevelt was looking for a U.S. ambassador of good will, he could have made no better selection. Indefatigable Eleanor Roosevelt attended receptions, teas, dinners, visited U.S. servicemen in hospitals

Eleanor Roosevelt greets a Maori in New Zealand. The First Lady is astonishing even in the land of the kiwi, wombat and dingo.

and clubs, autographed a wounded marine's leg bandage, got christened "Queen of the Great Democracy" by Maori chieftains, won friends and influenced people everywhere by her untiring kindness.

TEN-GOAL RATING: Handsome William Averell Harriman, SEPT. 27 whose father left him a railroad kingdom, a fortune of $100,-000,000 and a reputation of fearing "neither God nor J. P. Morgan," used to have an eight-goal polo rating. Then he went into diplomacy. Last week Washington said flatly that Averell Harriman's diplomatic rating had been raised to a ten-goal top, that Franklin Roosevelt would name him U.S. Ambassador to Russia.

Industrialist Harriman, 51, looked like a good man for the job. Despite his glittering social background, Harriman is no playboy. He has worked on a section gang, was a surveyor, once worked as a fireman on the Union Pacific. Now U.P.'s chairman of the board, he is known as one of the most liberal of U.S. industrialists, is also known as a hardheaded businessman.

In London since 1941 as Franklin Roosevelt's "defense expediter," Harriman became a Lend-Lease liaison officer between the U.S. and Great Britain, did a bang-up job, journeyed to Russia with Winston Churchill to confer with Joseph Stalin. He is said to have made a great impression on the Soviet leader. [Harriman was Ambassador to Moscow for more than two years, later served as Secretary of Commerce under President Harry S. Truman, Governor of New York, Assistant Secretary of State under President John F. Kennedy, and an Ambassador-at-Large under President Lyndon Johnson.]

YOUNG FRANK: "I know that Franklin D. Roosevelt Jr. is a NOV. 1 hero," said War Correspondent Quentin Reynolds, returned from Italy a month ago. In Palermo harbor Reynolds found a destroyer battered to a pulp, low in the water, listing badly. He boarded it and asked for the executive officer. A sailor said:

"Who, Big Pancho? That's him. The big guy in dungarees." Big Pancho turned out to be Lieut. Franklin D. Roosevelt Jr., busily trying to salvage his ship. The destroyer (nickname:

"The Mighty May") had turned up for the North African invasion and sank a bothersome Vichyfrench cruiser there. German Junkers 88s caught her ten miles off Palermo after the Sicily invasion and almost pounded her to the bottom. On the bridge, Executive Officer Roosevelt saw a gunner whose pants were rolled up, told him to get them down to avoid flash burns from enemy fire. The gunner had a bead on a bomber and could not comply; so Roosevelt unrolled one pants leg for him. At that moment a bomb fragment removed the gunner's other leg; Roosevelt suffered a slight hand wound. Big Pancho gave the gunner morphine, applied a tourniquet, lugged him below to sick bay. Says Reynolds: "His crew worship the guy. They say he's terrific in combat."

NOV. 29   **RENDEZVOUS WITH DESTINY:** The whole world, tongue aclack, waited only to hear *when & where* Roosevelt, Stalin and Churchill would meet. The Nazi satellite radios guessed at everything but Mr. Roosevelt's room number.

Wherever the Big Three decide to meet, the fate of millions living and yet unborn will be deeply affected by whether —after they have looked into each other's eyes for the first time and have taken each other's measure—a man named Roosevelt and a man named Stalin each decides that the other is a man to be liked, trusted and respected. If they do, a world Thanksgiving may lie ahead.

Joseph Stalin will meet a calm and confident man. Franklin Roosevelt still relishes jokes and wisecracks. He can still drop off for a cat nap anywhere, anytime. He still looks forward to a nightly old-fashioned or two in his study before dinner as a high point of his day. He has grown almost impervious to political criticism. He rarely becomes angry— and then it is usually when somebody snipes at him through one of his children.

DEC. 13   **MOMENT IN TEHERAN:** The declarations were signed, the toasts were drunk. Then the President reported to the U.S. people's true ambassadors to Teheran—the American soldiers being treated in a U.S. camp hospital near there:

"I came here to meet with the Marshal of Soviet Russia and the Prime Minister of England to try to do two things. The first was to lay military plans toward the winning of

President Roosevelt meets with Stalin and Churchill at Teheran. FDR moves into the Russian Embassy, where even the janitors are armed.

the war just as fast as we can. The other purpose was to talk over world conditions after the war."

The talks, he said, were promising. The plans must now be precise. "From west and south," he went on, millions of American soldiers must descend upon the continent, their lives staked against the hope of a better world. Many will never return. Then will come a world peace "to make it unnecessary for us again to have Americans in Iran just as long as we and our children live. I think that is worth fighting for, and even being sick for in Iran."

DECISION: The identity of the No. 1 U.S. soldier was settled. DEC. 27 Joseph Stalin had forced Franklin Roosevelt to make up his mind. Getting down to second front cases, he wanted to know who would lead the promised Anglo-American invasion of the continent. The Roosevelt-Churchill answer was General Dwight D. Eisenhower.

Earlier reports that General George C. Marshall would be assigned that supreme field command were not baseless. The U.S. Chief of Staff has long wanted to serve in the field as a tactician; and President Roosevelt had seriously considered able General Marshall for the invasion job. But he had excellent reasons for finally agreeing to keep the Chief of Staff at his vital post in Washington. The chief reason is that General Marshall has now attained the stature of a military statesman. Any successor would need many months to acquire his prestige, his experience in global strategy, and his smooth-working relationship with Congress and with his fellow members of the Combined Chiefs of Staffs— to whom General Eisenhower will be responsible.

THE TRIP: With Franklin Roosevelt's return to Washington, personal details of his epoch-making 25,000-mile trip came out. Some of them:

¶ In the C-54, the President slept on a rubber mattress stretched across two seats from which the backs had been removed. A green curtain hung about the improvised bed. The plane's remaining 26 bucket seats were for Presidential Assistant Harry Hopkins and Admiral William D. Leahy, for the President's naval and military aides, his physician, a masseur, and his valet. Also taken along were a corps of six Filipino cooks from the Presidential yacht *Potomac*.

¶ The night after arrival of the President's party in Teheran, Russian Foreign Minister Viacheslav Molotov telephoned U.S. Ambassador Averell Harriman, told him the *Ogpu* (Soviet Secret Police) had discovered a German plot on the lives of Roosevelt, Churchill and Stalin. He suggested that Franklin Roosevelt move from the American to the Russian Embassy. The President did so, the next day. Churchill remained at the British Embassy, just across the street. The Russians then threw a screen around the Russian and British Embassies, turning them, in effect, into one armed camp. Probable reason for the scare: week before, 38 German paratroopers had been dropped in the vicinity, and only 32 rounded up. Even the janitors in the Russian Embassy were armed.

¶ The President did all his Christmas shopping in U.S. Army post exchanges in Cairo and Teheran.

The Nation

JAN. 4 **BUTTER FACTS:** Housewives hurried from store to store, hunting butter. Sometimes they got a quarter pound for Christmas. Oftener they got the grocer's excuse: deliveries from his wholesaler had been cut a fourth or a half, and his small stocks had long ago been sold. Thus the housewives got an inkling of a bitter truth: they were face to face with the most serious butter shortage in the history of a country that once overflowed with milk. The huge stocks of butter in storage were almost gone.

Some of the reasons for the butter famine were: labor shortages on farms, transportation difficulties, mixups in the entire milk economy. But most important reason is bigger consumption: the Army & Navy are now eating some 200 million lb. a year—and will need more as the armed forces grow.

SUCH PLEASURES: The great American era of the automobile JAN. 18 came to a virtual end in 17 States along the Atlantic seaboard last week. Without any warning, the Office of Price Administration banned all pleasure and nonessential driving. Almost overnight nearly all private automobiles disappeared from the streets and highways. Outlying restaurants, dance halls, racing tracks folded up.

The reasons for this sudden action were as complicated as the rules for enforcing it. Partly it was the now well-known story of lack of tankers; partly it was new military demands in North Africa; and partly it was fumbling in OPA, which should have established more drastic controls earlier.

UNKINDEST CUT: In Hollywood, Twentieth Century-Fox last FEB. 22 week announced that, for the duration, it would cut all big banquet scenes from its films. In a world of rationing and black markets, sirloins, like sweater girls, have become a shade too seductive.

"IF I WAS A VIOLINIST . . .": Gimbels' Bargain Basement looked MARCH 8 festive. Some 750 New Yorkers were there to bid, with war bond pledges, on such precious items as Thomas Jefferson's Bible, a letter written by George Washington.

Glib, wild-haired Musicomedian Danny Kaye, working like a turkey gobbler, held up the auction's prize piece: Comic Jack Benny's violin, "Old Love in Bloom"—a $75 imitation Amati. Everyone present knew that only a war could have persuaded Benny to part with the old prop which had provided him with half his gags for the last 20 years. Before anyone could make a bid an attendant rushed up to Auctioneer Kaye with a letter. He opened it and gulped: "I have a bid for $1,000,000!"

That ended that. A solid, mild-mannered, aging gentleman in the rear of the basement rose and bowed. It was the first bow Julius Klorfein had ever taken.

The city-room files were bare of Julius Klorfein's name. At his penthouse apartment he apologized for this unfortunate anonymity: "I've just spent my life working hard and building up my cigar business, and I guess I didn't have any time to get in *Who's Who* or What's What or anything like that."

Julius Klorfein has been busy all his life. He came to the U.S. from Russia 40-odd years ago and began turning out his own cigars in the window of a little street shop in Brooklyn. His formula for a mild, cheap cigar caught on. Now 58, he is president of Garcia Grande Cigars, Inc., manufacturers of some of the U.S.'s best-selling nickel and two-for-a-nickel smokes.

Julius Klorfein with his wife. On behalf of the war effort, a two-for-a-nickel cigar maker bids $1 million for Jack Benny's famous fiddle.

Fondling the fiddle which had brought him momentary fame, he was asked whether he could play it. Said Julius Klorfein: "If I was a violinist, I wouldn't be able to buy a million dollars worth of war bonds."

REVEILLE FOR WORKERS: Slugabed war workers have had an MARCH 29 excuse, such as it was: in all the U.S. there was scarcely an alarm clock to be had at any price. WPB had closed the industry last July 1 to save metal. Now it was WPB's turn to be alarmed. War production might suffer. Last week clockmakers agreed on a victory-model alarm clock, sparing of metal, unsparing of noise. Some 1,700,000 will be produced.

THE BOMBING OF BOISE CITY: A fledgling from the U.S. JULY 19 Army air base at Dalhart, Tex. last week bungled his navigation by 45 miles: he mistook the lights of Boise City, Okla. (pop: 1,144) for his practice target. Aiming straight at the Baptist church and Forrest Bourk's garage, he loosed six practice bombs (each bomb: 4 lb. of powder, 96 lb. of sand and shell). The noise of the explosions roared through the sleeping town.

Boise City citizens, first in the U.S. to get a real blitzing, acted the way most civilians would act who had never been bombed before:

¶ Most of them ran like hell in no particular direction.

¶ Frank Garrett, light and power man, sprinted for the Southwestern Public Service building, pulled the town's master light switch.

¶ Air Warden John Atkins' big night had come. He phoned the FBI in Oklahoma City.

¶ Next day Fred Kreiger editorialized in the *News*: "What this place needs are some searchlights and antiaircraft guns."

BATTLEFRONTS ARE SAFER: AUG. 23

¶ War workers killed by traffic since Pearl Harbor: 22,500.

¶ U.S. war dead on all fronts: 16,913.

COMING HOME: One cold afternoon last week, at New York's DEC 20 Halloran (Army) Hospital, a long hospital train stood on the siding. Out of the hospital, walking, hobbling, on crutches, lying on stretchers, came the young wounded veterans of World War II. The men were just five days back in the U.S., just two weeks out of North Africa, veterans of Tunisia, Sicily, Salerno and Naples. The train would take them to Midwest Army hospitals, where they would be near home.

The train was clean and comfortable, with the antiseptic smell of a hospital. Each ward car had an operating room. Nurses in stiffly starched uniforms walked down the aisles. Just before it pulled out, chaplains came on, bringing cigarets and candy, magazines and books. Also on board was the New York *Times'* Meyer Berger, watching the faces of the wounded, listening to their talk as they came nearer & nearer home. It was a memorable ride. Next day Reporter Berger sent his newspaper a story which well & truly evoked the heart-breaking feelings of the returning soldier:

"The soldiers stared at the whizzing landscape. They dreamed on it with hungry eyes. One lad not more than 21, his leg amputated, told the soldier across the aisle: 'Even the dump piles look swell.'

"By and by the men started on rummy, pinochle, hearts and blackjack. Some read comics and newspapers. A soldier looked up from his paper and read names of brands from the sheet—names of cigarets, cigars, foods, liquors—and the card players grinned at the sound of them. Men called out the names of stations—Trenton, Philadelphia, Wilmington, Cumberland. A corporal spoke dreamily of the nights in Howie Dryman's Texaco Bar & Grill across the river from Vincennes, Ind. 'I'll smoke fresh cigarets,' he said, 'not cigarets that's beat up and spilling both ends.'

"There was talk of Arabs—A-rabs they all pronounced it —and desert storms. After 9 o'clock the nurses started alcohol baths for the litter cases. One nurse had to dig around for bread crumbs that had worked into a cast under a soldier's chest. Another cast case looked on and said: 'Wish I'd thought of that' and the car roared with laughter.

"Daylight was slow and wintry. At Dennison, Ohio, Pvt. Gerard Heil, a broad, red-faced soldier, couldn't contain his excitement: 'There's the Coca-Cola factory where I work,' he said. 'That woman with the books, that's Miss Cottrell. She's cashier at the Palace Movie.' The train moved on and Pvt. Heil named all the buildings that slid by."

The Congress

SESSION OF DESTINY: Milling Congressional veterans shouted JAN. 18
greetings to re-elected cronies, slapped backs, shook hands.
The 78th Congress was ready for business. The press had
warned the people of something they already knew—this,
more than any Congress heretofore, was a session of destiny.
Its deliberations would affect the state of the world and the
shape of the future for generations. Over all legislators,
short or tall, thoughtful or frivolous, hung a crushing responsibility. They must help prosecute the war—they perhaps
might help to write the peace.

BILLION-DOLLAR WATCHDOG: Anywhere but in a democracy, MARCH 8
the Senate's irreverent Truman Committee would be fair
game for liquidation. In a perfect state, free from but-
terfingers and human frailty, it would be unnecessary. In
the U.S., democratic but far from perfect, the Truman Committee this week celebrated its second successful birthday as one of the most useful Government agencies of
World War II.

Had they had time, its ten members might have toasted
their accomplishments all night. They had served as watchdog, spotlight, conscience and spark plug to the economic
war-behind-the-lines. They had prodded Commerce Secretary
Jesse Jones into building synthetic-rubber plants. They had
called the turn on raw-materials shortages. One single investigation, of graft and waste in Army camp building, had
saved the U.S. $250,000,000. Their total savings ran into bil-
lions.

The bigger the U.S. arsenal grew, the more important the
Truman Committee became. As the arsenal turned into a
modern-day Great Pyramid, most Washington officials still
lugged just one stone, and many carried it in the wrong direction. Senator Harry S. Truman and his Committee members had no power to act or order. But, using Congress's
old prerogative to look, criticize and recommend, they had
heard hundreds of witnesses, taken 4,000,000 words of testimony, given thick ears and red faces to Cabinet members,
generals, admirals, big businessmen, little businessmen, labor
leaders. Said one Washingtonian last week: "There's only

one thing that worries me more than the present state of the war effort. That's to think what it would be like by now without Truman."

APRIL 5   **PERFORMANCE:** John L. Lewis, last of the great ham tragedians of politics, strode to the witness stand with long, measured steps, bowed twice, sat down, sighed. Two tiny spring flowers, one white, one lavender, peeped from the lapel of his flowing black coat. His broad jowls were momentarily at rest, his eyebrows arched like innocent cupid's bows. Under subpoena by the Truman Committee, John Lewis had appeared gladly. There he sat, as guileless and patient as a volcano. He was ready to explain his threat of a coal strike.

First, what about absenteeism? John Lewis cleared his throat with a significantly explosive harrumph. "I have been told that absenteeism is higher in Congress than it is in industry." He leaned a little forward and added, with a slight, royal gesture of his labor boss' sceptre, a cigar: "I notice that absenteeism prevails on this committee this morning."

Chairman Harry S. Truman looked like a man who had expected the worst but not so soon. The missing Senators, he said, were busy working on another problem. Chairman Truman forced a chill smile. "I thought you might have some concrete statement that would be helpful."

"Yes," said John Lewis in solemn basso. "We have to fight this war with human beings. Human beings are subject to all the ills to which the flesh is heir."

The committee tried another tack. Would the witness admit that wage increases were inflationary? With majestic patience, he would not. On the contrary, the greatest danger to price controls was the Government's "excessive rewards to industry for producing war commodities."

There was always the excess-profits tax, said Maine's Senator Ralph O. Brewster. "We still hope the rich will not get richer out of this war."

"Hope deferred maketh the heart sick," rumbled John Lewis.

"You are a disciple of discontent with things as they are, Mr. Lewis," said Senator Brewster.

John Lewis knit his thunderous brows and growled: "One

Senator Truman to Lewis: "We don't stand for any sassy remarks."   *U.M.W.'s John L. Lewis to Harry Truman: "Who cast the first stone?"*

way to get cooperation is to give the workers of this country enough to eat."

"That's demagoguery pure and simple!" shouted Minnesota's young Senator Joe Ball. "You are not seriously trying to tell the committee that any large number of workers in the United States don't get enough to eat?"

The volcano erupted. John Lewis roared: "When you call me a demagogue before I can reply I hurl it back in your face, sir. When you ask me are the coal miners hungry I say yes, and when you call me a demagogue I say you are less than a proper representative of the common people of this country."

Snapped Chairman Truman: "We don't stand for any sassy remarks. I don't like that remark to a member of this committee."

"Who," asked Lewis, with righteous dignity, "cast the first stone?"

Three hours passed. John Lewis stepped off the witness chair, steamed majestically from the committee room. The echoes of his blank prose died: the stage emptied. The great tragedian had played another scene.

BLOW AT LEWIS: Ignoring Administration pleas for modera- JUNE 14 tion, ignoring organized labor's threats to purge them, come election time, the House members passed (231-to-141) the Smith-Connally strike-and-labor-control bill. Aimed squarely at John Lewis, the bill bristles with restrictions on labor and now goes before the Senate.

JUNE 28   **POSTWAR CATALYST:** "Resolved by the House of Representatives [the Senate concurring] that the Congress hereby expresses itself as favoring the creation of appropriate international machinery with power adequate to establish and maintain a just and lasting peace among the nations of the world, and as favoring participation by the United States therein."

This simple, concise, 50-word resolution made Congressional history last week. Introduced by a freshman Congressman, Arkansas' James William Fulbright, it proved exactly the catalytic agent that Capitol Hill has awaited. For the first time, global-minded Congressmen of varying political and economic chemistry were drawn together—and the world could see how fast has been the growth of sentiment in the U.S. for postwar world cooperation.

House Freshman Fulbright, unknown even to many of his colleagues, became momentarily the nation's most publicized lawmaker. A deluge of fan mail (10-to-1 in favor) descended on his desk. Interviewers discovered that the first-termer from Fayetteville was young (38), smart (Rhodes scholar), studious (onetime president of the University of Arkansas), aggressive (lacrosse), hardheaded (businessman, farmer). Asked how long it took him to write his one-sentence resolution, he replied philosophically: "Fifteen years."

JULY 5   **UPRISING:** In a dramatic, angry two and a quarter hours, Congress reasserted itself, and dealt Franklin Roosevelt the most stinging rebuke of his entire career, his worst domestic defeat of World War II. Congressional cloakrooms had buzzed with rumors about the Smith-Connally anti-strike bill: the President would sign, the President would veto. At last the Presidential message came. Wrote Franklin Roosevelt: he was "unalterably opposed" to wartime strikes. But he did not think this bill would stop such strikes. He also objected to the section forbidding union donations to political campaigns. This, said he, had no relation to wartime strikes. So—as organized labor hoped he would—he vetoed the bill.

The reading over, Texas Senator "Long Tom" Connally, one of the bill's major sponsors, rose to his feet. His face was flushed, his long grey hair unruly. His words rolled slowly: "I am sorely disappointed. The House is sorely disappointed. The people of the United States are sorely disappointed. Every soldier & sailor on the seas, on the land, in the air, is sorely disappointed. The Senate has a right to pass a bill over the veto. I hope the Senate will exercise its high constitutional privilege."

Franklin Roosevelt's veto had arrived at 3:13 p.m. At 3:30 p.m. the Senate voted 56-to-25 (two more than the necessary two-thirds majority) to override the veto. The House was fighting mad at John L. Lewis; it was fighting mad at the President—and it was fed to the teeth with inaction. The House demanded action.

When the news was flashed to the House pandemonium broke loose. Kentucky's labor-crunching Andy May choked with rage: "I shall expect the House to meet its responsibility in the interest of the men in the foxholes of Bataan and Guadalcanal and Kiska and Attu where the President's message has struck like a four-ton blockbuster." (Andy May was too angry to be accurate: Kiska is still held by the Japs.)

In C.I.O. headquarters, 17 blocks away, mimeograph machines whirred, turning out an appeal to the House to stop, think, do nothing hasty. Before the C.I.O. runners had reached the Capitol the House had already overridden the veto, 244-to-108 (nine more than the necessary two-thirds).

TRUMAN v. A GIANT: The Truman war-watchdog committee exploded in a new report, this time on a half-dozen phases of U.S. aircraft production, with a special shelling reserved for Curtiss-Wright Corp., second largest U.S. war contractor (first: General Motors).   JULY 19

On a flat greensward near Cincinnati sprawls the immense Lockland factory of Wright Aeronautical Corp., hailed in 1941 as the largest single-storied industrial plant in the world. The Truman Committee sniffed trouble there last January, reported it to Wright and the Army Air Forces. After four months, while Wright and the AAF found little wrong, Truman moved in, took 1,300 pages of testimony. Some points:

¶ Wright "was producing and causing the Government to accept defective and substandard material, by the falsification of tests, by destruction of records, by forging inspection reports.

¶ "More than 25% of engines built at the plant have consistently failed in one or more major parts during a test run.

¶ "Air Force inspectors were threatened with transfer if they did not accept engines which were leaking gasoline."

Truman's next punch was directed more at Air Force judgment than at Curtiss: "The Curtiss P-40 fighter planes have performed valuable work, but were relatively obsolete when we entered the war. The North American P-51 Mustang, characterized by both the British and the Army Air Forces as the most aerodynamically perfect pursuit plane in existence, was in production in 1941. It would have been preferable to increase production of Mustangs, decrease production of Curtiss P-40 Warhawks."

Dapper Guy Warner Vaughan, ex-automobile racer who heads giant Curtiss-Wright, answered Truman's attacks: "The P-40 has shot down from three to 20 enemy planes for every P-40 lost. The company emphatically denies that Wright has at any time sold products known to the company to have contained defective or substandard parts."

This week Under Secretary of War Robert Patterson minimized the Truman report, said the situation was much less sensational. He denied that any engines "known to be defective" were ever placed in service. But the U.S. public seemed well content that the Truman war-watchdogs keep on baying.

OCT. 4 **ISOLATIONISM?:** By a thumping nonpartisan majority, 360-to-29, the House had passed the Fulbright Resolution, pledging the U.S. to carry its full load in postwar international relations. Then the resolution went over to the Senate Committee on Foreign Relations, whose chairman is an old political gas-burner, Texas' Tom Connally. For 28 weeks this Committee had bottled up a batch of postwar resolutions. Connally now called his Committee together, emerged with a statement that it would not report out the Fulbright Resolution, either.

Argued Tom Connally: bringing the resolution to the floor of the Senate would only provoke a bitter debate, in which some Senators would have an anti-British, anti-Russian field day (ten out of 23 of his own Committeemen are pre-Pearl Harbor isolationists). In short, Tom Connally does not want to start the Great Debate. The result suggested by levelheaded Columnist Raymond Clapper: "Isolation has won the opening battle in the United States Senate."

MR. WHEELER'S FIVE HOURS: Montana's Senator Burton K. OCT. 11 Wheeler, great white hope of those who hate the prospect of fighting for their freedom, made another last stand. His colleagues slipped quietly out of the chamber. But the galleries were full of approving women and children. Burt Wheeler wanted to keep pre-Pearl Harbor fathers out of the draft, at least until next year. To the nearly empty floor he cried:

"I have said that no father in the United States should be called until the slackers are taken out of the Government bureaus. Fathers should not be called until the slackers are taken out of the industries where they are hiding today."

Senator Wheeler went off on a new tack: "There are in this country today over 3,000,000 men in the 4F classification. I have seen instance after instance of men who have been rejected subsequently going to work on the railroads or in factories, and demonstrating that they are just as strong as men in the services."

This was the signal for Administration stalwarts. Majority Leader Alben Barkley inquired innocently: "How does the Senator know that of his own knowledge?"

Wheeler—"Because I have seen them with my own eyes."

Barkley—"Did the Senator see them working on railroad tracks?"

Wheeler—"It is not a question of my seeing each and every one of them, because I do not imagine the Senator from Kentucky is able to see all the people of Kentucky."

Barkley—"No, and I am not going to imagine the condition of all the people of Kentucky whom I cannot see."

Thus, for five hours, Senator Wheeler spoke to empty seats and took his heckling. Though his evidence was hearsay, he had made three points: 1) many a Government bureau is overstaffed, 2) many a war plant has used occupational deferments to hoard workers, 3) if U.S. manpower were used more efficiently, fewer fathers would be drafted. But Senator Wheeler had changed no one's mind about his bill to defer fathers. At the unanimous urging of Army, Navy, Selective Service and Manpower Commission, Congress will do nothing to stop the drafting of fathers, which began officially last week.

OCT. 25 **ACCOUCHEMENT:** "Long Tom" Connally, whose Foreign Relations subcommittee sat like senescent setting hens on a nest of postwar resolutions for 202 days, last week hatched the egg—a 75-word Resolution which cheepingly proposed that the U.S. join in supporting international authority and international peace.

The Resolution: "That the war against all our enemies be waged until complete victory is achieved; that the U.S. cooperate with its comrades in arms in securing a just and honorable peace; that the U.S. acting through its constitutional processes, join with free and sovereign nations in the establishment and maintenance of international authority with power to prevent aggression and to preserve the peace of the world."

On the basis of statistics (one word per two and two-thirds days or every 65 hours), the Resolution seemed to many a Senator and citizen hardly to justify the 29 weeks spent warming it into being.

As a piece of statesmanship it offended at once the proponents of the more forthright B2H2 Resolution [which was named for Senators Ball, Burton, Hatch and Hill, and which had been pigeonholed]. Minor Statesman Connally explained feebly: "The best possible that could be secured. Unity and harmony are vital if the Senate is to pass a resolution by a substantial majority."

But the very timidity of Tom Connally's Resolution threatened to bring about the battle he had hoped to avoid. A group of Senators, including Joseph H. Ball and Carl Hatch of the B2H2 Resolution, served notice that unless the full Foreign Relations Committee make the Resolution more definite at once, they will take their fight for "strengthening and clarifying" amendments to the Senate floor.

85-TO-5: It had taken Texas' "Long Tom" Connally 29 weeks NOV. 15 to phrase his Senate Resolution for international cooperation. For ten days, insisting it should be stronger, Senators had hammered at it. Then came the Moscow agreement [at which U.S. Secretary of State Cordell Hull and the British and Russian foreign ministers agreed in principle to a post-war organization to help maintain peace and security]. Both Illinois' Scott Lucas and California's Sheridan Downey had the happy thought: Why not add the words of the pact to the Connally Resolution? Tom Connally was won over; so were the B2H2 supporters. The deadlock was broken.

There was a delay. On the Senate floor, the man who so long has symbolized "America, go it alone," was speaking. The voice was tired because California's Hiram Johnson is 77, and ailing. But it was tired, too, because the cause was lost. The voice croaked so feebly that only those who bunched up close could hear it:

"God save the United States of America. God preserve her in the days to come. God be good to us and permit us to resist, and permit us to be the country we have ever been."

The old man sat down again. He knew it was all over. Swiftly the Senate shouted down five delaying amendments. Then the voting began: Should the Senate resolve its willingness to join in establishing international authority to preserve peace? The final vote: 85 yes, 5 no, with 6 absent. (If all had been present, the final vote would have been 90-to-6.)

The Administration

TRUTH AND TROUBLE: When tranquil, white-topped Elmer MARCH 15 Davis went to Washington last summer as the people's choice for Director of War Information, his appointment was generally hailed. When he went to Capitol Hill, to ask for funds in well-rounded sentences full of common sense, modesty and "sirs," the House Appropriations Committee was moved to a rare compliment:

"The establishment of the Office of War Information is one of the most constructive steps which has been taken toward the coordination of agencies engaged in the war effort. The selection of Mr. Davis as director is equally gratifying."

But last week to Elmer Davis, as it must to all wartime officials, came pots of trouble. One cause: Davis' sprawling OWI had issued a cartoon booklet on the life of President Roosevelt, designed for distribution abroad. A U.S. soldier sent a copy to New York's Republican Congressman John Taber. Mr. Taber, who has a low irritation point, was moved to cry: "Purely political propaganda, designed entirely to promote a fourth term and a dictatorship."

There were dark hints of an investigation of Davis and his OWI. Many an OWIster was quietly looking for another job. The house might not yet be afire, but it was smoking. Elmer Davis, sitting on the smoking roof, was calm as ever. For the Roosevelt cartoons, Davis had a common-sensible explanation: the President "symbolizes the United States, both as a powerful nation and as a land of liberty and democracy. This fact is a national asset. A Government information agency would be stupid not to capitalize on it."

Davis' guiding principle is that "a free people has a right to know." He tries to base U.S. propaganda on plain truth, whenever he can dig it out. But the truth is not always palatable, either at home or abroad. The Allies do not enjoy hearing of strikes, Washington bungling, domestic political quarrels—but the Axis does. Thus one of his big problems is to explain the U.S. satisfactorily to the world.

This is a tremendous task. A totalitarian State can speak with one voice, its master's, can marshal all its logic, force and facts into one strong propaganda line. But a democracy, by its very nature, is a land of many voices. It cannot have a single propaganda line, because its only propaganda is that it has none. The U.S., as a free nation, can only propagandize its freedom—and freedom includes the right of men to dissent from their Government, to strike, to vote against it, to cry out against it. And the right of a free press is the right to print these doings as news.

In the summer of 1939, with World War II only days away, Elmer Davis was at his summer home in Mystic, Conn., writing the last chapters of a mystery novel for the *Saturday Evening Post.* He was a respected, reasonably successful author. But when CBS invited him to broadcast the news, as a fill-in for Commentator H. V. Kaltenborn, he put the mystery novel aside, hurried to Manhattan.

The trust of the U.S. people in Elmer Davis today is a tribute 1) to the power of radio, 2) to the power of common sense. At war's beginning, many a news commentator offered his audience little more than a 15-minute nervous breakdown. Not so Elmer Davis. His voice was calm, incisive, with a Hoosier twang as reassuring as Thanksgiving, as shrewd as a small-town banker.

OWI's front man, still solid and sensible, has kept his old habit and attitudes. (He had trouble getting used to a secretary, often typed out his own letters in the uneven, x'ed out style that is the mark of a working newsman.) And this week, the U.S. was glad to hear that Elmer Davis goes back on the air. Every Friday night henceforth he will broadcast to the people. This was what the U.S. wanted: there are lots of Administrators, Czars and such in Washington, but in all the U.S. there is only one voice on the radio with that dry, reassuring twang.

PENTAGON PIE: The War Department's mammoth Pentagon MAY 10 Building in Washington, the capital's most fabulous new sight, has eight cafeterias and two dining rooms which serve 40,000 meals a day. One day last winter ambulances clanged up, carted away 50 Pentagon diners griped by contaminated salad dressing. The Pentagon hastily changed cafeteria managers.

Last week ambulances rushed to the Pentagon once again. To the hospital went 36 servicemen and War Department employes woozy from another poisoning, this time apparently from the butterscotch pie. Said Manager Frank W. Hoover, unimpressed by talk of sabotage: "The place seems to be jinxed."

OPA MUST BE LOVABLE: Tanned, jut-jawed deputy OPAd- AUG. 9 ministrator Chester Bowles strode bravely into Washington. Reporters took a long, sympathetic look at an able new man in a jinxed job. After two years of rationing, OPA was still unworkable, still unlovable. Newcomer Bowles took a confident grip on his job. He had no illusions: "No sensible person would seek a job of this kind." He was modest: "Expect no miracles." He was reasonable: "There is no sense in rationing for rationing's sake." He sounded tough enough: "OPA will be no walking doormat."

Wealthy Yaleman Bowles, 42, started writing advertising copy 16 years ago, resigned last year as chairman of the board of Manhattan's potent advertising firm, Benton & Bowles. He has spent the last 18 months as a successful OPAdministrator for Connecticut. His program to make OPA more attractive:

¶ The "snooping, Gestapo approach" to enforcement must go.

¶ Black markets will get a crack-down.

¶ OPA cannot be run entirely from Washington ("I want to be reminded of this once a week").

Predicted energetic Chester Bowles: "We should make real progress in the next six weeks."

Sighed a reporter: "All right, give him six weeks." [Bowles stayed in the job until February 1946. He later served as Governor of Connecticut, U.S. Under Secretary of State and Ambassador to India.]

HOLD THAT LINE: When OPA asked restaurants to go back to earlier price levels, Manhattan's famed Stork Club pitched headlong into the battle against inflation, rolled back its price for coffee from 50 to 35¢ a cup.

AUG. 23 **A HOUSE DIVIDED:** One day last week, insiders said, two of the President's top czars consulted on the quiet with Secretary of State Cordell Hull. Subject: how to get rid of Under Secretary Sumner Welles.

All were agreed. Best idea was to send him on some very long and difficult diplomatic mission, possibly even to Moscow, as a kind of traveling Ambassador. In the meantime someone else could be inserted in his job.

Somehow the story leaked to the press. Perhaps it was planted. Insiders said that Sumner Welles then telephoned the White House to see if this deal had the Presidential blessing. Mr. Roosevelt is supposed to have answered no.

Thus, once again, a flare-up of long-smoldering hates and jealousies in the State Department illuminated the fact that the U.S. has at least three State Departments.

❡ Department No. 1 is presided over by stern, righteous, feudal old Cordell Hull, architect of the reciprocal trade agreements, believer in old-fashioned international law, a Cabinet officer who is politically unassailable.

❡ Department No. 2 is the province of chill, correct, intelligent Sumner Welles, whose ability is generally underestimated by the citizenry, who are either so awestruck or repelled by his attitude that they miss the man himself. Welles, product of Groton and Harvard, an ace career diplomat, is the author of the Good Neighbor Policy which Mr. Roosevelt adopted.

❡ Department No. 3 is that segment of U.S. foreign relations which Franklin Roosevelt reserves for himself, working through miscellaneous aides.

WELLES OUT: In factual terms the news was brief. Under Secretary of State Sumner Welles had resigned. In human terms the news was repetitious. Tough, old Cordell Hull had again got his man. SEPT. 6

Next day Welles slipped out of Washington, turned up at Maine's swank Bar Harbor, where he held to diplomatically correct silence.

If Sumner Welles was going into limbo, he would meet it with the good form a son of Groton and Harvard is expected to show.

No such considerations restrained the U.S. press. Its endorsement of Sumner Welles was surprisingly widespread, its condemnation of Franklin Roosevelt and Cordell Hull surprisingly severe:

❡ Said the New York *Herald Tribune*: "A fairly brutal sacrifice of American foreign policy to Roosevelt fourth-term politics. Mr. Welles has apparently had most of the ideas and the firmest grasp of any one in the State Department over the actual problems of the future."

❡ Said the Philadelphia *Inquirer*: "A disquieting indication of weakness on this country's diplomatic front."

❡ Said the Washington *Post*: "To be sure, Mr. Welles was one of the 'star-gazers,' as Mr. Hull stigmatizes the expositors of the Four Freedoms. But in terms of ultimate loyalties, surely no sin of disloyalty could be chalked up against Mr. Welles on that account."

Labor

MARCH 29 **ZERO HOUR:** Roared John L. Lewis to the soft coal operators: "Friends, Romans, millionaires. It is a safe assumption that without a negotiated contract the miners will not trespass on your property on April 1." He did not say "strike"—he had joined in the no-strike pledge given by labor shortly after Pearl Harbor. But his meaning was clear: he planned to turn his demand for a $2-a-day wage increase into an all-out assault on the Administration's Maginot Line against inflation.

Behind the line the Administration worked frantically on its defenses. First move: a delaying action designed to gain another month for negotiation. For if John Lewis gets his raise, he will have breached the War Labor Board's "Little Steel formula," which limits raises to 15% since Jan. 1, 1941. Ready to move into this gap are the vast forces of the C.I.O. and A.F. of L., which could not afford to stand idly by while Lewis gained a political victory. Thus Lewis may spearhead a pitched battle against the Administration cost-of-living controls.

MAY 10 **WEEK OF SHAME & WRATH:** This was a great week for John L. Lewis; a bitter hard week for President Roosevelt; and a week of shame, dismay and helpless wrath for the U.S. people. John Lewis had clearly, coldly and precisely outmaneuvered the President in a battle that was even more momentous than the people yet realized. John Lewis had not yet won that battle, but he had won a 15-day truce, in which he was prepared to bargain with his new employer, the U.S. Government, which had now taken over the struck coal miners. He had successfully by-passed the coal operators and the War Labor Board. As the week began, chances were he would win a guaranteed six-day work week for his bituminous miners ($7 a day for five days, $10.50 for the sixth), and perhaps even a guaranteed annual wage, which was his goal. The Government as an employer could afford to pay any amount, for the Government as a wartime customer needed all the coal the miners could dig.

The way he got the truce was a Lewis masterpiece. The President had given fair warning that he would address the miners and the nation on Sunday night. Sunday morning John Lewis and three henchmen slipped into Washington, worked out the details of the truce with Harold Ickes, now his boss as Solid Fuels Coordinator. Then Lewis entrained for New York. Naturally the truce could not be announced until the miners' policy committee had met. And somehow the policy committee deliberated just long enough. Twenty minutes before the President went on the air, John Lewis announced the truce, asked the miners to go to work Tuesday.

This act stripped the gears in the White House. The President did not have time to turn around and rewrite his plea that the miners go back on Monday. Doggedly, the President made his case, but the speech fell in a vacuum. It even confused many miners who were already all set to go back to work, and now heard the President plead that they do.

THE WORD IS TREASON: The War Labor Board came right MAY 24 out and said this week that John L. Lewis' defiance of the Government "gives aid and comfort to our enemies." The law has a word for giving aid & comfort to the enemy in time of war. The word is treason. If the Government meant what it said, its next step would be to place John L. Lewis under arrest.

Evidently the Government did not mean it. Instead of arresting John Lewis, the Government asked Mr. Lewis not to strike against it. Mr. Lewis, with a great show of patriotism, agreed to extend the truce another 13 days till May 31, sending out 5,000 telegrams over the overburdened telegraph lines to tell his lieutenants the strike was postponed. John L. Lewis had been playing with fire but the Government had been playing with John L. Lewis. It looked as if John Lewis was the more dangerous to play with.

CAT AND CANARY: John L. Lewis started out last week to re- MAY 31 draw the map of U.S. labor—and perhaps that of U.S. politics, too. Just eight years after he split American labor wide open by founding the revolutionary C.I.O., Lewis asked that he and his 600,000 miners be taken back into the older and more conservative American Federation of Labor. The news came as a mighty shock to millions: What was John Lewis up to now?

The move was the result of secret negotiations, mainly between Lewis and big Bill Hutcheson, head of the Carpenters' Union, who once called Lewis a big bastard and was forthwith knocked flat. And the announcement came, fittingly enough, from the lips of pious-faced Bill Green, whom Lewis originally made president of A.F. of L., and later denounced as a "faithless ingrate." Summoning reporters to his office, Bill Green took quiet revenge, smugly smiled a "cat-ate-the-canary" smile, stated that his executive committee was sympathetically considering Lewis' application.

If the Mine Workers do return to the A.F. of L. fold, however, John Lewis will be the cat, Green the canary. For A.F. of L. will immediately become the predominant labor bloc in the country, with a membership approaching 7,000,000 as against C.I.O.'s 5,000,000. And John Lewis will have boosted himself into a new strategic position to play politics in the election of 1944. His sudden switch back into A.F. of L., like his revolt from it in 1935, could be explained in one word: opportunism.

JUNE 28 **"DAMN YOUR SOUL":** Said an editorial in the Middle East edition of the U.S. Army paper *Stars & Stripes:*

"Speaking for the American soldier—John L. Lewis, damn your coal-black soul."

U.S. civilians were at no less a fever pitch than U.S. soldiers. Coal Strikes I & II (May 1-4; May 31-June 7) had already cost the country ten million tons of coal production; they had meant the loss of 16,000 tons of pig iron and 20,000 tons of steel in the western Pennsylvania steel district alone. That iron, thought the citizens, would have killed a lot of Japs and Germans.

Now came Strike III and the daily loss of two million more tons of coal for the steel mills and the arms plants. The nation, lathered into a rage, waited, not very patiently, for action from Washington. Bluff Harold Ickes, custodian of all the mines, stuck to his desk, plotting his course. His orders were to get coal mined, and he didn't much care how. On Franklin Roosevelt's desk still lay the Smith-Connally antistrike bill (he had until June 25 to act on it). Tension climbed like the U.S. thermometers.

When John Lewis began his war of nerves on the U.S. people he had two objectives in mind: 1) to get a raise for his miners—$2 a day if possible; 2) to blast the War Labor Board to smithereens. Midway in the battle he shifted tactics, demanded the raise on the basis of "portal-to-portal" pay, *i.e.,* money for time spent going to & from work. Then, twelve hours before Strike III's deadline, John Lewis shifted tactics again, announced, with an appropriate patriotic flourish, that his miners would be glad to work for the Government.

John Lewis well knew that the last thing the mine operators want is actual Government operation of the mines. Having failed in his other objectives, he would settle for federalization of the mines.

FIRST INDICTMENTS: For the first time the big, jagged teeth of AUG. 9 the Smith-Connally Act bit down. They caught not their intended prey, mastodon John L. Lewis, but 30 small-fry officers and members of United Mine Workers locals. John Lewis ordered his miners back to work. But in the captive mine region around Uniontown, Pa., where coking coal is dug for nearby mills that own the mines, Lewis' order did not stick. Groups of miners worked against union officials who were trying to get them back into the pits. At the height of the outlaw strike, 24,000 miners were on strike and furnaces stood idle at five big steel companies.

Pressure to crack down came not from Washington but, apparently, from the steel companies owning the captive mines, and from commercial coal operators who feared the strike would spread. Last week a Federal grand jury brought in the first indictments under the Smith-Connally Act, which makes it a criminal offense to attempt to strike a Government-operated industry. The indicted U.M.W. members have received no support from their union. John L. Lewis knows that aid for the indicted miners would infuriate U.S. citizens who consider such strikes near treason.

SPEECH ON A BUOY: Stocky Charlie Daggert knows how to AUG. 16 use his fists. During World War I, he punched his way to the featherweight championship of the U.S. Navy. But, as Daggert says, he also had "a bit of Irish wit." Last week Daggert called upon that wit.

Daggert, now 46, is president of a small, independent union at the Quaker City Iron Works, a Philadelphia plant engaged in secret war work. Last February the union petitioned the War Labor Board for a 10% wage increase, got no action. Despite the pleas of Daggert, the union voted unanimously to go on "a holiday."

Three days before the strike was to begin, Daggert went to Superintendent Robert Wilson, asked him to blow the quitting horn 30 minutes early. The men & women, their overalls soggy with sweat, hurried out of the sheds into the blazing sun. Daggert climbed on top a huge buoy he had been welding, stuttered a bit, then began booming in the voice he had used to referee many a Philadelphia fight:

"I'm not going to give you any patriotic spiel. You've had the flag waved in front of you for months to keep you on the job. All of you have sons in the service, brothers, husbands. If you walked out now you'd be going back on them. For instance, you'd be going back on Jimmy Morris. You worked side by side with him, and you all remember how he left here to become a flyer. You know how he was the pilot of a bomber on an important mission in the Mediterranean and how he brought back his plane and landed it. You know the rest of the crew got out and after a while looked around for Jimmy. But Jimmy hadn't come out of that plane. He landed the plane and died."

Jimmy's father shuffled his feet; greasy bandannas wiped away tears. Daggert's finger picked out one after another of his old friends.

"How about you, Big Joe?" Daggert pointed to Joe Milewski, whose son, Tom, is in North Africa.

"Or you, Sally?" Sally Lempa has two brothers in the Army, one, first reported killed, a prisoner of the Japs.

The vote to call off the strike was unanimous.

AUG. 23 **JOHN TAKES A TRIP:** Down the U.S. highway from Chicago moved a big Cadillac, bearing within it a big, black-browed majestic man. The car pulled into Decatur, Ill., stopped. Newsmen crowded around. What was John L. Lewis doing in this neck of the woods? And where had he got the gasoline?

John Lewis brushed aside all questions: nothing at all—

just going to Springfield—"for my annual visit with my mother." (Anna Louisa Lewis is 84.) This quote got into the
papers. Decatur residents, remembering that John L.
Lewis lived 750 miles away in Alexandria, Va., put in outraged
calls to their ration board. One complaint came from a citizen who had failed to get enough gas to visit his ailing
mother, who later died.

"THE ONE WITH THE DOUGH": The pudgy face of James Caesar   OCT. 11
Petrillo was wreathed in smiles. The boss of A.F of L. Musicians' Union strode through his big Manhattan office, sat
down to thumb happily through a neat nine-page contract.
His guests—officers of the nation's record companies—were
glum.

Boss Petrillo handed out copies of the contract, containing
the terms under which his 138,000 members will condescend
to make their first records for the U.S. public since August
1942. Representatives of Decca (half of all U.S. records)
meekly signed. Petrillo chuckled. A newsman asked which
paragraph of the contract he liked best. Said he, always ex-
plicit: "The one with the dough."

Thus Boss Petrillo won complete victory in the boycott
he has enforced against new recordings—despite an anti-
trust suit and a Senate investigation—for 14 months. The
"dough" was royalties ranging from $\frac{1}{4}$ ¢ to 5¢, a tribute
which Decca will pay into the union treasury for every record it sells. If all record companies sign, the union will
receive about $500,000 a year, perhaps as much as $3,000,000
a year when the wartime shellac shortage ends.

The money will go into a fund to pay unemployed musicians union rates for giving free concerts. Like all union
affairs, it will be administered exclusively by Mr. Petrillo—
who also now has the right to examine Decca's books to
make sure he is not being gypped. Thus Petrillo gains the
greatest power over management ever reached by a U.S.
union leader.

HOW TO BE A RACKETEER: Eight stony-faced men sat in Man-   OCT. 18
hattan's Federal Court last week and heard a veteran
blackmailer call them blackmailers. The Government had
charged that the eight men (seven ex-Capone hoodlums and

one Newark labor official) had shaken down the movie industry for $1 million. The Government's star witness: Shakedown Expert Willie Bioff, who was let out of jail to sing on his ex-chums. Dapper, wily Willie, nothing loath, sat calmly in a swivel-chair, hands clasped meditatively over his stomach —and sang.

Said Blackmailer Bioff: yes, he knew the defendants well. Seven of them were "The Syndicate" that had helped him filch at least $1 million in union dues, and blackmail the czars of Hollywood on a Hollywood scale. Staring coldly back at Willie Bioff's fat, pointing finger was an all-star police line-up: Gunman Paul ("The Waiter") de Lucia; pistol-packing ex-Capone Muscleman Phil D'Andrea; Beer-war Veteran Charles ("Cherry-Nose Joy") Gioe; Machine-gun Expert Louis ("The Man to See") Compagna; Frank ("The Immune") Maritote, alias Frankie Diamond; 14-time indicted Ralph Pierce; John Rosselli and Newark's Louis Kaufman.

For three days Willie Bioff prattled away about the troubles and triumphs of the shakedown industry. He told the Court how he worked a big Hollywood deal: "I told Nicholas Schenck [president of Loew's Inc.] to get together with other producers and get a couple of millions together. Schenck threw up his hands in the air and raved. I told him if he didn't get the others together we would close every theater in the country." The major studios eventually settled for $50,000 a year, the minor studios for $25,000 for the privilege of doing business. [Bioff, who had been convicted of extortion in 1941 and had served three years of a ten-year sentence for his part in the racket, was released from prison in 1944 as a result of giving testimony against the new defendants. Seven of the eight defendants were convicted; Ralph Pierce was not.]

NOV. 15 **END OF A BATTLE:** John Lewis, greatest labor tactician in U.S. history, captured his own Kiev last week. In the eight-month battle for higher wages he had campaigned like a Red general, scornful of the cost, his eyes fixed on the final objective. He began with a war of nerves, attacking with a demand for $2 a day more for every miner. He followed up with one strike threat after another—at a time when the U.S. considered a coal strike unthinkable. Three times, by strikes, his forces streamed through the suburbs and stormed the city's gates. Three times he was repulsed.

John L. had two opponents: the U.S. Government and the mine operators. Shrewdly he outflanked the operators, isolated the Illinois divisions, forced them to sign. Meanwhile he split the Administration forces, holding his fire from Fuel Boss Harold Ickes, but attacking the War Labor Board head on.

In the final battle last week, Lewis won from Harold Ickes a contract giving the miners an extra $1.50 a day for overtime, plus portal-to-portal travel time. This, together with an added 25¢ a day granted by WLB during an earlier delaying action, actually gave John L. more than he had asked for. He had demanded a weekly wage of $57.50; under the new and complicated contract, a miner working a full week will get a minimum of $58.87. John L. Lewis purred that it was a "satisfactory agreement."

John L. won his final victory by agreeing to cut the miners' lunch period from 30 to 15 minutes. Said a Washington gagster: "John Lewis signed a contract, and his miners lost their lunch." Cracked Scripps-Howard labor reporter Fred Perkins: "Meanwhile, Mr. Lewis may be found lunching daily in the Carlton Hotel, where it takes 15 minutes just to look at the menu."

Politics

GENE'S EXIT: Gallus-snapping Gene Talmadge was a bitter, JAN. 25 unhappy man last week as he turned over the Governorship of Georgia to stocky, ambitious Ellis Gibbs Arnall. With his coat collar turned up, his owl eyes staring straight ahead, he sat glumly on the platform throughout Arnall's inauguration; when the ceremonies were over he refused to shake hands, stomped off to his home in the hardwood swamps of Telfair County.

Ever since hustling Ellis Arnall trounced him in the Democratic primaries last September, vindictive Gene Talmadge has tried to embarrass his successor. With the near-dictatorial powers he had wangled from a supine Legislature, he arbitrarily raised schoolteachers' salaries 25% (added cost: $3,-500,000 annually). In a further attempt to gut the State Treasury he put 40,000 additional old-age pensioners on the rolls (cost: $1,600,000 annually); only a taxpayer's injunction suit stopped him from buying $1,600,000 of unneeded textbooks.

His last week in office capped the climax. When a guard at the State Prison at Tattnall testified that he had regularly delivered ham, eggs and chickens to Gene's home, Gene was unperturbed. Said he: "Sure I got the eggs and the chickens and I ate them. I'd advise the next Governor to try the same plan. It helps to keep expenses down."

Gene had one final job to do, and it was one he relished. While criminal lawyers jammed his office, he turned prisoners out of jail at the rate of 35 a day. The night before his retirement he proudly announced his achievement: in two years as Governor he had freed 2,941 convicts. Said Talmadge, with an eye on future elections: "I am sorry it couldn't have been more."

MARCH 1 **TERM IV & JIM FARLEY:** "President Roosevelt must run for a fourth term. As a matter of fact, the fourth term should not be an issue. The issue should, and I believe will, be: Is the President the best qualified man to do the job?"

Thus spoke Illinois' stanchly New Deal Representative Adolph J. Sabath last week. There had long been signs and portents that a Fourth Term movement was in the works: here was the first acknowledgment from a 100% New Dealer.

The line that Congressman Sabath was taking was too similar to that which preceded Term III to be overlooked. But if Franklin Roosevelt runs again, his opposition will be stronger than in 1940. One who has been laboring for months to block any attempt at Term IV is the man who twice put F.D.R. in the White House—James Aloysius Farley. Last week Jim Farley, who was once Roosevelt's Postmaster General and is now both New York State Democratic Chairman and board chairman of Coca-Cola Export Corp., returned to Manhattan from a five-week "business trip." But along the way Jim Farley had a lot of talks with Southern Democratic politicians—John Nance Garner, Georgia's Governor Ellis Arnall—which were not about Coca-Cola.

Jim Farley was mum about his trip. But along the way he had dropped some significant remarks. To the Texas Legislature: "I sincerely hope and trust by the time another Presidential election rolls around we'll have this war behind us so we will be able to decide the Presidency on domestic issues." To newsmen in Dallas: "I hope the voters pick the Democrats in 1944 but if they don't, it's all right with me."

BAEDEKER FOR THE FUTURE: Wendell Willkie saw his trip APRIL 12 last year to the Middle East and Asia as a trip into the future. This week, in a book-length report called *One World*, he sets forth the guideposts he found.

The one great signpost which Willkie saw required courage to follow. Says he:

"Freedom is an indivisible word. If we want to enjoy it, and fight for it, we must be prepared to extend it to everyone, whether they are rich or poor, whether they agree with us or not, no matter what their race or the color of their skin.

"America must choose one of three courses after this war: narrow nationalism, which inevitably means the ultimate loss of our own liberty; international imperialism, which means the sacrifice of some other nation's liberty; or the creation of a world in which there shall be an equality of opportunity for every race and every nation.

"Three things seem to me necessary—first, we must plan now for peace on a world basis; second, the world must be free, politically and economically, for nations and for men, that peace may exist in it; third, America must play an active, constructive part in freeing it and keeping its peace."

FOREGONE: Term IV talk was past the news stage; it was MAY 3 now a foregone conclusion that Franklin Roosevelt was going to run. The hot news upcoming was the next Democratic Vice-Presidential candidate. One thing seemed fairly sure: just as Franklin Roosevelt had dumped John Nance Garner as a political liability in 1940, so is he likely to dump Henry Agard Wallace in 1944. Practical Democrats took him in 1940 only at Franklin Roosevelt's insistence. Henry Wallace lost his own farm state of Iowa; by 1942 the whole farm belt was solidly Republican.

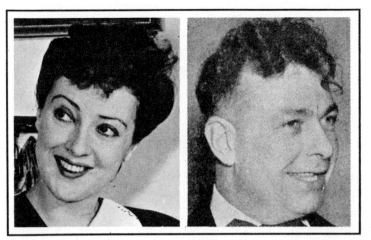

Gypsy Rose Lee. She hasn't kissed a baby in years.

Rep. Everett Dirksen. A tousled lawmaker throws in his hat. Page 53.

The race to be Franklin Roosevelt's running mate was wide open. Jokesters even suggested Stripteuse Gypsy Rose Lee. Said Miss Lee: "I'd like to run, but I haven't kissed a baby in years."

SEPT. 20 **UNFILIAL:** Iowa's stern Democratic Senator Guy M. Gillette addressed himself this week to the subject of Term IV. Said he: "I would oppose a Fourth Term for my own father."

SEPT. 27 **MR. CURLEY, THE FAMED UNDERDOG:** "It's just a political move. I'm being persecuted."

The mellifluous voice was familiar. The 225-lb. body, superbly carried, the pouched eyes, the air of expensive splendor were familiar too. Most familiar of all was the role. Massachusetts' former Governor and present Democratic National Committeeman, Boston's three-time Mayor, Congressman James Michael Curley has again been indicted, is again the underdog.

This time Curley wriggled under the hottest spotlight he has yet faced—indictment by a Federal grand jury. The charge: Curley and five other men used the mails to mulct suckers through a war-contracts racket called Engineers Group, Inc. The company claimed an ability to wangle fat contracts for new clients. Fees as high as $9,000 were accepted. Actually, the Government charges: Engineers Group has no contracts, no legal ability to get contracts.

For scandal-scarred Jim Curley this is indictment No. 3. At the age of 29, while a Boston alderman, Curley was sentenced to 60 days for taking a letter carrier's examination under another man's name. After he had thrice been Mayor of Boston, the State Supreme Court ordered him to pay back to the city treasury, at the rate of $500 a week, $42,629 which he had been found guilty of accepting as graft. But Curley, oozing martyrdom, turned both cases into political assets. Campaigning from jail, he touched many an Irish heart by telling how he perjured himself on the civil service exam in order to get a job for a destitute friend with a wife and four children. On the second occasion, he let Boston know that he was selling the family silver. Promptly the local teamsters union held a giant testimonial dinner to pay off the debts of its great & good friend. Curley, rising to speak his thanks, was overcome by emotion.

Hurrying to Washington to meet the latest indictment, America's most successful underdog missed no cue. Now, after a lifetime of oppression in Massachusetts, he was being crucified in Washington. Explained Curley, his ruddy, liverish face messianic: "I have refused to be a rubber stamp while serving as a member of Congress. Indictments, threats or pressure of any character shall not deter me from doing what in my judgment is best for the American people." [Curley was convicted of using the mails to defraud in 1946, a year after he had been elected mayor of Boston for the fourth time. In 1947 President Truman commuted Curley's 6-18 month sentence to the five months that he had already served. He died in 1958.]

DEADLY EFFICIENT: As man, District Attorney or Governor NOV. 1 of New York, Tom Dewey is calm, neat, painstaking and deadly efficient. For ten months, the former racket-buster has held the most important job of his life. And at his desk in the New York State Capitol at Albany, he is all business. Appointments are arranged at 15-minute intervals. The telephone, hidden inside the desk, seldom rings. The only interruption comes from the flies sucked in occasionally by the air-conditioning system. Dewey extracts a rubber swatter from his desk drawer, waits, pounces as if he were swooping down mercilessly on another New York gangster. He rarely misses.

DEC. 13 **PRIDE OF PEKIN:** The U.S. got another GOPresidential candidate last week—a man who has little chance for the Republican nomination, and knows it. But he had a good reason for his candidacy. The man was Everett McKinley Dirksen, 47, a big, tousled farm-minded Representative from Pekin, Ill. The Pride of Pekin told the Washington press that 36 fellow Congressmen from 13 states had signed a petition urging him to try for the Republican Presidential nomination. He insisted that he was a serious candidate.

DEC. 20 **CLEAR TRACK:** Senator Arthur Vandenberg, of Michigan, main booster of General Douglas MacArthur for the GO-Presidential nomination, last week wangled from the Army and Navy a special statement that no regulation forbids an officer's being elected to public office. This also cleared the track for Minnesota's Republican Lieut. Commander Harold Stassen. [The Republican candidate in 1944 was Thomas E. Dewey, who lost to Franklin D. Roosevelt by three million votes.]

Races

JUNE 28 **DYNAMITE IN DETROIT:** On Detroit's lush, leafy Belle Isle, thousands of Negroes and whites nervously held their Sunday picnics under the trees. They had reason for nerves: rumors of race trouble poisoned the June air. As the sweltering thousands jammed the bridge to the mainland on the way home, they were ripe for explosion.

A sudden fist fight touched it off, sent fighting, cursing whites and Negroes battling across the bridge, spilling through the city. Like wildfire, the rioting spread to "Paradise Valley," Detroit's downtown Negro section, washed over Woodward Avenue, Detroit's main street. Gangs of whites and Negroes roved the streets, smashing windows, tipping cars, looting stores, seizing guns and ammunition in pawnshops. Courageously Negro leaders toured the Valley in sound cars. But their pleas for peace were drowned by jeers. Thirteen elementary schools were closed. Many a decent citizen stayed at home, afraid to go outside.

Governor Harry F. Kelly called out 1,000 state troops, rushed in 500 state police, asked Fort Custer for 1,000 military police, and decreed a "state of emergency." Under the decree, all bars and restaurants were shut, a 10 p.m. curfew established. Still the rioting continued. Finally, after a proclamation by Franklin Roosevelt ordering the rioters to disperse, Federal troops marched in, cleared the streets.

After 24 nightmarish hours, Detroit was quieted down, counted the toll of one of the worst riots in modern U.S. history: at least 23 dead, over 700 injured, over 600 jailed. Of the dead Negroes, police had shot as least eight. By next day the city was searching for the real roots of the trouble. Detroit had been warned only two weeks ago that the Ku Klux Klan was fomenting trouble. Nearly a year ago LIFE had warned: "Detroit is Dynamite."

THE TAUT STRING: In too many U.S. communities this week, AUG. 9 whites and blacks tiptoed stiff-legged around one another, watching, waiting and a little afraid. The ugliest strand of the U.S. fabric had tightened under wartime pressure. In New York City's Harlem, a white policeman arrested a Negro woman for disorderly conduct. A Negro soldier, on leave, tried to stop him. Both went to the hospital, the policeman with a battered head, the soldier with a pistol wound in the shoulder. The story, much garbled, spread quickly through Harlem. Twenty-four hours later six Negro rioters were dead, 543 rioters and police injured; a curfew was clamped on Harlem.

WORLD BATTLEFRONTS

Battle of Africa

It was in North Africa that American soldiers engaged in their first World War II combat against German troops. After landing in Morocco and Algeria late in 1942, the Americans moved on into Tunisia to join with General Bernard Montgomery's British forces in an all-out effort to crush German Field Marshal Erwin Rommel's Afrika Korps.

FEB. 1 **THE LONG ROAD:** The Road is a ribbon along the fair, azure sea. It wanders past graves inscribed "This is hallowed ground. They died in the service of their country." It streaks, hot and straight, for miles across the desert sands. At the Road's end last week stood a wiry man with pale, piercing eyes, hawk's nose and cadaverous cheeks. General Sir Bernard Law Montgomery had traversed half the continent of Africa, leading a victorious army on the heels of a beaten one. To his troops he had proclaimed: "Nothing has stopped us. Nothing will." This week he was in Tripoli and driving on.

The long trek had started at El Alamein. Now, after eight days of fierce fighting against rear-guard troops left behind by Nazi Field Marshal Erwin Rommel, the British had persevered and Tripoli fell in flames and smoke. Montgomery had shattered the last vestige of Italy's African Empire. He had opened up a new base for Allied ground and air forces from which the Axis' slipping grip on North Africa could be pounded and attacked. He had ended the longest chase in military history—1,300 miles in 13 weeks.

It was on a sweltering summer's day, some five months ago, that Bernard Law Montgomery had walked into Cairo's crowded Shepheard's Hotel. Few people noticed the man who had come from England to boss the demoralized Eighth Army. Outside military circles, the scrawny, gimlet-eyed little man was unknown. Montgomery did not stay long at Shepheard's. At 5 o'clock in the morning the day after his arrival, he rode into the desert with a young cavalry aide. Weeks went by while he mercilessly pounded his army into shape. Supplies poured in to the Eighth. Montgomery attacked.

Montgomery made sure that every man down to the last blue-eyed boy private understood his intentions. In his Order of the Day he declared: "When I assumed command of the Eighth Army I said that the mandate was to destroy Rommel and his army, and that it would be done as soon as we were ready. We are ready now. The battle which is now about to begin will be one of the decisive battles of history. It will be the turning point of the war."

An hour before the Eighth let loose its first shattering artillery barrage, the General went to bed. He read his Bible, as was his custom, and slept. At 1:30 a.m. an aide awoke him to make a report. Montgomery listened, issued some orders and went back to sleep. He rose at his customary hour of 6, while the British barrage was splitting open the sky.

Twelve days later newsmen met Montgomery in his desert headquarters. He sat through the interview with a fly whisk balanced steadily on one finger. "I have defeated the enemy. I am now about to smash him," he asserted flatly, relaxed and asked: "How do you like my hat?" Then, wearing a tank corps beret which he had picked up, he climbed into a tank and rumbled off after his troops like a skinny avenging angel.

WORST DEFEAT: U.S. soldiers clung like goats to the rocky Tunisian hillside, dug into shallow holes, anxiously watched the German positions on the opposite ridge. From the German rear, 88-mm. guns coughed. A lieutenant on the rocky ridge pulled a U.S. infantryman down, saying curtly: "A man lying down looks like a rock. A man standing up looks like a man."

Early Sunday morning, hours before daybreak, General Dwight Eisenhower rode up in a Jeep to inspect the Allied positions. The whole situation was precarious. Eisenhower had been maintaining this mountainous front largely by bluff. Even now the fresh, inexperienced U.S. troops under General

Lloyd Fredendall were inadequate for any real defense. Fredendall knew that he was holding the bag. Eisenhower rode off to inspect the next point in the U.S. positions.

Three and a half hours later the Germans called his bluff. A canopy of screeching *Stukas* shook U.S. soldiers, experiencing dive-bombing for the first time. Thirty German tanks poured out of Faïd Pass, overran the positions of green U.S. artillerymen, who sometimes scarcely had time to fire one round.

In the end U.S. forces had to abandon Gafsa, swinging their whole line north and westward to escape annihilation. Great columns of smoke rose over abandoned and burning munition dumps. In the valleys of olive groves lay more than 100 wrecked U.S. tanks, numbers of Jeeps, motor transports, huge quantities of ammunition. Valiant Allied air support kept the retreat from turning into a rout. But when weary U.S. troops tried to hold Kasserine Pass, the cocky Germans kept jabbing at them.

Despite a storm of U.S. artillery fire, the Germans seized the pass, swept on through. For the first time in this war, on a battlefield of their own choosing, U.S. troops had been thoroughly defeated.

MARCH 8 **TURNABOUT:** From Kasserine Pass, Major General Lloyd Fredendall's weary young U.S. infantrymen, artillerymen and tankmen had fled across the valley. They abandoned their dead and their equipment along the muddy, bloody roads. They were handicapped by a lack of motor vehicles. Some of them fought blindly in small isolated groups. But there appeared to be no stopping the Germans.

A great opportunist, like all good soldiers, Rommel was ready to exploit any gain. And he was a gambler. If he were lucky and could crack the Allied line, he could pour troops onto the flatland and drive against the flank of the British First Army which sprawled across the top of Tunisia. Then the whole Allied strategy in North Africa would have to be recast. This was the crisis when the weary young men braced themselves and Allied reinforcements rushed up to give them aid.

The story of the next few days was the story of a desperate Allied stand. British artillery and lumbering new

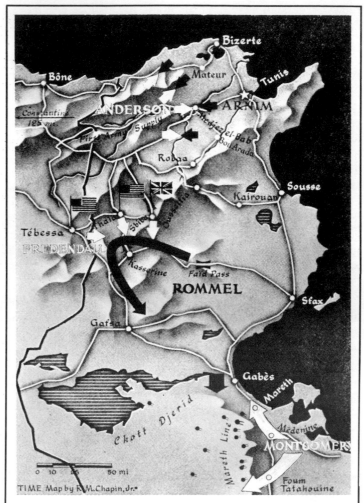

This map from the March 8 issue of TIME *shows the area of Africa, some 230 miles wide and 350 miles long, in which U.S. and British forces eventually trapped the Afrika Korps. Less than five months after breaking out at El Alamein (off the map) some 1,500 miles away, General Bernard Law Montgomery is about to crash through the Mareth Line with his British 8th Army. Meanwhile, other Allied units have begun consolidating their positions in French North Africa and Tunisia. U.S. troops under General Lloyd Fredendall have suffered a serious defeat at the Kasserine Pass, but they will soon rally under the command of General George S. Patton. The Tunisian port city of Bizerte will fall to the Allies in May, and the last elements of the Axis forces in Africa will be wiped out.*

Churchill tanks rolled up. U.S. cannon and armor, supported by strong air units operating in dubious flying weather, pounded and slashed at the German onrush. Then, as suddenly as they had started their drive ten days before, the Germans turned tail and withdrew. Rommel's troops had become exhausted, overextended and overtaxed. And perhaps there was another explanation for the turnabout: Fredendall's young men had learned their lessons fast. Said Eisenhower of the U.S. troops: "All complacency has now been dropped."

Rommel left Italians to fight a rear-guard action, pulled his precious *Panzer* troops south along the roads over which Fredendall's U.S. troops had beat a hasty retreat northward only two weeks before. At week's end the Axis was still in flight.

MARCH 22 **GRAVEYARD OF PANZERS:** In the fine, slanting rain of an early Tunisian morning General Erwin Rommel sent his tanks charging south toward the little town of Médinine, which the Eighth Army had occupied. From the foothills, Rommel's cannon laid down a barrage to cover the advance.

In a dried-up river gulch yellow-haired Sergeant Ivor Andrews watched 17 German tanks file up a slope, let the first four go by toward another gun crew, knocked out the next three. When TIME Correspondent Jack Belden visited the battlefield after it was all over, he counted 52 German tanks left on the arid, rock-strewn plain. Turrets were torn off, fronts were blown in. They were casualties of Rommel's most earnest attempt to hit back at the British Eighth Army since the Eighth had chased him out of Egypt. [Although the Allies were not aware of it for some time, after this battle Rommel went home to Germany because of ill health and never returned to his *Afrika Korps.*]

MARCH 29 **"THE LIONS TREMBLE":** Major General George Smith ("Old Blood and Guts") Patton Jr. became a lieutenant general a fortnight ago. Last week he took command of the central sector in Tunisia, where U.S. troops got an ignominious licking a month ago, and celebrated his appointment by advancing. Patton replaced 59-year-old Major General Lloyd R. Fredendall, an infantryman and tactician who may have been the unluckiest general in the North African campaign. He had said at the time, "I am holding the bag," and he was.

George Patton's favorite motto (expurgated) is "Grab 'em by the nose and kick 'em in the tail." In 1916 he was a dashing, cocky young cavalryman and aide to "Black Jack" Pershing in Mexico. When he went to France in World War I he organized the first U.S. tank brigade, returned to study that new wrinkle in modern warfare, and to help develop it for the U.S. Army.

In 1942, Patton snorted off to California to organize the Desert Training Center. In the 120° heat he whipped a desert fighting force into shape. Most of the men he trained followed him overseas. He was assigned to seize Casablanca, which he did after four rip-roaring days. At the end he strode into French headquarters with a pair of pearl-handled .45-caliber pistols strapped to his legs and a tommy gun under one arm. So impressed was the Sultan of Morocco that he presented Patton with the special order of Ouissam Alaouite, with the citation: "*Les Lions dans leurs tanières tremblent en le voyant approcher*" ("The lions in their dens tremble at his approach").

"Soldiers," says Patton, "fight primarily for two reasons: hero worship for a commanding officer and the desire for glory." He used to inspire his men with four-letter oratory

General Montgomery. "Nothing has stopped us. Nothing will." Page 55.   *General Patton. "Grab 'em by the nose and kick 'em in the tail."*

and assurances that he, Georgie Patton, would know what to do when he got those German so-&-sos in his gunsights. General Patton now has the Germans at gun point.

APRIL 5 **IN THE DUST OF THE KHAMSIN:** The khamsin, the hot African wind, filled the air with the sands of the Sahara. Through the thick of it roared General Montgomery's planes. The mountains thundered and echoed with his artillery barrage. His infantrymen, like the point of a crowbar, jabbed into Rommel's suddenly faltering defenses. Montgomery's armor poured through, levering the crack until it was a wide and shattered hole. The Mareth Line, southern bulwark of the whole Axis position in Tunisia, collapsed.

APRIL 12 **AT HEADQUARTERS:** The General was restless. George Smith Patton Jr., who had long ago boasted that nothing would please him so much as to get in a tank and joust, medievally and to the death, with a single tank commanded by Erwin Rommel, was now confined to a single room behind the lines by his lord and master, battle. The room was on the second floor of his headquarters. The General paced it, went out on the balcony, peered up and down the street, went back in, sat down, crossed his legs, uncrossed them, rubbed his big hands over his face, yawned (he had been up since 5:30), stood up, paced again.

He was no longer a man approaching battle. Now he was a man running a battle, the very battle he had wanted for years—against Rommel. Now he must forsake his reputation for impetuousness, and be careful; this was a battle that would not tolerate error. At one moment Patton, who is said to be a pretty tough fellow, told about the death of 27-year-old Captain Richard Jenson, who had been his aide for three years. "Captain Jenson," he said, "had volunteered to go to the front as an additional officer in our tank force on the Gabès Road. When *Stukas* came over this morning he was standing only a few feet from one of our generals. Both dived into slit trenches. A heavy bomb landed almost at the edge of the one in which Jenson lay. He was killed instantly. . . ."

The general's voice broke. His eyes overflowed. He pulled out a handkerchief. "I'm acting like an old fool," he said.

TO THE TROOPS: Monty sat down and wrote to his men: APRIL 19
"I doubt if our empire has ever possessed such a magnificent fighting machine as the Eighth Army; you made its name a household word all over the world. Let us make the enemy face up to and endure a first-class Dunkirk on the beaches of Tunis. The triumphant cry now is: Forward to Tunis! Drive the enemy into the sea."

THE STORMING OF TAKROUNA: Ahead, across 1,500 yards of MAY 3 moon-bright plain, lay the hill called Takrouna. Men differed in describing Takrouna. Some of the British Highlanders, staring at it through the moon-sifting mist, said that it looked like Edinburgh Castle. Other men said it looked like terrain on the moon. The height was held by some of the best Axis troops, for Takrouna was the beginning of the last natural wall before Tunis. For 90 minutes, beginning at 9 p.m. the Eighth's guns winked at the enemy. Then infantry crept forward and began the awful climb.

"I have never known anything like it," said a young officer who was there. "The Germans came yelling like demons. Grenades seemed to be exploding everywhere. It was raining heavily and all over the place bombs were bursting in the rain. We slipped and rolled in the mud. Some of our lads are expert wrestlers. They lopped down dozens of the enemy with machetes. Then we would dive on them and crash to the ground, arms locked, trying to find their throats or get our knives working. In the occasional flash of grenades you could see our boys whirling the bodies of Germans over their heads and flinging them over the cliffs on to the rocks below."

Takrouna was taken. The Eighth Army moved on toward Tunis.

THREE STARS, TWO FRAGMENTS: Lieut. General Lesley J. McNair, in charge of training all U.S. ground forces, went on a tour of command posts in Africa last week to get a feel of war. As he stood on a hill watching troops move forward, a shell exploded close by. A four-inch fragment tore across his left shoulder and smashed the tip of his collar bone. A splinter about an inch and a half long pierced his helmet and came to rest against the base of his skull. The

General walked to a Jeep, rode three hours to a hospital, was operated on, said: "I'll be back there soon. I'm looking for my clothes now." But his doctors thought that the first U.S. lieutenant general to be injured in World War II would be out of action for several weeks. [General McNair was killed in Normandy in 1944 when a U.S. bomb accidentally hit his observation post.]

MAY 10 **IN PASSING:** In a Tunisian town, American soldiers who could speak Italian heckled a batch of Italian prisoners. Finally, one Italian could contain himself no longer. "All right, laugh," he said, "but we're going to America. You're only going to Italy."

MAY 17 **HOW IT WAS DONE:** A German staff officer, wearing the Iron Cross around his neck, stepped to the tent of a U.S. general at 9:50 a.m. on Sunday, May 9, 1943 near Bizerte and said: "What are your terms for surrender?"

"Tell him," the general said to his interpreter, "my terms are unconditional surrender and no attempt at evacuation by sea. We will kill all who try to get out."

The emissary and a U.S. colonel carried the terms to the headquarters of Major General Fritz Krause, commander of the sector. General Krause accepted the terms, got in the colonel's Jeep. On the way back to U.S. headquarters, the colonel saw Germans setting fire to their trucks. He told General Krause to order them to stop. The general did. One of the Germans snapped: "Why should we give the damn Americans all this equipment?" General Krause pointed at the U.S. colonel in the back seat. The German grew confused, ordered his men to stop firing their trucks.

At German headquarters another Nazi major general broke into tears. "I am a general without a command," he said. "I have seen my division split in two and my *Panzers* wiped out. I have no *Panzers,* no artillery, not even a grenadier."

Thus, suddenly, breathtakingly, the battle of Tunisia was decided. It was U.S. infantry, supported by superb artillery fire, which unbuttoned the first button along the front—a tough position known as Hill 609. The men hit this hill with courage and craft, and took it. Executor of the breakthrough was Major General Omar N. Bradley, a top-notch infantry soldier. Tall, wiry and grey, General Bradley is as tough as his hardest top-kick. But probably the greatest factor of all in the victory was the unity of all arms, of all nations, of all commanders, of all units participating on the Allied side. This unity was largely the handiwork of General Dwight D. Eisenhower.

Battle of Italy

With the end of Axis resistance in North Africa, the next Allied move was an invasion of Sicily, which preceded the assault against Italy itself. The Sicilian campaign was relatively quick and easy, and so were the first landings in Italy, during which the Italian government surrendered to the Allies. The German units occupying Italy, however, decided to fight it out, and when the main Allied landing was made later at Salerno, some 200 miles up the coast from the initial invasion, it met fanatical resistance.

SEVEN LUCKY COINS: The assault on Sicily had begun. Two JULY 19 thousand warships, transports and landing boats churned the dark waters of the ancient sea. Planes roared off to the north, loaded with paratroops or towing gliders packed with infantrymen. General Dwight D. Eisenhower, Allied commander in North Africa, had set in motion the largest amphibious military operation ever attempted. Now he had to live with the bleak inner loneliness that comes to a commander when he must wait for the fall of the dice, wondering what will go wrong, how well reality will fit the shape of plans. But Ike Eisenhower stood the ordeal so well that excited Correspondent John Gunther compared him to "a perfectly confident and unworried father awaiting the birth of a healthy baby." Like an expectant father, the general was up most of the night. Later he got three hours of sound sleep on a cot, awoke at 4:30 a.m. to have tea with the Royal Navy men and hear the news: landing operations were going according to plan. Then the general went back

This map from the June 21 issue of TIME *shows Allied bombs falling on Sicily and Italy in preparation for the invasion of Italy that September. The smaller Italian islands of Pantelleria and Lampedusa have already been knocked out of the war, and the bombing of Italy is being carried out not only from the British stronghold of Malta but also from former Axis bases at Tunis and Bizerte. Allied troops will land on Sicily in July and then move on, across the Straits of Messina, to the toe of Italy itself.*

to his quarters for a fresh uniform. His only propitiatory gesture to the gods of war had been a judicious rubbing of his seven pocket pieces—a collection of old coins which includes a cartwheel silver dollar, a British five-guinea piece and a French franc.

HOW THE INVASION BEGAN: The first U.S. troops to set foot JULY 19 on Axis Europe were paratroops. Their high half-boots hit the enemy soil early in the moonlit night of July 9, 1943— hours before Allied landing barges disgorged infantry, tanks and artillery on Sicily's shore. In one of the planes was Photographer Robert Capa, who took pictures and later described the flight:

"Soon they were bumping through rough air over the Mediterranean. Some of the men got sick. The men knew that they, a handful only, must plant a cancer amidst the enemy and make it grow. They knew this even before the colonel spoke: 'Well, boys, we are truly the first men of America tonight. We will be the first to land in Axis Europe. There will be enemies all around us and over our heads. We must do our best.'

"The flak was some, not so much," said Photographer Capa. "The formation came over its objective. Inside the plane the red light winked on. Now the men rose quickly, hooked up their release lines. Each man bulged with 100 pounds of gear—tommy gun, pistol, grenades, rations, cigarets, medical equipment, knife-bayonet. Over the side they could see the flat, rocky terrain of Sicily and islands of fire— the fierce circles of flame left by Allied aerial barrages."

Bob Capa saw the chutes float down "like strings of diminishing pearls" in the moonlight and flarelight. That was how the invasion began.

BOMBERS OVER ROME: The summer sun, climbing toward JULY 26 warm noon, had started the heat waves dancing from the seven ancient hills, from the dusty brick and weathered marble of the Colosseum and the Forum. Now out of that sun came the sound and the sight Rome had long been spared: the drone, the wings of hostile bombers.

Perhaps three million stunned people, jampacked in a city that normally houses about 1,000,000, scanned the sky or scurried to the shelters they had hoped never to use. At 11:13 a.m. the first bomb bay opened. Chief target was the immense railroad marshaling yard about four miles from St. Peter's. Before the last bomb had fallen in the first raid on the Eternal City, the Allies broadcast the news. The world— particularly the Catholic world inside and outside the

Axis fortress—was told how Allied airmen had carefully trained for this mission, how they studied huge maps, absorbed repeated instructions, took unusual risks in daylight, all to avoid as far as possible the damaging of religious and cultural buildings. Many of the airmen—as many as possible —were Catholics and aboard their planes were seven correspondents to vouch for the meticulous care with which the bombs were aimed.

AUG. 30 **WINDUP IN SICILY:** Cautiously, under a butter-colored moon, U.S. 3rd Division patrols reconnoitered the last eight miles to Messina. The stony Sicilian landscape flashed now & then with snipers' fire. The road was edged with the menace of mines, booby traps and demolition chasms. But clearly the stubborn, skillful, beaten enemy had pulled out. At 5:30 a.m., Aug. 17, Lieutenants Jeff McNeely and Ralph Yates led patrols into Messina. The Battle of Sicily, 38 days after it had begun, was over.

Then in a little vineyard hidden from German eyes across the Messina Strait, a U.S. battery commander brought up one of the 155-mm. rifles that the Allies have dubbed "Long Tom." A truck hauled the heavy gun into position. The crew wrote their names on the first shell. A red-haired Tennessee private was about to yank the lanyard when the colonel came up and said: "Do you mind, son?" The private answered: "That's all right, sir." The colonel yanked. Seconds later the shell crashed into the San Giovanni rail and ferry terminal.

It was the first artillery shot fired on Italy, some two miles across the strait.

SEPT. 13 **"AS ONE NATION":** General Eisenhower went to Messina last week and decorated the commander of one of the five U.S., British and French armies now serving under him. That commander was General Sir Bernard Law Montgomery. On Sept. 2, Montgomery had gone to bed at his usual time, 10 p.m., having already issued an order to his troops:

"The time has now come to carry the battle on to the mainland of Italy. To the Eighth Army has been given the great honor of being the first troops of the Allied armies to land on the mainland of the Continent of Europe. We have a good plan, and air support on a greater scale than we have ever had before. Forward to victory. Good luck, and God bless you all."

That night Monty's troops moved to their landing boats and toward the near shore of Italy. The night was clear and starry. There was little resistance. Italian defenders in pillboxes fired several rounds, then came out with their hands in the air. The Germans had left three days before.

As the battle began, Eisenhower was back in his Allied Headquarters in North Africa, following its progress and planning the next move. His headquarters is fantastically enormous. Attached to it are some 1,100 officers and 15,000 enlisted men to work its communications, cook its meals, drive its cars, guard its billets and offices on more than 2,000 pieces of Algiers real estate. Its signals center handles 1,000 code messages a day.

Literally atop this maze, in the hilltop St. George Hotel, Eisenhower spends most of his working days. In off hours, he lives in a pleasant Algiers villa with three companions: his devoted "dog robber" (orderly), Sergeant "Micky" McKeogh; a Scottish terrier named Telek; his principal aide, Navy Commander Harold Butcher, a friend from Washington days who used to be a broadcasting-company executive. To his little-known, unbloodied workers, the Staff Officers, Eisenhower recently said: "The job is a hard and a thankless one. You will not go down in the pages of history. But we have shown and will continue to show the world one thing— that the Allies can fight under one command and as one nation."

THE SHAPE OF HELL: For the men who fought the battles, Salerno was hell. At some points the Germans let the first forces come smoothly ashore and cluster on the white beaches, then blanketed them with artillery fire from the near hills. At others, naval landing craft bore the troops landward in the face of continuous fire. Everywhere the men of Lieut. General Mark Clark's Fifth Army had to make their first moves inland amid shells, bombs, confusion, fear. SEPT. 27

As the Americans marched inland to seize the high ground and try to forestall a German attempt to split the beachhead,

German tanks suddenly appeared on the road ahead of them. Atop a bare ridge, Sergeant Stanton Dobbins and his men got set with rifle grenades. When the tanks were 60 yards away Dobbins cried: "Let 'em have it." The first volley set one tank afire, knocked the treads off another. Other tanks came up, concentrated their fire on the slopes where the Americans lay. Some of the soldiers fled. Three more tanks were hit; the rest turned away.

German artillery raked the battalion the rest of the day. A shell from a German 88 hit a company commander point-blank, hurled his body 60 feet. But the men clung to the hills, awaiting reinforcements. The help did not come; the regiment was trapped. By dusk two battalions with their artillery had been completely cut off, and another was in danger. Their 105-mm. guns were turned around, faced the way the regiment had marched the night before. Only 15 rounds remained for each gun, and they were silent.

For reasons unknown, the Germans did not attack that night. Next morning artillery thundered in the distance, an American relief column appeared under German fire, and the 105s spat their hoarded ammunition. Cabled TIME Correspondent Will Lang:

"The regiment had been sleepless for two nights. Now it had only a deep and bitter hatred. There is still fierce fighting for this bridgehead, but this regiment will now avenge its dead."

The dead were avenged. At the height of the German threat, Allied warships shelled the Nazi positions and Allied air forces threw in hundreds of planes. The German spearhead was stopped within three miles of the sea and thrown back. On the eleventh day a reporter flying over the lines saw columns of Germans retreating inland.

OCT. 11 **"VEDI NAPOLI":** It was a white city on a blue gulf. Beside it rose Vesuvius, breathing a plume of smoke. Cicero had loafed among the villas. It was a pile of palaces, churches, an opera house, university, museum, an aquarium where famous pale octopuses swam in tanks. Its citizens had a proverb: *"Vedi Napoli e poi Muori."* ("See Naples and die.") But last week, ravaged and gutted, Naples was dead.

Allied shells and bombs had wrecked the waterfront. The

retreating Germans had done the rest. They had destroyed warehouses and dock installations, had stripped the steel works, the glass, wool, linen, silk, even macaroni factories of their machinery and left the buildings charred and gutted. With Nazi ruthlessness the retreating army had wrecked the waterworks.

Gaunt, thirsty women & children roamed the streets looking for water, in desperation dipped into sewers. Out of sheer spite against the ally who had deserted him, the Germans even destroyed his palaces and his public buildings. The aquarium was wrecked and the famous octopuses thrown in the street.

MONTY'S BREECHES: Chilled by Italy's rains, the Eighth Army's DEC. 27 General Sir Bernard Montgomery last week asked London for water-proofed pants and jacket.

The package was made up, sent. Its custodian: the Bishop of Southwark (pronounced suth'erk), who was beginning an inspection tour of military stations. Ahead went a message to "Monty" from the Imperial General Staff:

> *We've dispatched pour La Guerre,*
> *A mackintosh pair*
> *Of trousers and jacket, express;*
> *They are coming by air,*
> *And are sent to you care*
> *Of the Bishop of Southwark, no less.*
>
> *According to Moss,*
> *The outfitting Bros.,*
> *'Twon't matter, so stout is their fibre,*
> *If you happen to trip*
> *And go arse over tip,*
> *Like Horatius into the Tiber.*
>
> *And you'll find, so we hope,*
> *When you call on the Pope,*
> *That his blessing's more readily given,*
> *On learning the news,*
> *That your mackintosh trews*
> *Were brought down by a Bishop from Heaven.*

Battle in the Air

During 1943 the long-awaited buildup of large-scale bomber and fighter forces in England was accomplished, and for the first time really heavy air attacks were launched against German cities, and also against Nazi installations in France, in preparation for the invasion that would be made the following year.

FEB. 1 **RETALIATION:***"Wir haben unsere Bomben gerade dorthin geschmissen wo wir sie haben wollten."* ("We dropped our bombs just where we intended to.") Thus Captain Schumann of the *Luftwaffe* described for German radio listeners the daytime air attack on London last week by way of retaliation for the two poundings the R.A.F. had given Berlin. Perhaps Captain Schumann did not know when he made his boast that 42 children (aged six to 16) and six teachers had been killed by a bomb which crashed through the roof of a four-story schoolhouse.

The bomb was dropped at noon, when the students were lunching in the school cafeteria. Ordinarily many of the children would have gone home for their noonday meal, but on this day they had stayed to see a performance of *A Midsummer Night's Dream.*

MARCH 29 **BOMBS AWAY!:** Down in the nose, Jack Mathis was ready. He was a country boy from Texas, slow but sure, not very excitable and yet pretty excited now. This was the biggest daylight raid the Eighth Air Force had ever carried to Hitler. The target, the U-boat works near Bremen, was nearly lined up in the bombsight. Suddenly a burst of flak punched the plane, Jack Mathis was hit in the chest, side and back. The plane shuddered but went right on into the groove. Jack picked himself up, crawled in a widening path of his own blood back to the Norden bombsight, made his final adjustments with his left hand (his right was limp). At the proper moment, he let go.

He tried to say "Bombs away!" All he could get out was "Bombs. . . ." He did not live to see the bombs split the target. He did not live to hear, as the others in the outfit did, of Winston Churchill's calling the raid "a brilliant exploit."

THE NINTH STRIKES OIL: This was the big target. Nearly a AUG. 9 third of the petroleum for the Axis war machine was drawn from Ploesti, Rumania. To attack it properly the Ninth U.S. Air Force, in the Middle East, built up a powerful group of Liberator bombers, its pilots and bombardiers specially trained for low-level bombing. One day this week more than 175 of the bombers took off on the long (2,400 mi.) mission. Droning over Greece and Bulgaria, they crossed the Danube just before 3 in the afternoon and dropped low above the villages and farms of Rumania.

The Germans had strong air defenses. The Liberators shot down at least 51 enemy fighters, lost 20 U.S. planes over the target and eleven more on the return. Over Ploesti's 19 sq. mi. of oil derricks, refineries, storage tanks and cracking plants, the bombers dived within 500 ft. of the ground, and often through flames from the fires. One Liberator was destroyed by a bomb blast. Behind them earth and air trembled, patterns of black smoke blossomed and merged into one massive pall.

Gloated Major General Lewis Brereton, commander of the Ninth: "It is reasonable to suppose that the gallant action has materially affected the course of the war." [This was a famous and dramatic raid, but it was not decisive. U.S. losses totaled 54 bombers, and damage to the oil refineries was slight.]

DEAD CITY: As nearly as any German city has ever been in AUG. 16 this war, Hamburg was dead last week. Its streets were twisting lanes through tumbled wreckage. Cars equipped with loud-speakers called on the population to leave, for Hamburg had no gas, no electricity, no water, little food. In the ruins, on the streets, in the branches of trees where bombs had blown them, lay the dead, their eyes wide open, staring.

Foreign workers returning home to Denmark and Sweden brought descriptions of the Reich's second city, blasted by 10,-000 tons of bombs in seven night raids by the R.A.F., two daylight attacks by U.S. bombers. Dante's Inferno, said one, was incomparable with Hamburg.

DEC. 6 **THE HEART STILL BEATS:** Last week, as never before, the R.A.F. hammered at the bone and spirit of Berlin with five raids in five successive nights. In these five nights, Berlin became the most heavily bombed city in the world, taking three-fifths the tonnage dropped on London in nine months of 1940 and 1941.

Amid the dust of shuddering walls, a woman in labor delivered her child, then shook her fist at the smoky ceiling and gasped: "God damn the English."

All night long, dull explosions continued as time bombs went off or workmen dynamited weakened walls. By morning smoke hung over the town. At week's end Berlin could take stock of the damage: nearly a third of the city lay in ruins. On the Wilhelmstrasse Hitler's residence gaped to the sky, its roof burned. The Foreign Office was burned, Propaganda Minister Paul Joseph Goebbels' house gutted, Foreign Minister Joachim von Ribbentrop's house gone. Gone too was Reich Marshal Hermann Göring's proud, block-like Air Ministry.

In a comparatively undamaged wing of the Foreign Office Von Ribbentrop and his press chief, Dr. Paul Schmidt, held their conferences as usual. The Foreign Minister was grimy-faced; Schmidt had his arm in a sling. Both wore steel helmets pushed down over their heads. Glass crunched underfoot and the wind blew cold through the broken windows. But the city lived on. The Battle of Berlin will continue, said the R.A.F.'s Air Marshal Sir Arthur Travers Harris, "until the heart of Nazi Germany ceases to beat."

Battle of the Atlantic

JAN. 25 **JUMP FEET FIRST:** A newly published British Government pamphlet, called *A Guide to the Preservation of Life at Sea after Shipwreck,* tells in simple, sometimes grim language the personal lessons learned in World Sea War II. Sample lessons:

¶ "If you do not get away in a boat, go over the lower side if the ship has listed. If you go over the upper side you will be in danger of being badly hurt by barnacles."

¶ "If you have to swim through a patch of oil keep your head and eyes high and your mouth closed. If you have to jump into burning oil jump feet first through the flames. Swim as long as you can underwater, then spring above the flames and breathe, taking a breast stroke to push the flames away; then sink and swim under the water again."

¶ "The danger of injury from underwater explosion is lessened by swimming or floating on the back."

BURY THEM AT SEA: Two U.S. passenger-cargo ships, cramfull MARCH 1 of servicemen and civilians on war missions, started eastward across the Atlantic in early February. Somewhere at sea, U-boats, probably using wolf-pack tactics, picked them up, kept snapping at their keels. By night, a torpedo sank one of the ships; four days later, the other was sunk. Each ship went down in less than 30 minutes.

This week Washington, announcing the sinkings, also announced the death toll: more than 850. The horror came home with Signalman Robert Weikart, whose ship was the first to reach the spot where one of the torpedoed vessels went down.

Said Weikart:

"We saw hundreds of bodies in the water and lifeboats full of men swirled about us. It took me a while to figure out why we did not stop to pick any of them up—they were frozen to death at the oars of their lifeboats. I saw the sea dotted with bobbing heads in life jackets. I started counting, but realized there were hundreds so I gave up. We left them there—that's the best thing. All sailors want to be buried at sea anyway."

IN WHICH WE SWERVE: In August 1941, Prime Minister MARCH 15 Churchill visited his namesake vessel, a former U.S. four-stack destroyer, and promised to come aboard again if the H.M.S. *Churchill* ever sank a U-boat. The destroyer's crew did not forget. One night last June, as the *Churchill* patrolled off Venezuela, a dark shape loomed ahead. Men sprang to action stations. The *Churchill* swerved, tried to ram the foe. Luckily, she missed. What looked like a hulking U-boat turned out to be tiny Lasola Island, ten feet high, 200 feet long.

JUNE 7 **"SCRATCH ONE HEARSE!":** At 3 a.m. one morning last month, the raucous bell-and-siren of General Quarters routed officers & men of the U.S. Coast Guard Cutter *Spencer* from their bunks. In the distance a huge Atlantic convoy was silhouetted in a streak of silvery light. Somewhere in the darkness was an enemy submarine. Aboard the *Spencer* was TIME Correspondent William Walton, whose account of what followed was released by the Navy this week:

"The seconds dragging by seemed an age. 'Jesus, why don't we do something?' muttered a gunner's mate. The tension grew.

" 'He's submerging,' whispered a man with headphones.

" 'Son of a bitch,' said the gunner's mate. 'We won't get to fire.'

"Another order from the bridge: 'Stand by K guns! Ready! Fire!'

"The squat little guns on either side of the quarter-deck sent TNT-laden depth charges hurtling into the dark sea. The ship's stern bucked like a blooded stallion. From the sea came a lightning flash and muffled thunder, then the water fountained. It was over for the moment. Results: uncertain.

"At 7 o'clock, in the dazzling morning light, the same pattern of action was repeated. Results: again uncertain; but the enemy was still near.

"At 11 o'clock, it came again. The deck plates rattled as depth charges thundered in the *Spencer*'s wake. The tension was less than during the attack in darkness. Then, without warning, a shout came: 'Submarine breaking water off the port quarter!'

"Then we saw it: a long grey U-boat not more than 600 yards away, deck awash, conning tower, guns and even men plain to the naked eye. It had evidently been hurt by depth charges.

"On the *Spencer,* first into action was the forward 3-in. gun. A splash foamed beyond the submarine. Then big 5-in. guns fore & aft plowed furrows of water near the U-boat. The air reeked of cordite fumes as stocky, gruff Captain Harold Sloop Berdine kept his ship in a course that gave the gunners a maximum chance.

"The sub was dead ahead, so close it could be rammed.

But there was no need to ram when it could be smashed with gunfire. The U-boat's conning tower by now was badly smashed.

But the crippled submarine was still dangerous, and its deck guns were firing. On the *Spencer's* bridge a radioman dropped, clutching his belly. In his eyes was the hurt surprise of a man looking into unexpected death (it came within the hour).

"As the *Spencer* passed beyond the submarine, firing slackened. A patch of water was alive with struggling figures, black dots surrounded by bright orange lifejackets, bobbing and pitching in the waves. The sub's conning tower was dented and broken. Waves washed over her decks. She was done.

"'Cease firing!'" came a hoarse command from the bridge.

"Reluctantly the gun crews halted. Smeared with grease and smoke, they celebrated, forgetting for a moment the days and months of bitter cold.

"To nearby ships went a victory message: 'Scratch one hearse! Scratch one hearse!' (In Navyese, a U-boat is a hearse.) As an afterthought, the message added: 'Pallbearers in the water!'

"From Captain Berdine came an order to pick up survivors. White-knuckled Nazis were clinging to the *Spencer's* ropes. One survivor gasped a weak 'Heil Hitler' and an angry seaman threatened him with an oar. But soon mess stewards were passing hot coffee to Americans and Germans alike.

"Next day six German officers paced the wet, misty quarter-deck while armed guards stood by. The U-boat's captain had been killed, so the executive officer had become their commander.

"Whatever the leader did, the rest did. When they halted in the lee of a gun shelter to light cigarets, he got the first match. Yesterday he had been sullen and silent. Today he spoke English.

"'You must pardon my English. You see, I have not used it for some three years,' he said with a half-smile. 'You Americans do not understand Germany. You should visit our cities after the war. Then you would know. We just want a little room, a little sunshine, that is all.'"

Battle of Russia

The great German land offensive into Russia was finally blunted early in 1943 with the failure of the Wehrmacht to hold Stalingrad after a siege lasting 66 days. This victory gave the Russians the initiative, and they spent the remainder of the year pushing the Germans out of one key city after another.

JAN. 11 **ORPHANS' WINTER:** The Russians have a phrase for the winter of their greatest success. They call it "Orphans' Winter" because, as Russian winters go, this has been a mild one, kindly to the thousands of homeless children in Russia. The snows have been deep—but not too deep for tanks. It has been cold—but not so cold as it was last winter, when Germans froze at their guns.

FEB. 1 **THE BRIDE'S LAMENT:** A mournful, melodious song, *The Ballad of the German Soldier's Bride,* has been haunting BBC's shortwave listeners in Germany. The words are by Bavarian Bert Brecht. English translation:

> *And what did he send you my bonny lass,*
> *From Paris the city of light?*
> *From Paris he sent me a silken dress,*
> *A dream caress of a silken dress,*
> *From Paris the city of light.*
>
> *And what did he send you my bonny lass,*
> *From the deep, deep Russian snows?*
> *From Russia he sent me my widow's weeds,*
> *From the funeral feast my widow's weeds,*
> *From the deep, deep Russian snows.*

[Bertholt Brecht, the German poet and dramatist, who fled his homeland in 1933, is best known for his play, *Mother Courage,* and the lyrics of *The Threepenny Opera.* He died in East Germany in 1956.]

FEB. 8 **100,000 HAND GRENADES:** This week the battle of Stalingrad approached its end. The Red Army had killed or captured

The major section of the Russian front is shown on this map taken from the February 15 issue of TIME. *After breaking the Nazi siege of Stalingrad in late January, the Soviet armies have gone on the offensive and pushed the Germans back along a 500-mile front all the way from Rostov, gateway to the Caucasus in the south, to the outskirts of Smolensk in the north. The cities of Rostov and Kharkov will fall to the Russians a week later. By the end of the year the Germans will be in full retreat.*

most of the troops that had been hammering the city since last August.

Not until last week did the Russians reveal how nearly the German Sixth Army had come to capturing Stalingrad. In September the Germans actually occupied the central part of the city. Often the opposing lines were only 15 yards apart. Most of the fighting was done with hand grenades, one Russian division using more than 100,000 of them in a single month's fighting.

THE RUSSIAN VIEW: Joseph Stalin said this week in an Order MARCH 1 of the Day celebrating the 25th Anniversary of the Red Army: "The beginning of the massed drive of the enemy from Soviet lands has begun." The Order also said: "In view of the absence of a second front in Europe, the Red Army alone is bearing the whole weight of the war."

SEPT. 27   **HE ALSO FIGHTS WHO BAKES:** For its heroes, grateful Russia has created many a new decoration. The newest, reported Moscow's *Pravda,* are intended for: chauffeurs and cooks, road builders and bakers. To win his red-and-gilt medal the heroic baker has to observe these stern commandments: bake excellent bread; build field ovens quickly; economize in the use of flour, butter and firewood; take good care of the equipment; utilize camouflage; be clean.

OCT. 4   **HITLER SLEPT HERE:** Since the Red offensive began in July, the Russians have rolled forward 50 to 200 mi. along a 700-mi. front, recaptured 95,000 sq. mi. of Russian earth. They have cleared the Caucasus, reoccupied almost half of the Ukraine, imperiled the Crimea, reached the borders of White Russia. They have bled the *Wehrmacht,* destroyed the bulk of its *Panzer* forces. Last week the Red Army captured Smolensk, the northern anchor of the last major defense line available to the *Wehrmacht* in Russia. Its fall marked a victory as important as that at Stalingrad.

NOV. 1   **TRIUMPH ON THE DNIEPER:** In Berlin, the *Wehrmacht*'s spokesman addressed the correspondents: "I am sorry I have to announce a Russian breakthrough on the German front." In these 14 words, the German Command last week admitted a grave defeat. The Dnieper River line, on which Hitler had ordered his army to stand or die, was pierced.

NOV. 15   **THE OUSTING IS AT HAND:** "Comrades," said Joseph Stalin in his calm, dry voice, "we have turned the course of the war. The complete ousting of the Fascist invader is at hand." A few hours earlier Stalin had announced the year's richest victory: the recapture of Kiev. Moscow's walls echoed the jubilant salvos of 324 guns, the pealing of the Kremlin's bells, the happy tumult of the crowds. Now, in Moscow and all over the land, men huddled before the loudspeakers to hear once more Stalin's voice: "Victory is near. But to achieve victory a new mustering of all forces and decisive action of the Red Army are necessary."

VICTORY AND BLOOD: In the murky dawn hour when Kiev fell, the battle for the Dnieper had ended, the battle for western Russia had begun. The Red Army had thus beaten the *Wehrmacht* in its prime. But it had taken Russian lives and steel. Both Moscow and Berlin last week totaled up the cost to each other of the summer and fall offensive, came out with incredible figures:

	RUSSIANS SAY GERMANS LOST	GERMANS SAY RUSSIANS LOST
Killed	900,000	1,300,000
Wounded	1,702,000	1,570,000
Prisoners	98,000	130,000
Planes	9,900	10,200
Guns	13,000	9,529
Machine Guns	50,000	14,499

When the people of Moscow went into the streets on Nov. 7 to celebrate the 26th anniversary of the revolution, their hearts were glad with victory. But they were also heavy with sorrow. For few Russian families had not sacrificed lives to keep their country free.

ATTA BOY: A Red flyer named Pokryshkin roared head on at NOV. 22 a slim-bodied German *Junkers,* shot upward, swerved right, then banked sharply, with his guns blazing. The German bomber fluttered down, trailing smoke. At a Red Air Force headquarters, a 35th digit was marked against the name of Major Alexander Pokryshkin. Across the breadth of Russia, men & women grinned and muttered: *"Molodets paren"* ("atta boy"). For to them, Alexander Pokryshkin is one of the war's top air heroes.

Russia's Pokryshkins did not save her, as the R.A.F. saved Britain in 1940. For in the vastness of Russia's plains the infantryman and the artilleryman bore the biggest burden. But Pokryshkin and his comrades helped to win an uphill fight for the control of Russia's skies, contributed much to this year's victories. [By the end of the war Pokryshkin had shot down a total of 59 German planes and was one of Russia's great aces. He became a lieutenant general and was three times named a Hero of the Soviet Union.]

ARMIES OF THE FOREST: In peacetime Russia, Peter and Ele- NOV. 29 na Ignatov led a quiet, homey life. But the war altered all that. Killing has become their trade; they pursue it with the matter-of-factness with which Peter once tinkered with engines and Elena mended her sons' torn garments. Today, Peter is the leader of one of Russia's busiest guerrilla "armies"; Elena is one of his killers.

Their exploits have made them national figures. *Pravda* honored the Ignatovs in an editorial. The same issue announced that seven partisans had been made Heroes of the Soviet Union. Two of the seven were Peter's sons: they had died blowing up a Nazi ammunition train.

Peter and Elena Ignatov. Once they led a quiet life; now killing Germans is their trade.

When the *Wehrmacht* retreats, partisans like the Ignatovs retreat with it—harassing, dynamiting, killing, raiding villages and towns, ambushing supply columns, cutting telegraph lines. In the Army of the Bryansk Forest alone, 3,200 men and women won decorations. Most of the partisans fight with captured rifles, hand grenades, machine guns. An air shuttle service flies doctors and Army officers into guerrilla territory, flies the wounded out. The bigger "armies" even operate their own bakeries, hospitals, community bathhouses. Many mimeograph and distribute their own newspapers.

In its effort to root them out, the *Wehrmacht* has burned down entire forests where guerrillas lurked. It has razed villages, killed or imprisoned thousands of suspects, offered big rewards (for the head of Guerrilla Chief Mikhail Ro-mashkin: 15,000 rubles, a house, 32 acres of land, two cows, a horse).

THE WOUNDED SLEEP WITH GUNS: Famed U.S. surgeon Elliott DEC. 13 Carr Cutler, chief consulting surgeon of the European Theater of Operations, went to Russia last summer. Colonel Cutler last week recounted some of his impressions:

"The Russians are very practical. When a soldier comes out of anesthesia, they throw a machine gun in bed with him, and he spends his time taking it apart and putting it together again. There are no Red Cross girls around to rub the backs of the wounded soldiers, no basket weaving."

Colonel Cutler met Russians who had earned eight wound stripes since the war began. "I am not sure that the Anglo-Saxon nervous system could go into trenches eight times and be wounded in that period. But that's the way to win the war, and that's the way the Russians like it."

Battle of the Pacific

Having won two critical sea battles at Midway and in the Coral Sea in 1942, and being in position to drive the Japanese out of their key base at Guadalcanal as 1943 began, U.S. forces were now about to continue their amphibious operations against islands closer to Japan. The toughest struggle of the year proved to be the capture of Tarawa in the Gilbert Islands.

THE SPARROWS OF TIMOR: One of the most gallant guerrilla JAN. 11 stories of the war was brought out of Timor, an island in the Dutch East Indies, last week: An Aussie unit, whose nickname was the Sparrow Force, was driven to the hills when the Japs attacked Timor with a superior force in February. The Sparrows had rifles, a few machine guns, a little ammunition and 400 miles of open sea between themselves and a safe refuge. Their only hope was radio contact with Darwin.

A young Tasmanian signalman named Joe Loveless went

to work. While the force settled in bamboo huts, taught natives to sing *Lambeth Walk* and *Lead, Kindly Light,* Joe Loveless came up with a weird machine assembled from parts of a weak transmitter, a native's receiver and a few pieces of wire. But it worked. Joe Loveless called Darwin. Darwin, suspicious of a message from an outfit given up as lost for two months, radioed: "Is Jack Sargent there?"

Replied XYZ: "Yes, he is."

Darwin: "What is his wife's name?"

XYZ: "Kathleen."

Now Darwin believed. XYZ radioed: "FORCE INTACT STILL FIGHTING BADLY NEEDS BOOTS MONEY QUININE TOMMYGUN AMMUNITION." Soon the needs were flown in and the Sparrows went to work. They dynamited bridges and burned camps. They sniped and rushed and potshot until by last week they claimed 30 Jap officers and 500 men. They lost exactly three Sparrows.

Their most embarrassing lack, for a time, was toilet paper. They had to use cigaret papers, bamboo bark and banana leaves. Then one day the considerate Japanese showered the bivouac with printed broadsides demanding surrender. The Sparrows were grateful.

MARCH 29 **SOLDIERS IN THE SEA:** Fortnight ago the Japs lost 22 ships in the Bismarck Sea to a U.S. air attack, and last week the Japanese Government announced by radio that all Japanese soldiers would be taught how to swim. "The scheme has been prompted," said Tokyo Radio, "by the fact that war operations in Greater East Asia are closely connected with water."

APRIL 5 **JIU-JITSU IN THE SEA:** Four of the pluckiest ships in the U.S. Navy were old destroyers which had some of their guns taken off and boilers taken out, and then were camouflaged to look like palm-fringed jungle, so that they could shuttle Marines to the Solomons in the first phases of the campaign. All four were sunk. What it felt like to be on—and later off— one of them, the *Gregory,* was vividly described last week by Machinist's Mate George Thomas Rhodes:

"Just as we started to go overside a shell hit the stacks over our head. Two of my friends were killed and I was wounded. I dove about 20 ft. to the water. I swam along for a short while when I came to a group of guys from the ship. After swimming with them for a while I got separated from them. I don't know how it happened but I was alone. Gosh, I was thinking about everything. I was thinking about home mostly and whether I'd ever get back there and whether I'd ever get to see the baby that was coming.

"After a couple of hours in the light from burning ships I saw someone floating in the water, I thought he was one of my shipmates who had been wounded. I swam over to see if I could help him. I was pretty weak from loss of blood. My jaw was torn open—about three and one-half inches— and I had two other wounds, one on my thigh and one on my ankle. But I didn't know about them then.

"As I came up I called out, 'Are you hurt?' He came toward me. Then he made a grab for me—right for my throat— and he was mumbling something. I knew it was Japanese. Afterwards I figured he was trying to get my lifejacket. The Japanese kept clawing at my throat, trying to choke and scratch me. He tried to gouge my eyes out, and he dug his nails into my cheek. I felt as though I were being entangled by an octopus. His arms and legs were all around me. I tried to grab his hair, but it was cut too short. He knocked me under several times, like he was trying to drown me. Every time I came up I got big gulpfuls of air.

"I remembered something about lifesaving, and so I tried to place myself so I could put my feet against his stomach, catch him by the shoulders and shove him away. Well, I got hold of him somehow. Then I swung an overhead blow right into his face. He loosened his hold and I didn't see him any more. I guess he sank."

A TRIP TO JAPAN: Eight of Major General James H. Doolittle's MAY 3 fliers who bombed Tokyo last year were captured by the Japanese. Fifty-five made their way back to the U.S. Five flew to Russia and were interned there. One was killed, two are missing. Eight stayed in China to fight with Major General Claire Lee Chennault. Last week those eight told their story to TIME Correspondent Theodore H. White:

"We just lay around the ship [the U.S. aircraft carrier *Hornet*] playing poker, shooting craps. We had Easter service aboard the ship. It was surprising how many people showed up. The morning of the 18th we noticed a little Japanese shipping boat about 7:30 and a cruiser with us sank her right away. We were about 740 miles off the coast of Japan, but decided to take off right away because all those little ships had radios and we thought they might have warned the Japanese.

"That was 8 o'clock in the morning. Doolittle was off first at 8:20. The only formation flight was with Doolittle. All the other planes took off singly with specific targets— power plants, ammunition dumps, oil storage, the Mitsubishi aircraft factory, docks, water supply.

One of Doolittle's bombers takes off from the "Hornet." The fliers shot craps and celebrated Easter, then headed for Tokyo.

"We hit the coast north of Tokyo, had to look for the city quite a while. We were 30 feet off the ground. We passed a training field with lots of planes taking off and landing. We flew right down one side but they didn't pay any attention. We lined up on a power plant way off to our left. We got three hits out of four. Doolittle says he saw the stuff go higher than our planes.

"We were running right along over the streets, just above roofs and could even see a couple of soldiers leaning against a lamppost. The antiaircraft got bad with lots of black puffs but we passed over the whole bay with warships, a weather ship, seven subs there, and nobody fired at us. There were a bunch of people sunning themselves on the beach. They waved to us. By this time our planes were hitting targets all over the city. There were big scattered clouds of smoke and flame, some terrific block-long fires. We had orders not to bomb the Emperor's palace.

"One plane headed out to the bay with fishermen on small boats waving at them as they passed. As we were heading for China a miracle of tail winds sprang up behind us, pushing us along to the west. At about 10 o'clock at night, it was raining like hell. All over a 70-mile radius our planes were coasting down, red danger lights on the instrument panels indicating there was no gas reserve left.

"The sky for the next hour was full of our boys parachuting down. One boy landed beside a mountain ledge, lit a cigaret in the dark, flicked the burnt butt on the ground beside him. He looked down and saw the butt dropping hundreds of feet below him into what seemed a bottomless void. He didn't move another foot until daylight.

"The area we landed in was under Japanese threat but was thoroughly infiltrated by Chinese guerrillas. Peasants everywhere were hospitable. One couple even made one of the pilots crawl in bed and spend the night on the marital couch with them."

General Doolittle with a few of his pilots and friendly Chinese after the Tokyo raid. A miracle of tail winds pushed the raiders over China to safety.

In 1943 the peculiar Japanese campaign in the Aleutian Islands off Alaska came to an end. During the critical days of 1942 the Japanese presence there had seemed to threaten an invasion of the American continent, but the attack never materialized. U.S. forces did meet stubborn resistance in a counterattack against the island of Attu in 1943. Then they set out to recapture the Japanese base on Kiska, and discovered that the enemy had vanished.

AUG. 30   **JANFU:** The cold rocks of Kiska had been gavelled under 106 bombings and 15 shellings from the sea since the first of the month. When U.S. and Canadian troops landed on Aug. 15— expertly primed for perhaps the strongest single operation the U.S. had yet undertaken in the Pacific—they found no living creature except a lonesome dog. The timing must have been hairline: invading Allied troops found a container of hot coffee. Victory it was, but seldom has a victory been acknowledged with such wry humor. The Jap garrison had been neatly evacuated just before the attack, and among the echoing cliffs of Kiska a new word was born: JANFU ("Joint Army-Navy foul-up").

From TIME Correspondent Robert Sherrod came this firsthand report:

"The Canadian and American soldiers found no Japs, but they did get a good look at the installations our planes and naval guns had been shooting at. What they found: gun emplacements, ammunition, living quarters and other evidence which indicated that at one time nearly 10,000 Japs had been on Kiska. There was a submarine base (evidently abandoned weeks ago) and a long-neglected seaplane base and hangar. Telephone lines strung around the eastern side of the island led to a fair-sized power plant. The Japs were also victory gardeners and had planted several small patches of vegetables. The Japs did not leave Kiska because they were in danger of starving.

"Evacuation involved destroying equipment and installations. In some cases the Japs did a good job. Three midget submarines, which long ago had been taken out of the ocean into pens, had their bellies blown out. Many containers of food had been jabbed with bayonets and stank from spoilage. There were land mines and booby traps. Most of the booby traps were crude and not up to the fictional standard of Japanese cunning. However, a few Allied soldiers were killed. I was disappointed at the apparent ineffectiveness of our aerial bombardment. Not one of the 6-in. coast artillery guns had been hit, though they had been prime targets for months. The sooner we acknowledge the relative ineffectiveness of precision bombing on small, well dug-in, expertly camouflaged positions, the better off we will be."

The assault on Tarawa came after bombardment to soften up the atoll, but when the Marines went ashore they met with furious resistance. TIME *Correspondent Robert Sherrod was with the Marines. The story based on his report follows.*

ONE SQUARE MILE OF HELL: The little landing vessel was loaded with silent prayers. Then the boat boss said: "From here on you can walk in." The men in the boat, about 15 in all, slipped into neck-deep water. There were at least 700 yards to walk, and as the waders rose on to higher ground, they loomed as larger and larger targets. Those who were not hit would always remember how the machine-gun bullets hissed into the water inches to the right, inches to the left. But on they crawled, past countless fish killed by concussion. DEC. 6

Once they got ashore, a Jap ran out of a coconut-log blockhouse into which Marines were tossing dynamite. As he emerged a Marine flame-thrower engulfed him. The Jap flared like a piece of celluloid. He died before the bullets in his cartridge belt finished exploding 60 seconds later. From treetop concealment and from pillbox slits Jap snipers and machine-gunners raked the Americans.

The first night passed perilously. For every Marine who slept in a foxhole, two kept watch through the darkness. Next morning low tide bared the bodies of many Marines, some hunched grotesquely, others with arms outstretched. At regimental headquarters, located 30 yards inland against a Jap blockhouse, Colonel David Shoup, huge, bull-necked commander [and 17 years later Commandant of the U.S. Marine Corps] reported: "We're in a tight spot. We've got to

On the beach at Tarawa, a U.S. Marine stands by a blasted pillbox among Japanese dead. For a while it was touch and go.

have more men." It was touch-&-go whether the Marines would all be killed, be pushed back into the sea.

The turning point came about 1 p.m. on the second day after strafing planes and dive-bombers had raked the island. Tanks fired point-blank into the slots of the enemy forts. Then artillery got ashore, laid down a pattern over every yard of the Jap positions. But the decisive factor was the fighting spirit of the U.S. Marines themselves. Lieut. William D. Hawkins, a Texan, led his platoon into the coconut palms. Though twice wounded, he refused to retire. He personally cleaned out six machine-gun nests.

That afternoon, Colonel Shoup wiped his red forehead with a grimy sleeve, said: "Well, I think we're winning, but the bastards have got a lot of bullets left. I think we'll clean up tomorrow." The Colonel was right. On the third day the Marines advanced inland at a mounting pace, overran Betio's valuable airfield, bottled the Japs in the island's tail. Some, when they realized that further opposition was useless, removed their jungle shoes, placed rifles against their foreheads, pulled triggers with their big toes. But most fought to the death. Then, on the third afternoon, the waterlogged bodies on the coral flats were gathered up, the crude island graveyards were filled with the American dead. The U.S. Marines had proved they could take it as superbly as any fighting men had ever taken it in the history of warfare. They also proved at Betio that no amount of bombing and shelling can guarantee a victory in the Pacific. It will also take brave men.

POSTSCRIPT: DEC. 13
❡ More eloquent than words was the record of the carnage in the Gilberts. Capture of the atolls had cost the U.S. 1,092 men killed, 2,680 wounded. Most casualties (95%) were Marines who fell on Betio island.
❡ Surveying Betio's defenses after the battle, Marine Major General Holland ("Howlin' Mad") Smith, chunky, bespectacled commander of amphibious operations, said: "It looks beyond the realm of human possibility that this place could have been taken."

Battle of Asia

Things went badly for the British and American forces on the Asiatic mainland in 1943. Their theater was immense, extending all the way from India, through Burma and Malaya up into central China. Their forces were small and largely uncoordinated, and they were obliged to remain so because the chief Allied priority was being given to the military effort in Europe and in the nearby Pacific.

ELEPHANTS HATE WAR: The Indian Army, which is playing a   APRIL 12
leading role in the battle for Burma, is forced to fight over terrain which will not tolerate motor transport. Result: the Army has turned to elephants as military transport after a lapse of 40 years.

Elephants can carry 500 lb. loads over country too difficult even for mules. They cross the stiff country at the lordly rate of ten miles a day. They also help sappers build bridges. But elephants hate war. The Burmese elephant is an especially sensitive beast who loathes mechanized transport of any kind. He refuses to go near trucks, and he trumpets, shies and runs away when he hears even a distant airplane motor. The most famous elephant assisting the Indian Army is Bandula, named after a famous Burmese general. Bandula's mahout receives "danger pay" because the elephant has already killed two keepers.

MAY 31 **WINGATE'S RAIDERS:** By last week it was clear that the five-month-old British attempt to retake the west coast of Burma and open up the Allied supply route into China had ended in disheartening failure. The British troops had been trained for the desert, had only a few weeks' jungle experience. They never solved Japanese tactics, never exploited the jungle. Casualties through disease and action approached 100% and the replacements had even less training; hence the troops became rawer and rawer.

But the whole ledger was not written in red ink. An action reported last week was a hopeful note for the future. Out of the tangled jungle across the saw-toothed range on the Indian frontier came a ragged band of men who for three months had fought the Japs on their own terms and come back alive. Led by small, unorthodox Brigadier Orde Charles Wingate, they had shown on a small scale that the ordinary British and Indian soldier can learn jungle fighting.

Supplied by plane and what they found to eat in the jungle, these British raiders operated over 10,000 square miles of Burma, cutting Jap lines of communication, raiding Jap outposts, throwing the enemy into confusion far behind the front lines. The troops were highly trained; for six months Brigadier Wingate had worked them in the Assam jungles. One of Wingate's officers, who had left a staff job and even taken a demotion in order to lead a column of raiders, watched a railway bridge rise in a cloud of smoke and then settle into the gorge. Said the Major softly: "Now I know that all my life I've wanted to blow up bridges."

SEPT. 6 **LORD LOUIS IN TO BAT:** For the biggest present vacancy in United Nations Commands—the much-talked-about Southeast Asia Command—Prime Minister Churchill and President Roosevelt last week picked much-publicized Lord Louis Francis Albert Victor Nicholas ("Dickie") Mountbatten.

Lord Louis, 43-year-old, 6-ft.-4-in. second cousin to King George VI, is best known as the Chief of Britain's savage, knife-wielding Commandomen. In previous years he had earned the reputation of a blooded, moneyed playmate of the Prince of Wales. And for various high jinks, he was blackballed from the haughty Royal Yacht Squadron. But behind the gaiety was a lot of earnest attention to naval matters.

Two years ago Lord Louis was made a Vice Admiral and given honorary titles in the R.A.F. and the Army. Combined Operations, as his commando organization was called, was then a stepchild, frowned on by Colonel Blimps, struggling along in hand-me-downs. Smooth Lord Louis made drastic changes, used his influence to get matériel and facilities, lifted Combined Operations to glamor and renown.

As Commander of Southeast Asia Lord Louis acquired another stepchild. He will be based in India, where the British have an army, mostly Indians, totaling an estimated 1,000,000 men. Mounting stock piles of U.S. matériel, and the recent appointment of Major General George E. Stratemeyer to the command of U.S. air forces in Burma, India and China, meant that Lord Louis would have active U.S. aid there.

ON THE PLAINS OF DELHI: In India's capital this week there NOV. 29 was a beginning of military unity. Over New Delhi, long a cauldron of inter- and intra-Allied intrigue for military power and prestige, floated the flag of Admiral the Lord Louis Mountbatten. Lord Louis' command embraces a conglomerate collection of British, Indian, Burmese, Chinese and American soldiers, sailors and flyers. His job was to coordinate their functions, curb jealousies, instill discipline, create unity. The handsome, confident Admiral began his task last month when he flew to Chungking. He consulted with Generalissimo Chiang Kai-shek, bluntly asked for his advice on continental strategy, had an initial success such as no other British military leader had attained in China. When Lord Louis returned to New Delhi, he established his headquarters in the palace formerly occupied by a Sikh maharaja. To insure greater harmony and constant exchange of ideas, Lord Louis insisted on having the highest ranking U.S. and British officers live and dine with him.

And soon another precedent was shattered. Batches of

"pukka sahib" generals, brigadiers and colonels, wise in the ways of frontier outposts and native rebellions, but notoriously untutored in modern jungle warfare, were ordered home to Britain. Replacing them were the bright young men of Admiral Mountbatten's old commando command.

DEC. 6 **THE HAWK:** It is Claire Chennault's face that stops a man, meeting him for the first time. The skin is burnt and leather-beaten by the sun to a permanent brown, cut and scarred by razor-sharp lines that drop perpendicularly about his mouth. About the eyes sky-strain has woven a lacework of crow's-feet. Within this network, two coal-black eyes brood and smolder. Said an artist assigned to do a portrait of the General: "That man has the face of a hawk."

Back in 1920, as a first lieutenant in the Army Air Corps, Chennault was already a pilot with ideas. His famed stunt team (the "Three Men on a Flying Trapeze") thrilled air-meet crowds. But its purpose was serious: to impress on the Air Corps the value of precision pursuit operation. The conservative Air Corps command paid little or no attention to these and other Chennault ideas. Russian military observers offered him $10,000 a year to go to Russia as military adviser and pursuit instructor. He turned the offer down, stuck with Billy Mitchell and a few other pioneers through years of frustration.

Finally, in 1937, the Army retired him when he was 56—officially, because of his partial deafness. That same year the dark, determined Louisianian went to Shanghai and became Chiang Kai-shek's air adviser. In a few months, the Japs almost wiped out his infant air force, but Chennault proved his theories, and his pilots and tactics wrote a never-to-be-forgotten record across the skies of Asia.

In 1942, he was called back to active duty in the U.S. Army with the rank of brigadier general. "I don't want to be a general," Chennault sighed, "but I can't fight without planes." For a while he almost had to fight without them anyway: in the summer and fall of 1942 his bomber force sometimes averaged five B-25s, his fighter force was down to 20 P-40s.

Chennault taught his pilots to minimize the disadvantages of the slow, cumbersome P-40 and utilize its advantages:

greater fire power, heavier armor, sturdier construction, a much higher diving speed. He discouraged dog-fighting by individual pilots. Essence of his teaching: hit hard, hit precisely, hit as a team.

Now, after six years in China, Chennault is as American as a baseball bat. With eyes narrowed and cheeks twitching, he can discuss the quickest way to kill in battle and the next moment tell of his longing to return to Louisiana to shoot ducks. He likes to dig in his garden, pitch for the headquarters' softball team. His indoor game: poker. His ever-present companion is a dachshund, Joe.

ON THE NOSE: "There she is, right on the nose!" Lieut. Colonel Joseph B. Wells had to shout to TIME Correspondent Theodore H. White; thunderous twin engines were driving their B-25 bomber over the turbulent waters of the South China Sea. Wells pointed a finger at an airdrome on Formosa, one of Japan's great nests of air power. The only newspaperman to accompany the mission, White cabled:

"The mission was to be at almost suicidal level—even five minutes warning would give the Zeros enough time to take off, climb and turn to the attack. We had to come in from the sea precisely—an error of two degrees, a miss by ten miles or more, would warn the entire coast.

"We dropped down until the ocean surface almost touched the bellies of our planes and the props lifted spray into the air, filling our mouths with a salty taste. Almost within spitting distance a green Zero with red balls on its wings came up bravely beneath our tail before the pursuits chased him away. The P-38s had preceded us over the airport by a matter of seconds, diving to strafe the field. I peered out the side blister as we made our run and counted 14 Jap planes burning, bursting like brilliant red buds and then flowering into orange and black coronas.

"When we left eight minutes later, we had literally devastated the great airdrome, shattered ground installations, strafed startled and fleeing Jap ground troops. We destroyed or damaged in the air or on the ground an estimated 50 Japanese bombers and fighters. Every American plane returned safely and not a single American or Chinese on the raid was injured."

FOREIGN NEWS

Great Britain

APRIL 5   **SPRING ALWAYS COMES:** Britain last week lifted a ban on the railway transport of spring flowers. From Scotland the first boxes of snowdrops went south. London's Hyde Park was carpeted with purple crocuses which lovers crushed, unmindful of the grunts of passers-by, and botanists haunted bomb cavities for London rocket *(Sisymbrium irio),* which flourished after the great fire of 1666. Already 95 types of flowers and shrubs unknown for decades before the blitz have been found in holes where nitrates from burning bombs have enriched the soil.

JUNE 7   **HIT & RUN:** TIME Correspondent Wilmott Ragsdale cabled this account of *Luftwaffe* hit & run raids which have done little military damage but have made village life both dangerous and exciting:

"Twenty-five German planes swept out of the sea mist, their guns wide open. They came in so low that they had to bank to avoid church steeples. While their machine guns and cannon sprayed indiscriminately over the town, they dumped high explosive and incendiary bombs. In less than 60 seconds it was over.

"The church steeple crashed to the ground. Children walking home from Sunday school were carried from the streets with pulverized glass and cement ground into their cheeks. A department store was in flames.

"Housewives caught table-setting were driven to emergency wards to have chunks of their own glass and dishes dug from their flesh.

"Bombs and bullets do strange things when dropped and fired at random. In an East Anglia town Joan Smee was sitting in a municipal office 'when a tracer bullet came through the window and went through my hair, setting it on fire.' Somebody in the office put the fire out."

THE LUFTWAFFE INTERCEPTS: The British Overseas Airways JUNE 14 station at London knew the weather had roughened over the Bay of Biscay. But it was nothing unusual for the regular flight of the big Douglas liner from Lisbon. Then, suddenly, came the voice of the Dutch pilot over the radio: "I am being followed by strange aircraft. Putting on best speed. We are being attacked. Cannon shells and tracers are going through the fuselage. Wave-hopping and doing my best." Then silence.

Next day a Berlin communiqué claimed an enemy transport downed over the Atlantic. London announced the Douglas overdue and presumably lost, with a four-man crew and 13 passengers, including Actor Leslie Howard. Britons regarded last week's casualty as an incident in a Nazi hunt for Winston Churchill, known to be enroute to England from North America and North Africa. For Leslie Howard, this probability had made a tragic curtain.

THE MASTER'S VOICE: As long as the English language lives, NOV. 22 its users will be reminded that Winston Churchill said: "I have nothing to offer but blood, toil, tears, and sweat. . . . Never in the field of human conflict was so much owed by so many to so few. . . . We shall fight on beaches, we shall fight on landing grounds, we shall fight in fields and in streets, we shall never surrender."

Unlike Franklin Roosevelt, who pores over and polishes one draft after another, Churchill often chisels the splendid phrase as he speaks. In preparation, Churchill dictates ideas directly to a typist (who uses a machine with very large type). These notes frame what he intends to say, but they are no more than a frame. Once on his feet he improvises, digresses, shapes his points as he rolls along.

In delivery he grunts ("and-ah"), gropes for the next phrase, glares at his notes (if he is using them at all), peers pugnaciously over his big-rimmed spectacles, often thumbs his lapels. Usually, it is only after he is done that there can be an accurate written version. Whether heard or read, that version usually is a work of art.

ONE MORE CLOSE CALL: This week the tension eased. Small DEC. 27 showers of memoranda began dropping on the desks of military and civil leaders. Winston Churchill was getting well, was working again. The Prime Minister had lingered on in the Middle East, picking up loose ends of the Cairo and Teheran conferences. Suddenly, it was announced, a cold had developed into pneumonia, the second such attack he has had this year. During the next four days the world waited for each bulletin. Occasionally it was stirred by rumors that the end had come. Although the people knew that on Nov. 30 Churchill had entered the last year of his Biblical allotment, it was unthinkable that he might die now, before his mighty job was done.

The illness was one more close call for Churchill. At the age of nine, he had double pneumonia. There were no sulfa drugs then. The physician who attended him remarked, when he saw the recovery, that Churchill had a charmed life. At twelve, at Harrow, he fell 30 feet off a bridge, broke his shoulder instead of his head. At 21, in Cuba, he walked untouched through a rain of bullets. At 23, in India, he jumped from boat to dock, misjudged, smashed again his once-broken right shoulder (on this occasion he is reported to have uttered "most unChristian oaths").

In World War I, German shells demolished a dugout five minutes after he had left it. Shortly after that, he was in a Flanders farmhouse when a shell came through the roof, wounded only his adjutant. He had an acute appendix operation in 1921. Ten years later a New York taxicab knocked him down, gave him lacerations and pleurisy. He recovered with the aid of 3,000 units of anti-tetanus serum. Only ten months ago he had another attack of pneumonia.

The record seems to show that Churchill is susceptible to lung ailments. There is a limit to the capacity of an aging, though apparently tireless body to fight them off. And last week in the House of Commons there was strong talk of making sure that henceforth the Prime Minister stay at home.

France

JAN. 4 **END OF AN EXPEDIENCY:** The afternoon sun was streaking the white porticoes of the Palais d'Eté in Algiers. It was

3:30 p.m. on Christmas Eve. Before the pretentious entrance an official car drew up. Out of it stepped Admiral Jean François Darlan, High Commissioner for French North and West Africa, followed by his orderly. Through the dark corridors to his office the Admiral strode briskly. He approached the anteroom where visitors waited for interviews. The door opened; a young man stepped into the hall. He aimed a revolver at the Admiral's face and pressed the trigger. The Admiral staggered, lunged forward, blood spurting from his mouth. A second shot. He fell, and lay still.

The small, stocky form of Admiral Darlan was lifted from the bloody floor. Outside his car still waited. He was carried into it, driven to a hospital. But it was too late. When he was taken from his car, Jean François Darlan, the turncoat collaborationist, was dead.

Death came to the Admiral just six weeks after he had taken over the government of French North and West Africa with the backing of the U.S. command. His swift change of allegiance was one of the war's greatest surprises. And in his brief career at the side of the anti-Axis powers, the progress of the U.S. campaign had been sped. But Darlan's assumption of power had also unleashed a storm of anger and criticism, widening dangerously the already existing split between the supporters of Vichyfrance and General Charles de Gaulle. It had involved the U.S. in a tangled skein of international politics which was becoming more & more involved. Termed by President Roosevelt a "temporary expediency," the Darlan regime was gaining a firmer foothold with each day.

Now the assassin's bullet had brought the opportunity for a new beginning. In death Admiral Darlan opened the way for French unity, which he had rendered impossible as long as he had a voice in French affairs.

SUCCESSOR: There was one man on whom the Fighting French, the British and the U.S. could agree: General Henri Honoré Giraud had been picked for this role before the U.S. forces landed. But when he reached North Africa Darlan was there ahead of him and he had voluntarily yielded to Darlan. Now Giraud was once again chosen to carry on.

General Giraud was no politician, but, as a soldier, he

could perhaps bring unity to France as no politician could. His political stand was clear. In an interview granted just before Darlan's assassination he had promised French cooperation with the United Nations. "Most certainly," he said, would the French African Government cooperate, if not consolidate, with General Charles de Gaulle and his Fighting French. For himself, he had renounced all political ambition, saying simply: "I am a soldier."

THE KILLER: Darlan's assassin was Fernand Bonnier de la Chapelle, 20, member of the French patriotic youth organization *Chantiers de Jeunesse,* which aided Allied landings in North Africa but became embittered when Collaborationist Darlan emerged as chief of what many Frenchmen considered a Fascist North African regime. When informed that the Admiral was dead he had said only: "So much the better. You may kill me now."

Sentence was summarily delivered: death by firing squad. Next day it was announced that the sentence had been carried out at dawn in the midst of a German air raid, when the air was filled with the sound of ack-ack. Said a Fighting French spokesman: "Admiral Darlan's actions have finally caught up with him."

FEB. 1 **"WE HAVE MET":** Franklin Roosevelt and Winston Churchill did not have to go to Africa to bring General Giraud and General de Gaulle together. But the conflict between Giraud and De Gaulle was indicative of a basic disagreement between U.S. and British foreign policies. And every time De Gaulle and Giraud had seemed on the point of agreeing on some form of cooperation, butter had got in the works. Latest blob of butter was the appointment by Giraud of Marcel Peyrouton as Governor General of Algeria. In 1940 Peyrouton was a Minister in the Vichy government; before that he was Vichy Resident General in Tunisia; to General de Gaulle he was unpalatable.

But when Roosevelt and Churchill went to Casablanca, Generals de Gaulle and Giraud could both go without loss of face. The fact was that they had to go, so as not to be left out of the plans that were made there. What passed at their meeting was as secret as other decisions in Casablanca,

President Roosevelt presides as two feuding Generals, Giraud (left) and De Gaulle, come together at Casablanca. There was no Gallic kiss as they met.

but they shook hands for cameramen. Their official announcement said only: "We have met. We have talked. We have registered entire agreement on the end to be achieved, which is the liberation of France and the triumph of human liberties by the total defeat of the enemy."

RESISTANCE: As wild and angry as when Frenchmen had MARCH 22 cried *"à bas la Bastille!"*, the voice of French resistance echoed last week from the Pyrenees to the Swiss Alps. In its violent aspects it was still a minority resistance. But it spoke with gunfire in Paris, with hand grenades in Lyon. The immediate cause of the outbreaks was Germany's attempt to drain France of manpower. The Germans sought French workmen to build up the fortifications of Hitler's *"festung Europa,"* to labor in German factories, to help move supplies behind German lines in Russia.

Frenchmen hid out in cities. Many fled to the Alps. They dug up buried guns and ammunition. The Fighting French, in contact with French partisans, reported 500 Germans killed throughout France last week. Saboteurs blew up a troop train near Dijon, killed 250. In Lyon a German detachment was ambushed and scattered with hand grenades. Bombs killed 23 Nazi officers at a Lille café.

JUNE 7 **UNION IN ALGIERS:** With no Gallic kiss, but a handshake, sensitive General Henri Giraud (five stars) greeted sensitive General Charles de Gaulle (two stars) at Maison Blanche airport near Algiers this week. Then, in a blue Packard sedan, Generals Giraud and De Gaulle rode off to the long-awaited parley for a united France.

JUNE 14 **THE PEOPLE WIN:** Charles de Gaulle has a well-deserved reputation for being difficult to deal with: H. G. Wells has called him "an artlessly sincere megalomaniac." De Gaullism is something else again. To many a Frenchman, De Gaullism stands for the France that never surrendered, the France that was betrayed by her leaders. General de Gaulle, the individual, derives his strength from the people of France, who are his potent political weapon.

This hard fact dominated last week's parleys in Algiers. There were times during the week when a unified France seemed impossible. Slander and counter-slander muddied the Algiers atmosphere. The mudslinging began even as General de Gaulle arrived to receive a correct but unenthusiastic welcome from General Giraud, an ovation from the people. To the cheers, the Fighting French leader responded by raising his arms in a V sign. Anti-De Gaullists sneered that such a gesture hardly differed from a Hitler salute.

The job of these men was to constitute themselves a French Committee of National Liberation, the central power that would rule until France could choose her own government. When they gathered, General de Gaulle stood adamant on two principles: 1) the North African administration must be purged of ex-Vichyites; 2) the military must be subordinated to the civilian authority of the central power. The Giraudists rocked back on their heels. They held out against a purge. The meeting broke up.

Then the sticky atmosphere cleared suddenly and the impossible became a fact. After three hours behind closed doors, the conferees announced that the French Committee of National Liberation had begun to function. By week's end it was clear that De Gaullism would dominate. For at

De Gaulle's insistence, notorious ex-Vichyite General Auguste Noguès (he had opposed the U.S. landing at Casablanca) stepped out as Resident General of Morocco. The purging process had begun.

EXPEDIENCY AGAIN: Allied secret diplomacy last week made JULY 5 its second major decision in French North Africa. The results were as politically disturbing to the United Nations cause as the first decision nine months ago, when the U.S. had used turncoat Admiral Jean François Darlan on the ground of expediency. Now the U.S. and Britain insisted that control over the French armed forces in North Africa must go to General Henri Honoré Giraud and not to General Charles de Gaulle, on the ground that it would be militarily dangerous to risk a sudden reform in the French army. The Allies let their wishes be known as the French Committee of Liberation met for a showdown over the issue of military control. Out of a three-hour session emerged a makeshift compromise. General Giraud remained as Commander in Chief of the North and West African troops (300,-000), with his own army, navy and air chiefs of staff. General de Gaulle remained as Commander in Chief of forces (90,000) elsewhere in the Empire, also with his own chiefs of staff. The two commanders and their staffs would operate as a committee to supervise military reform.

From Algiers TIME Correspondent Jack Belden cabled this estimate of the compromise:

"Within the French Empire there now exist two armies responsible to two different commanders who are not responsible to one war minister. In terms of the hopes of a few days ago, this is a turning back of the French political clock. And hollow sound the recent words of De Gaulle and Giraud: 'Frenchmen, the unity you have been waiting for has been achieved.' Viewing this struggle, it is not surprising that French unity has not been achieved. North Africa has not been pregnant with a new France, but has only had a miscarriage."

THE TERROR: Occupied France was aflame last week. Cried OCT. 25 pro-Nazi Jacques Barteaud over Radio Paris:

"Harvests are burning, railway lines are being blown sky-high, trains are being derailed. Everywhere the army of terrorists is moving about."

Vichy was slipping, and the Nazis knew it. They did what they could. A specially trained German army rumbled to the revolt areas to clean out the underground at any cost. The death penalty was decreed for all Frenchmen caught aiding grounded Allied flyers. At last, all else failing, German authorities told the Vichy Government that the long-threatened "Plan A" would be put into effect.

The Germans had been saving "Plan A" for Allied invasion. Salient features: arrest of all officers of the French armistice army, internment of all army reserve officers, disarmament of the *Garde Mobile,* the arrest of all Jews and suspected foreigners. But the hour was late. Frenchmen, awaiting the invasion, would know how to deal with "Plan A."

NOV. 22 **COUP:** General Charles de Gaulle last week swept into full power. Out of the Liberation Committee went General Henri Honoré Giraud, former Committee Co-President, and three of his Committee appointees. Simultaneously seven Gaullists entered the Committee's ranks. Giraud kept his job as chief of the French armed forces. But his retreat from power had not necessarily ended. De Gaulle spokesmen said that the General would continue as military chief "for the time being."

De Gaulle's ascendancy pointed up a looming question: Who will administer France in the early days of its liberation? De Gaulle last week said that when France is liberated, his Committee alone will be valid on French soil.

Germany

JAN. 25 **THE HELMET MAY COME IN HANDY:** Reich Marshal Hermann Göring was 50 years old and weighed 270 lbs. last week. From all over Europe presents poured in. They filled three halls in his palatial Karinhall, and included a long-buried Roman helmet found in Milan after a recent excavation by an R.A.F. bomb.

DAY OF JUBILEE: It was Naziism's tenth birthday. In the Hall FEB. 8
of Honor at Berlin's Air Ministry building meaty, perspiring
Reich Marshal Hermann Göring scowled at the pages of
his carefully prepared speech. In a moment the Marshal
would step to the microphone. But in far-off England moni-
tors on the German frequencies, listening for Göring's
guttural voice, heard instead the sudden crump of bombs, a
confusion of muffled shouts. A flustered voice announced
that Marshal Göring had been delayed for a moment. A military band brayed out.

High over the capital of the Reich droned planes of the
R.A.F. Swift, light bombers, in the first daytime raid on Berlin, were dodging ack-ack, fighting off the astonished *Luftwaffe* and raining 500-lb. bombs on a now noisy and
exploding city. It was 45 minutes before Herr Göring could
speak.

"Today we are united," he shouted desperately. "We
shall fight to the very last for our way of life. Hitler has led
us from poverty and impotence to victory and is now leading us to the greatest of all victories. Our leader—our
beloved leader—*Sieg Heil!"*

---

*In May of 1941, Deputy Führer Rudolf Hess, who was Adolf
Hitler's close personal friend and his choice—after Hermann
Göring—to succeed him, commandeered a Luftwaffe fighter
plane and flew to Scotland on a mysterious mission. His apparent
motive was to negotiate a peace between Germany and Great
Britain. He was interned by the British, and in 1946 he went
on trial at Nürnberg and was sentenced to life in prison for
war crimes.*

DREAM WORLD: Last week London's *Daily Mail* printed a full SEPT. 13
account of the condition and activities of Britain's No. 1
War Prisoner, Rudolf Hess. The *Daily Mail*'s story, amplified
by information given to a TIME correspondent:

The moment he hit British soil, Hess demanded to see
King George and "the Dukes." He wanted to tell them that
Germany was about to invade Russia, to urge them to
make peace and join the crusade. He was certain that, once

the King and the Dukes decided on peace with Germany, the peace would be immediate. British officials who interrogated Hess found him hopelessly saturated with Nazi propaganda. If Hess could be taken as accurate evidence, even top-rank Nazis lived in the unreal world their propaganda had created. Hess could not believe that the "plutos" of a "plutodemocracy" would ally themselves with Communist Russia. Hess did finally understand that his mission was no go, and so he decided to fly back home. When British authorities refused, he was indignant. He accused them of discourtesy.

In captivity Hess grew moody, despondent; he exploded in fits of anger. One British official saw Hess alone one day. Said the official: "There's something that has always interested me. In the Battle of Britain, British communiqués said Germany lost about 2,500 planes and we lost about 750. Now your German communiqués said just about the opposite—that we lost 2,000 planes and Germany lost only about 650. How do you account for this wide difference?"

Hess: "The *Luftwaffe* communiqués are absolutely accurate. We shot down 2,000 planes and lost only 650."

Official: "But, Herr Hess, do you know how many planes we had during the Battle of Britain?"

Hess: "You never had more than 1,000 planes."

Official: "Don't you think there is something of a contradiction between the number of planes you say we had and the number you say you shot down?"

Hess: "You're trying to trap me! Get out!"

Hess is a developed paranoiac. His head jerks; he listens anxiously for voices from corners; under cabbage leaves on his plate he slyly hides pieces of meat he thinks have been poisoned. His only game is darts. He hurls the dart violently; then, when collecting his darts from the board, he is apt to duck, dodge, cower—expecting someone to throw a dart into his back.

SEPT. 20   **ONE TIRE BLOWN:** An hour and a half after the people of the United Nations began celebrating Italy's surrender, Radio Berlin was still soothing its listeners with a musical program called *Let Us Go On Dreaming*. After sufficient time had passed for hard-pressed Dr. Paul Joseph Goebbels to concoct his explanations, the German radio let out the big, bad news:

¶ From the Nazi press: "Mussolini was too great a person for a nation like that."

¶ Dr. Paul Schmidt, German Foreign Office spokesman: "Yes, one tire has blown out of the Berlin-Rome-Tokyo tricycle."

¶ Dr. Goebbels: "There is only one deadly sin and that is cowardice. In critical situations one must keep one's heart in one's hand and jump over the threatening precipice."

¶ Adolf Hitler: "The withdrawal of Italy means little in a military sense because the struggle in that country has for months been sustained and carried on mainly by German forces. We will now continue the struggle free of all burdensome encumbrances."

LA FORZA DEL DESTINO: From Essen's *National-Zeitung:* In OCT. 4 the cities of Lintfort, Rheinberg and Rheinhausen there will be no performances of Italian opera this season—"owing to recent political events."

Occupied Europe

Only rare bits of news filtered out of that part of Europe that lay in Hitler's grasp. The following stories were among the items that did.

FEE: Onetime Chief of Staff Lieut. General Hendrik Alexander FEB. 15 Seyffardt was the only Dutch general who aligned himself with the Nazis when his homeland was invaded. Last week he got his fee. He was shot and killed by the underground in front of his home in The Hague.

TOTAL MURDER: Last week the American Jewish Congress MARCH 8 asked the United Nations to do what could be done to save 5,000,000 Jews in occupied Europe from extermination this year. Anyone who thought that the Congress exaggerated the danger had only to read Adolf Hitler's prophecy to

Nazi Party members last week: "This struggle will end with the extinction of Jewry in Europe." In a report drawn from Nazi statements, smuggled accounts and the stories of survivors who have reached the free world, the Congress told what was happening in Poland, slaughterhouse of Europe's Jews.

By late 1942, the Congress reported, 2,000,000 had been massacred. *Vernichtungskolonnen* (extermination squads) rounded them up and killed them with machine guns, lethal gas, high-voltage electricity and hunger. Almost all were stripped before they died; their clothes were needed by the Nazis. A typical massacre: "In the town of Otwock two companies of German soldiers were dispatched from Warsaw with the assignment of slaughtering every Jewish man, woman and child. The massacre started at midnight and lasted eight hours. The dead were later collected and buried."

The ghettos established by the Nazis in Poland and the Baltic States are ghost towns today, decimated by deportation and execution on the spot. "The Warsaw ghetto is empty. The streets crowded only a year ago with 500,000 Jews are silent now. Last month gunfire was heard in Warsaw for several days. When it stopped, the Germans had finished their task. The last of the Jews were gone."

The Congress said that about 150 children managed to escape, roamed Warsaw's streets begging for food. An eyewitness described them: "They look less human than little monsters; dirty, ragged, with eyes that will haunt me forever. They trust no one and expect only the worst from human beings. They slide along the walls of houses, looking about them in mortal fear."

MAY 24 **PARIS IN THE SPRING:** Parisians in the spring of 1943 know hunger, humiliation, the fear of air raids. Life in all of France is hard and ugly. But the French, and particularly the French of Paris, still have their old genius for softening the hardness and hiding the ugliness.

An American girl who recently escaped from Occupied France to London gave an authentic account of life under the Germans. She said that women can still buy chic dresses for 5,000 francs and up without ration coupons. But only the darlings of Nazis, grafters, collaborationists can afford such luxuries. The only unrationed foods are rutabagas, *topinambours* (Jerusalem artichokes) and cabbage. The combined butter, fat and oil ration is about three and a half ounces a week per person (compared to eight ounces in Britain). For five precious coupons, a Frenchman supping at a restaurant is lucky to get watery soup, a dab of meat, an inch-square wafer of cheese. Trading in the black market is an act of patriotism, for when Frenchmen trade with each other, *les boches* get nothing. Well-off townspeople buy direct from farmers at astronomical prices: 2,000 francs for a ham; 800 francs for a goose; 500 francs for a chicken; 300 francs for a rabbit (with hind feet left on to prove that it is not a cat). Cats have almost entirely disappeared.

HOPE & HUMOR: The sudden Allied victory in Tunisia set up a clamor of urgency over all of Europe. Once again it had been proved that the German *Wehrmacht* was not invincible. To peasants and patriots in occupied countries the certainty of eventual Allied victory was a staff to lean upon until guns could be used again. In the meanwhile, there was room for humor to bolster the hope:

¶ In Brussels, German soldiers stormed that impudent Belgians asked them: "Have you packed your bags yet?"

¶ In Copenhagen, a Danish bookseller put two huge portraits of Hitler and Mussolini in his window. Between them, he placed a copy of *Les Misérables*.

THE FAÇADE CRACKS: A German officer was stamped to death SEPT. 6 by Danish boots in Odense. A German troop train exploded on its way north to Aalborg. Night fires broke out in Copenhagen's port and three locomotives were wrecked at Varde. After 40 months' service as Hitler's "model protectorate," Denmark was coming of age: sabotage was turning professional. Said the Nazi-controlled radio: "The patience so long exerted by the occupying authority has been exhausted as from today."

Germans machine-gunned Danes in Copenhagen's *Raadhusplads* to teach them not to congregate. But angry Danes seized girls who continued to walk out with German soldiers, stripped them, slapped swastikas on them, drove them screeching through the streets. And one Sunday morning Copenhagen woke before dawn to the sound of firing from the port. Denmark's tiny Navy was committing suicide. Some were trying to escape to Sweden, some were scuttled by their crews where they lay. German planes caught and sank at least one that fled, but nine reached Sweden.

International

Although President Roosevelt and British Prime Minister Churchill had met six times since the beginning of the war to discuss joint strategy, there had been no attempt to bring in the other Allies until 1943. In that year Roosevelt and Churchill met in Cairo with Chinese Generalissimo Chiang Kaishek and at Teheran with Marshal Stalin of the Soviet Union.

DEC. 13 **THE BIG PARADE:** At Cairo the Generalissimo and Mme. Chiang Kai-shek were the first to arrive, flying in from Chungking aboard a four-engined U.S. transport plane. Winston Churchill and Franklin Roosevelt, with their separate parties, traveled to Africa by ship, made the last leg of the trip by plane. Tenants had been cleared out of the fashionable Mena House hotel, out near the Pyramids, and troops moved in, setting up barbed-wire barricades around an area of three square miles. When the President drove in, his limousine, with curtains drawn, was led by two motorcycle outriders, two Jeeps carrying four soldiers with submachine guns at the ready, a command car mounting a machine gun.

The top staffs settled down in villas and houses surrounding the hotel. There were 34 villas altogether, divided into seven "defensive zones." Around them bristled antiaircraft guns, searchlights, pillboxes, gun emplacements, fire-watcher towers. The Chiangs were virtually inseparable, Madame acting as interpreter for her husband. Afternoons they strolled hand in hand in the gardens of their villa and talked over the day's events.

Heading the U.S. delegation were the joint chiefs of staff: Admiral William Leahy, General George C. Marshall, the

Navy's Admiral Ernest King, Air Forces General Hap Arnold. General Dwight Eisenhower came up from Algiers; Generals Joseph Stilwell and Claire Chennault flew in from China.

Formal entertaining ranged from small teas to elaborate dinners; President Roosevelt gave a Thanksgiving Day feast, with turkey and cranberries. The bar on the hotel's main floor did a rush business from 9 a.m. to midnight. Scotch ran out the first night, but there was no repetition of that disaster; the Government hospitality fund had shipped 35 cases out from Britain, also provided 500,000 cigarets and 1,250 cigars.

After the Cairo agenda had been completed, Roosevelt and Churchill flew on to Teheran and the Chiangs returned to China. The President arrived at Teheran late Saturday afternoon, Nov. 27, and went straight to the handsome American legation. That night he was invited to move into the main building of the Russian Embassy, where the meetings were to be held. Foreign Minister Viacheslav M. Molotov and Marshal Klimenti Voroshilov had accompanied Stalin on his first trip outside Russia since the Revolution.

Next day, after lunch, Franklin Roosevelt and Joseph Stalin met face to face and spent their first hour together. By blocking off all entrances, hanging up big cloth screens at the end of the street and opening the wide iron gates, guards converted the two embassies and their grounds into one big compound. For the four days of the conference, the Big Three lived and worked there, dining together each night, never more than 200 yards from each other.

Molotov started the Teheran social ball rolling with a tea at which the delegates showed some awe of one another, and Stalin took it on himself to move around and get everyone talking. But the ice was broken with a vengeance at dinner, and stayed broken. Stalin enthusiastically sipped Roosevelt's special martinis. Toasts were mostly in champagne, but Churchill stuck to his favorite still wines.

Kingpin social event of all turned out to be Churchill's birthday dinner (he was 69) at the British Embassy on Tuesday. Winnie had been planning it all day. He insisted on checking his party's place cards before dressing, then by 8:15 was back, impeccable, in jacket and black tie, nervously puffing a cigar and peering at his watch. Stalin and party arrived five minutes early—precisely enough time for one drink. At dinner Churchill announced that toasting would follow the Russian style—everyone toasting everyone else. Later estimates of the toast total ranged from 35 to 50. Stalin gave toasts to "My fighting friend Churchill" and "My fighting friend Roosevelt." Churchill responded with toasts to "Stalin the Great" and saluted the President twice over, as "Roosevelt the President" and "Roosevelt the Man."

"IN FACT, IN SPIRIT, IN PURPOSE": President Roosevelt, Generalissimo Chiang Kai-shek and Prime Minister Churchill declared at Cairo:

"The three great Allies are fighting this war to restrain and punish the aggression of Japan. It is their purpose that Japan shall be stripped of all the islands in the Pacific which she has seized or occupied since 1914, and all territories stolen from China shall be restored. Japan will be expelled from all other territories taken by violence and greed. With these objects in view, the three Allies, in harmony with those of the United Nations at war with Japan, will persevere in the serious operations necessary to procure the unconditional surrender of Japan."

Roosevelt, Churchill and Stalin declared at Teheran:

"We—the President of the U.S., the Prime Minister of Great Britain, and the Premier of the Soviet Union—have shaped and confirmed our common policy. We express our determination that our nations shall work together in the war and in the peace that will follow. We have concerted our plans for the destruction of the German forces. The common understanding which we have here reached guarantees that victory will be ours. We are sure that our concord will make it an enduring peace. We recognize fully the supreme responsibility resting upon us and all the United Nations to make a peace which will command the good will of the world and banish war for many generations. We came here with hope and determination. We leave here friends in fact, in spirit and in purpose."

DEC. 20 **BIG LITTLE MAN:** Americans and Britons, going home from Teheran, took with them an unforgettable figure: Joseph Stalin.

Never before had he been viewed by so many of his allies; never before had he loomed so sharply. Those who had seen him conveyed a vivid impression to the world:

Marshal Stalin is 5 ft. 5 in. tall. But there was magnetism and a certain majesty in the figure with the brushlike mane, iron-grey mustache, a bright Marshal's uniform which was slightly too large for a perfect fit. In all that he did and said, he was quiet, impassive, at times almost immobile. He walked smoothly, effortlessly into every reception and meeting of the Conference. Sophisticated diplomats said that when he passed them in the gardens their hair rose and they quivered.

The Bahamas

THE GREAT OAKES: In the cool, labyrinthine Nassau house he JULY 19 built above the quiet sea, Sir Harry Oakes was found dead in bed. There were four blows on his head, burns on his body. The Duke of Windsor, Governor of the Bahamas and a friend of Sir Harry's, called in detectives by plane from Miami.

Sir Harry was a splendid character for a murder mystery. He was born in Sangerville, Maine in 1874. After graduation from Bowdoin College he heard about the Yukon gold strike and rushed off to prospect. In the next 13 years of a persevering search he found no gold in Alaska, the Philippines, Australia, New Zealand, West Africa, the Belgian Congo, South Africa, Mexico, California or Nevada. By 1911 he was in Canada, broke. A conductor kicked him off a train at a junction called Swastika, in northern Ontario. A down & out Chinese was sitting there, and when Oakes said he was a gold prospector the Chinese said that if gold was all he wanted there was plenty of it all around the place. Oakes found it, staked out Lake Shore Mine. It became the second-richest gold mine in the world.

In 1932 Oakes married Eunice McIntyre, whom he had met during his Australian prospecting days. They built a modern palace on the Canadian side of Niagara Falls, bought show places at Bar Harbor and Palm Beach, a house in London and a shooting box in Sussex. There were five children. Their 18-year-old daughter Nancy eloped last year with Alfred de Marigny, a slick weekend guest. Sir Harry did not approve.

In 1937 Oakes got hopping mad at Canadian taxes, announced that he was moving to Nassau because it would tax him only 5%. There he bought the Bahamas' largest hotel, built a private airport, rebuilt the Bahamas Country Club, got himself elected to the Bahamas House of Assembly. For his contributions to St. George's Hospital in London, Oakes was made a baronet. When death came last week, Sir Harry Oakes was 69 and worth about $200,000,000. His wife and family were summering in Bar Harbor. But Son-in-Law Alfred de Marigny was in Nassau. And it was he the detectives arrested at week's end. The charge was murder.

SEPT. 6   **NANCY & FREDDY:** At 19, Nancy Oakes, Countess de Marigny, is a dignified married woman, a fabulous heiress and a student at outdoorsy Bennington College. Her husband is in jail, held on suspicion of the murder of her father. Somebody killed Sir Harry Oakes during a tropical thunderstorm on the night of July 7. Nancy is sure it was not her thrice-married husband, Count Marie Alfred de Fouguereaux de Marigny. "Freddy could not have done this terrible thing," she has explained over & over. "I am the only person who can help him."

Soon after their 1942 elopement, Nancy and Freddy went to Mexico City. Nancy came down with typhoid and trench mouth. Her parents flew to her side. Freddy came every day to the hospital, twice gave blood for a transfusion. But there was still strain between Freddy and Sir Harry. Then, in Miami, Nancy told her mother that she was pregnant. On doctors' advice the pregnancy was terminated: Nancy was too weak. Sir Harry forbade the Count to enter his house. At about this time Sir Harry and Lady Oakes changed their wills. In the spring Nancy left Nassau, enrolled at Bennington.

Sir Harry had planned to go North July 6 but postponed his trip. On the 8th he was found dead, in a twisted position on a charred bed, his head crushed, his body covered with blisters. Said Nancy: "I want the murderer of my fa-

Sir Harry Oakes. Four blows on his head cause an international mystery.

Grisou, the cat. He wouldn't let the suspect sleep.

ther found." She had already seen a web of circumstance develop around her imperturbable husband.

It distresses Nancy and Defense Attorney Godfrey Higgs that Freddy still refuses to take his plight seriously. Before the bar he lolls, stretches his long legs, traps flies, winks at friends, strokes his shiny Vandyke and spins in his swivel chair. Beyond a formal denial of guilt, he has said nothing.

THE RUFFLED SHEET: Beyond the town and the deep blue NOV. 1 water of the Gulf Stream there was a world at war, but in Nassau this week interest was focused on the legal battle for Freddy de Marigny's life. Sir Oscar Bedford Daly, the Chief Justice of His Majesty's Supreme Court for the Bahamas, interrupted his reading of testimony when he came to a statement that the sheets on Harold Christie's bed were ruffled and the pillow dented. "Ruffled?" mused the Justice. "I think 'rumpled' is a better word. However, we shall leave it 'ruffled.' "

Harold George Christie, 47, Bahama born & reared, wealthy, unmarried and a close friend and real-estate associate of Sir Harry Oakes, spent the night at Westbourne, in a room 18 feet away from the murder. No servants slept in. He testified that a storm awakened him, but that he knew nothing of the tragedy until he went to call his friend

Count Alfred de Marigny. Are there singed hairs on his hands?

Nancy de Marigny: "Freddy could not have done this terrible thing."

for breakfast. Police Captain Edward Sears stated that he saw Christie downtown in a station wagon after the time dinner guests Dulcibel Effie Heneage and Charles Hubbard left and Sir Harry and his friend retired. When Defense Counsel Godfrey Higgs pressed him on his movements that night and his actions after discovering the crumpled body, Christie began to shout.

During the first week witnesses were offered by the prosecutors and evidence collected at preliminary hearings last summer was presented again: singed hairs on De Marigny's hands, arms, face and chest; the mark of his little finger on the smoke-smudged white screen that stood by Sir Harry's bed; the light that a neighbor saw burning in the Count's bedroom that night; the fact that the shirt Freddy wore has never turned up.

But the evidence did not go unchallenged. Defense Attorney Godfrey Higgs, the unseen but active Private Detective Raymond Schindler, from New York, and the unwavering support of Nancy Oakes de Marigny made themselves felt. Doubt was cast on the case of the singed hairs; the possibility was opened up that De Marigny might have touched the screen two days after the struggle in Sir Harry's bedroom, and the name of Grisou, an ash-grey Maltese cat, was introduced to explain away the light in Freddy's bedroom.

Grisou really belongs to the Marquis Georges de Visdelou-Guimbeau, Freddy's boyhood friend from Mauritius in the Indian Ocean. The night of the murder Freddy and Guimbeau gave a party for friends. Afterwards Freddy drove two wives of R.A.F. pilots home and, he says, went to bed. This was just after 1.

At 3 Guimbeau drove his friend Betty Roberts home, returning 15 minutes later to find Freddy having trouble with Grisou, who would not let him sleep. Guimbeau put Grisou out and went to bed. It remained to be seen whether all this would be capped with a conviction.

KILLER AT LARGE: For all that anyone in Nassau could say NOV. 22 with assurance, the man who killed Sir Harry Oakes might even now be sipping a whiskey & soda at the Prince George bar, or racing a fleet sailboat before the Royal Nassau Sailing Club—or resting, full fathom five, beneath the clear waters off Hog Island. Or he might not be in the Bahamas at all.

Few in Nassau had doubted the outcome of the trial of Count Alfred Marie de Fouguereaux de Marigny for the murder of his rich father-in-law. The evidence of the burnt hairs withered. The fingerprint which De Marigny was supposed to have left on the screen beside Sir Harry's bed became hopelessly confused with other prints. The mystery of how the mosquito netting over Sir Harry's bed could burn without smudging the white ceiling was left unsolved.

Like actors in a well-worn play, the black-robed, white-wigged attorneys had waded through the tangle of circumstantial evidence. Like playgoers, Nassau's lush sun set had paid early rising natives a pound a day for places in the tiny courtroom. Between sessions Count Freddy waltzed by himself in the police station, read books on sailing.

When Chief Justice Sir Oscar Daly finished his summation and the jury retired, Freddy had his chauffeur park his car beside the courthouse. But he managed to look vastly relieved when the words "not guilty" were read. In a sea of shrieks and yells and jumping natives, Freddy kissed his wife and his friend, the Marquis de Visdelou-Guimbeau, whose coat of arms is three wolves with their tongues hanging out. Then he dove into his car, told the driver to race for home.

There Grisou, the Maltese "alibi" cat, stood on his hind legs at the window making strong noises in his throat.

Freddy had not stayed long enough to hear the rest of the jury's recommendation: immediate deportation. Next day the Count consented to discuss his plans. "The war?" he asked. "I do not follow the news. I am only interested in the fishing trip Nancy and I plan for next week. I am staying in Nassau. It is my home."

Briskly the Colonial Executive Council decided to honor the jury's recommendation, invite the Count and his friend the Marquis to move on. This action was taken without the participation of the Governor, the Duke of Windsor, who with the Duchess had gone to the U.S. a month before the trial opened, and had stayed there since. Attorney General Eric Hallinan grimly declared the search for the murderer closed.

In the dank odor of suspicion which tinged the pre-season gaiety, one hostess suddenly said: "Why! Now I'll always have to wonder whether I'm dancing with the murderer of Sir Harry Oakes." [The murder was never solved. Nancy Oakes' marriage to De Marigny was annulled in 1949.]

India

FEB. 22   **WATER AND THE SPIRIT:** Inside the palace of the Aga Khan at Poona, wizened, rebellious, mystical Mohandas K. Gandhi last week began his tenth hunger strike since 1918. At the age of 74, Gandhi said that he planned to live on a diet of fruit juice and water for 21 days. (Gandhi had gone through two previous 21-day fasts, had twice broken "fasts to the death." The rest averaged three to seven days.) He thus embarrassed the British, who have branded Gandhi as a traitor at worst, a troublesome mystic at best. For his own Congress party followers (including at least 60,000 who have been arrested since last August) the fast was an effort to bolster sagging morale and stiffen the fraying fibers of resistance to British rule. Immediate results were a spate of factory strikes, one bombing which killed three men, the start of a wave of riots.

"POLITICAL BLACKMAIL": Each morning inside the guarded MARCH 1
Palace of the Aga Khan, the Mahatma (Great Soul) was
wheeled on his bed to a palace bathroom to be shaved and
washed. He was massaged twice daily, had mud packs
placed on his head. He was given occasional enemas. At the
age of 74, in a land where life expectancy is only 27, Gandhi after twelve days of his fast was sinking rapidly. Said
an Indian physician, Dr. B. C. Roy: "Only a miracle"
could see him through. During the first days he took only cit-
rus juice and water. Midway through his ordeal the act of
drinking water exhausted him. A panel of nine doctors announced that Gandhi's "uremic condition deepens and if
his fast is not ended without delay it may be too late to
save his life." He was too far gone for blood transfusions
or glucose injections to be of help. Government bulletins prepared Indians for news of his death.

*Mohandas Gandhi with followers. When the old leader refuses everything but
fruit juice the whole British Empire quivers.*

Crowds gathered outside the Palace each day, peeping
through the grilled gates to the sunburned lawns and neglected flower beds. They caught no glimpse of Gandhi but
they felt closer to him. Other followers, disavowing the Mahatma's creed of nonviolence, rioted, stoned police, burned
state buildings. The British Viceroy, Lord Linlithgow, held
Gandhi legally responsible for the deaths that had occurred,

the damage done. In the Viceroy's words, Gandhi's fast was "political blackmail."

Between Gandhi's will and that of the Viceroy the final clash had come. Like a Greek tragedy the action moved inexorably toward the climax. A frail little bag of bones had decided he would drink only fruit juice for three weeks, and the whole British Empire quivered.

MARCH 8   **ONLY ONE ANSWER:** Mohandas K. Gandhi last week survived a crisis that had caused a panel of nine reputable doctors and the people of India to believe that this time he would die. At week's end Gandhi's condition improved. He was more cheerful, weak but "perky." This week it appeared that his aged but surprisingly resilient body would last out his 21-day fast. Doctors said that a change in Gandhi's diet from sour lime juice to sweetened juice on the 12th day had stopped his nausea and possibly prevented his death. Gandhi himself said: "God intends me to live."

The British view, from Winston Churchill on down, was that Gandhi's "failure" to die merely showed that the irascible Mahatma's bluff had been called at last. Most Britons applauded a New Delhi White Paper: "Only one answer can be given to the question as to who must bear responsibility for the mass uprisings and individual crimes which have disgraced and are still disgracing the fair name of India. That answer is—the Indian National Congress under the leadership of Mr. Gandhi."

MARCH 15   **FAILURE:** Lord Linlithgow, tall, stern symbol of British policy, unbending in his scarlet-carpeted marble palace, had stood his ground and defeated Mohandas Gandhi, frail symbol of India's ceaseless struggle for her independence. Gandhi had survived a fast of 21 days without wringing a single concession from Linlithgow. From the standpoint of the Indian Government, the triumph of Linlithgow was complete, the failure of Gandhi was unqualified.

To Linlithgow, the victor, went Britain's praise for being the first Viceroy to withstand the pressure of a Gandhi fast without budging an inch. Gandhi, thinner than ever, his head propped on pillows, was again just a prisoner, held incommunicado and charged with inciting revolt in wartime.

Lord Linlithgow. He stands firm against the Gandhi fast. Page 119.

Field Marshal Wavell, new Viceroy. His daughters are late to breakfast.

NEW RULER OF 390,000,000: "The politician, who has to persuade and confute, must keep an open and flexible mind, accustomed to criticism and argument; the mind of the soldier, who commands and obeys without question, is apt to be fixed, drilled, and attached to definite rules. That each should understand the other better is essential for the conduct of modern war." JUNE 28

Britain's versatile Sir Archibald Percival Wavell, essayist as well as general, spoke these words in prewar 1939 while lecturing at Cambridge. It is doubtful if he even dreamed then that he would ever play the politician's part. Last week the opportunity came: he was named Viceroy of India. By putting a military man in the post, Britain broke a precedent standing since 1858. At 60, the scion of a family of generals, the trooper who lost an eye at Ypres, who studied desert tactics under Lord Allenby and applied them triumphantly in the campaign of 1941, the reader of Socrates, Shakespeare and Browning—this close-mouthed, wry-humored Briton took over the Empire's most complex, burdensome political post and became ruler of 390,000,000 people.

When his appointment was announced, Field Marshal Wavell was in Britain. Monocle in eye, he motored around in a black Packard. He revisited his old school, Winchester, talked to the boys about India, saw the movie *Colonel*

Blimp, and complained: "One word of command from me is obeyed by millions but I cannot get my three daughters, Pamela, Felicity and Joan, to come down to breakfast on time." In India he was likely to have more troubles than that.

AUG. 2 **SOLDIER'S CHOICE:** Soon after Field Marshal Sir Archibald Wavell was appointed Viceroy of India King George VI elevated him to the peerage. Last week, Lord Wavell selected his title: Viscount Wavell of Cyrenaica (his old battleground) and of Winchester (his old school).

OCT. 18 **THE RAJ HAS FAILED:** Smoke pillars writhed skyward last week from Calcutta's five burning ghats. Emaciated Indians shoveled at least 100 Hindu dead into the ancient fires each day, victims of a bitter, ten-month-old Indian food shortage now grown to famine proportions.

Through Calcutta's crowded streets a destitute army of more than 100,000 roamed foodless, homeless, hopeless. Families were jerked apart as mothers peddled daughters for a few rupees. Sons committed suicide to conserve scanty family stores. All around lay the hunger-shriveled dead awaiting, sometimes for hours, the arrival of corpse-removal squads. In London, Food Secretary Lord Woolton said that ships were at sea bearing "thousands of tons of cereals" to India. But his words did not allay a nation's conscience. Said the liberal *New Statesman and Nation:* "The British Raj has failed in a major test."

Italy

FEB. 1 **THE EMPEROR IS DEAD:** Last week the one Italian venture into empire that was worthy of the name was gone, along with Ethiopia and all the rest. Ancient Tripolitania, gleaming with modern roads, watered by giant aqueducts, colonized with thousands of eager peasants, had fallen to the Allies. Italians had only the sands blown across the Mediterranean by the sirocco to remind them of the 1,239,112 sq. mi. of African empire they had once owned.

To the Italian people Tripoli was a proud name, a "jewel city." They saw logic in Mussolini's empire-mongering when Tripolitania produced olives, grapes, barley, wheat, almonds and figs for the homeland. There was a glamor about Tripoli. Since 1912, when the Italians wrested it from the Turks, it had bolstered the Italian ego. And since 1933, when Mussolini began exploiting its riches, it had further inflated Italian pride. Losing it was a shock. And for "El Piccolo," King Vittorio Emanuele, who had docilely hitched his destiny to Mussolini's bombast, the loss meant that he could no longer call himself "King-Emperor."

By the summer of 1943 the Italian people were fed up with the war. They had lost their African empire, had seen the Allied invasion of Sicily in July and were suffering from serious food shortages. The Fascist Grand Council met for the first time since the war and produced what amounted to a vote of no confidence in Benito Mussolini, who had ruled Italy since 1922. King Vittorio Emanuele was thus in a position to ask for the dictator's resignation.

IL DUCE FALLS: Over the Rome radio, at 11 p.m. of July 25, AUG. 2 1943, came 47 words:

"The King has accepted the resignation from office of the Head of the Government, Prime Minister and State Secretary, tendered by His Excellency *Cavaliere* Benito Mussolini, and has appointed as Head of the Government, Prime Minister and State Secretary His Excellency *Cavaliere* Marshal of Italy Pietro Badoglio."

For the first time in more than two decades, the Fascist hymn was replaced by Italy's *Marcia Reale,* the old royalist anthem. No longer was there a Duce. But more than 20 years of Fascist power and preachment could not be wiped out in a day. Mussolini, as much as any man, had planted the cancer of fascism that had spread beyond his homeland into Germany, Spain and Central Europe. The removal of the Italian dictator was, in a sense, preliminary surgery on the malignance still afflicting mankind.

In Mussolini's place stood no democrat. Aging (71), stiff

backed Martinet Pietro Badoglio had opposed Mussolini's war against Greece, had sided with high Italians who resented the alliance with Hitler and the swelling Nazi arrogance in Italy. Yet, since 1936, he had been a member of the Fascist Party. He had masterminded the Fascist victory in Spain, defeated the Ethiopians and accepted from a grateful Mussolini the title of Viceroy and Duke of Addis Ababa.

King Vittorio Emanuele. The emperor has lost his empire.

Premier Badoglio. He announces the death of a pact, age 6. Page 125.

Now Pietro Badoglio accepted from his King the task of governing Italy and proclaimed: "Italians! By order of His Majesty I take over the military government of the country with full powers. The war goes on. Let us close our ranks around the King Emperor, the living soul of the fatherland. Long live Italy! Long live the King."

Swiftly the new Premier decreed martial law, with a ban against all public gatherings and a dusk-to-dawn curfew. He formed a new cabinet sprinkled with military names. In every action Pietro Badoglio and the aristocratic, clerical faction he represented showed the core of their ambition: They wanted a conservative, disciplined, monarchial Italy.

AND NOW, SILENCE: Benito Mussolini had studded his gaudy years with gaudy phrases:

¶ "I shall make my own life a masterpiece."

¶ "I am desperately Italian. I believe in the function of Latinity."

¶ "Better to live one day as a lion than 100 years as a sheep."

¶ "Imperialism is the eternal and immutable law of life."

¶ "War is the normal state of the people."

¶ "Democracies consist of people who are in a decline."

¶ "If I advance, follow me; if I retreat, kill me; if I die, avenge me."

Benito Mussolini's people had had enough of such phrases. Of late the trains had not even run on time.

LOVE AND POLITICS: The Badoglio dictatorship was still mum SEPT. 13 on Benito Mussolini's whereabouts. But now the controlled Italian press began to talk volubly on Benito Mussolini's love life. Practically every paper added details to a tale long familiar to gossips:

Quite by chance, in a Roman swimming pool, Benito Mussolini met voluptuous, curly-haired Claretta Petacci, daughter of an obscure but ambitious Roman family. Swiftly he put aside his other mistresses. There were many, including a pink-&-blonde German, of whom the Paris gossip-sheet, *Aux Ecoutes,* had once reported: "The new favorite discharges her delicate mission all too well. The doctors are said to have limited the daily. . . conversations with the Duce to three. The medical profession is rather lenient to a man of 56." Now Mussolini enthroned the newly-discovered Claretta in a resplendent villa. She quickly flaunted her power. She managed the Duce's fan mail, dragged him on shopping tours, hired & fired officeholders. Infatuated Benito Mussolini even followed Claretta's counsel on foreign policy. When the time came to attack Greece, for instance, Claretta approved the plan because the Greek Ambassador had snubbed her at diplomatic receptions.

FINIS: Over the North African radio came a Texas soldier's SEPT. 20 voice:

"This is General Dwight D. Eisenhower, Commander in Chief of the Allied Forces. The Italian Government has surrendered its armed forces unconditionally. I have granted a military armistice which becomes effective this instant."

The "instant" was 6:30 p.m., Sept. 8. All that day the wave lengths down the Mediterranean from Rome had berated the Allies, promised a big battle against their invasion armies. Now General Eisenhower and his staff listened for a proclamation of surrender from the Italian Government. The minutes slipped away to 7:30 p.m. Then spoke the Piedmont soldier's voice of Premier Marshal Pietro Badoglio:

"The Italian Government, with the object of avoiding further and more grievous harm to the nation, has requested an armistice from General Eisenhower. This request has been granted. The Italian forces will therefore cease all acts of hostility against the Anglo-U.S. forces. They will, however, oppose attack from any other quarter" [i.e., the Germans, who seized Rome and continued the war]. Thus death came to the Rome-Berlin Axis—six years, ten months, 14 days after it had been born.

HITLER RESCUES MUSSOLINI: With a fanfare of trumpets the Berlin radio announced:

"Members of the armed *SS* Guards and Secret Security Service, aided by parachute troops, today carried out an undertaking for the liberation of the Duce, imprisoned by a clique of traitors. The coup was a success. Mussolini is at liberty and his delivery to the Anglo-U.S. Allies has been frustrated."

All next day the Nazi propaganda mill ground thrilling details: how the loyal Führer "himself prepared the plan for freeing his friend"; how Italian guards had orders to shoot the ex-Duce if anyone tried to free him; how "*SS* Commandos" whisked off their man "without a scratch"; how grateful Mussolini had movingly phoned the Führer after his release. The Berlin claim fitted into Adolf Hitler's unfolding scheme for Italy under Nazi control. That scheme called for a puppet Fascist regime, set up in Mussolini's name.

SEPT. 27 **THE PUPPET SPEAKS:** The Germans set the stage with care. For a week they plugged the new "Republican Fascism." Then, they played a muffled recording of the Duce's voice, followed by brisk translations in all important languages. Said Mussolini in his supervised 15-minute comeback:

"Blackshirts! Italians! I am sure you will recognize the voice that called often to you in the most beautiful days of the Fatherland. I needed some time before again appearing in public. It had never been heard of that a man who had served his King absolutely loyally for more than 20 years was arrested on the steps of the King's private house and taken from one barracks to another at great speed.

Adolf Hitler & friend. "I had a sure feeling," says the rescued Mussolini, "that the Führer would look after my person."

"Although cut off from the world, I had a sure feeling that the Führer would look after my person as a brother. The word loyalty reflects the spiritual world of the Germans. It was about 2 p.m. when I saw the first German parachutist coming down to rescue me, followed by others who were resolved to break any resistance. The liberation will live in history—will in the future become legendary."

The flat, weary voice climbed to the old balcony swagger as it recounted the rescue. Then it fell again and croaked:

"It was not Fascism that betrayed the monarchy. It was the monarchy that betrayed Fascism. Take up arms again. Eliminate the traitors. Give Italy a place near the sun. Long live the new Fascist Republican party." [Mussolini remained in Nazi hands until Germany's final defeat in 1945 when he and his mistress, Claretta Petacci, were captured by Italian partisans and summarily executed.]

Yugoslavia

Ever since the fall of Yugoslavia to the German army its mountains had contained two separate guerrilla organizations. One was called the Chetniks and was under command of a Royalist officer, Draja Mihailovich, with official connections in London. A second and more effective group was led by a Yugoslav Communist with the underground name of Tito.

NOV. 22   **SALUTE FOR TITO:** General Sir Henry Maitland Wilson, Commander in Chief in the Middle East, had heard enough. For a year the rival claims of General Draja Mihailovich's *Chetniks* and Comrade Tito's Partisans had blurred the picture of resistance in Yugoslavia. For a year the Yugoslav Government in Exile had sought to bury the fact that its War Minister, Serb Mihailovich, was doing little or nothing, that all or most of the pressure on the Nazis was coming from Tito's guerrillas, who call themselves the Army of Liberation. Each band has accused the other of working with the Germans.

Across General Wilson's desk flow reports from all U.S. and British liaison officers attached to Balkan guerrilla bands. Last week Cairo radio beamed at the hills and valleys of Yugoslavia General Wilson's considered judgment:

"I salute the notable successes of the Yugoslav forces of liberation. But I have learned that in some areas certain men are dishonoring the *Chetniks* and helping the Germans in their vain attempts to subdue the forces of liberation. These men are shamefully betraying the cause of their country and adding to this shame by claiming that their actions have British approval. This claim is entirely false."

The blunt words fell hard on the youthful ears of King Peter II, patiently waiting in Cairo for a chance to resume his overturned throne in Belgrade. Last month Peter had announced that his war minister, the *Chetnik* leader Mihailovich, had promised not to fight Tito's Partisans again unless attacked.

But liaison officers recently in Yugoslavia had reported only one possible wartime solution: separate areas for the rivals to defend.

TITO ACCLAIMED: Partisans with tommy guns stood guard DEC. 13 where the village's steep and darkened streets leave the town for the mountains. The Germans across the ridge might know of the meeting, try a night attack. Inside the shabby hall sat 142 sweating, cheering men, engaged in founding a government.

Before the delegates stood the man called Drug (pronounced "droog," it means "Comrade") Tito. He heard them acclaim him Marshal of Yugoslavia, the first in history. Now he could drop his incognito, step forth officially as Josip Broz, Croatian metalworker, Communist labor leader and fighter for Loyalist Spain against Francisco Franco. The new Marshal's first act: substitution of the conventional army salute for the Partisans' greeting—the clenched fist.

Solemnly the ragged men proclaimed themselves a National Committee of Liberation, assumed the powers of a temporary Government for the freed areas of Yugoslavia. The variety of figures at the head of this Government reflected Yugoslavia's historic groupings, now partly fused by war: the Roman Catholic Croats; the hardy, heady, Orthodox Serbs; the minority Slovenes. The Partisans made Marshal Broz president of the Committee and chairman of a special Defense Committee.

There was consternation in Cairo. The new Government, the first to be formed of men who had endured Nazi occupation, ignored young King Peter and his War Minister, Draja Mihailovich, leader of the quiescent Serb *Chetniks,* and also ignored the fact that the King's Government in Exile had been recognized by the Great Powers, including Russia.

PEOPLE

"Names make news." In 1943 the following names made the following news:

Contralto MARIAN ANDERSON finally scored her triumph over the Daughters of the American Revolution. After four years of brush-offs she sang in Washington's Constitution Hall, to the first non-segregated audience in the hall's history. Some 40% of her 3,844 listeners were Negroes, who sat among Washington's social and political bigwigs. "I'm so thrilled," said the singer, "I don't know how I feel."

Yam-nosed, publicity-wise JIMMY DURANTE let it be known that he was insuring his neb for $50,000.

"I've tried all my life to drink," HELEN HAYES told a Manhattan interviewer, "and I don't like it. I consort with nobody but drinkers. I married a good two-fisted drinker [Playwright Charles MacArthur]. Once I felt I had found something I could drink—vodka. But it was the same as with every other drink. I just got sleepy and had to be taken home."

CAPTAIN CLARK GABLE, on his third operational flight, stood for seven hours in a bomber named *Ain't It Gruesome* to take training pictures while the Fortress led a raid on Gelsenkirchen, Germany.

From GERTRUDE STEIN in France came a manuscript, *Mrs. Reynolds,* to Manhattan Publisher BENNETT CERF. She had mailed it to the U.S. by mysterious means—to spare suspicious censors the task of trying to decode it. The publisher said he looked at the manuscript, could make nothing of it, thought it could probably be read from either end, decided to publish it.

Button-nosed, publicity-wise SONJA HENIE applied to Lloyd's for $250,000 insurance on her last five pairs of skates. [Ice skates were out of production because of the war.]

A few days after 18-year-old OONA O'NEILL [daughter of Playwright Eugene O'Neill] had described her eight-month acquaintance with CHARLES CHAPLIN as "entirely on the esoteric side," the comedian packed sleek, sloe-eyed Oona into a car, picked up the certificate and a case of champagne at Santa Barbara, sped to coastal Carpinteria, nervously found the finger for her first and his fourth wedding ring. Among the newlyweds' first callers were OPA agents who wanted to find out why Chaplin had used two cars for the wedding party, how he had filled their tanks.

ELEANOR ROOSEVELT, who had lately christened a barge at Port Angeles, Wash., got a phone call after she arrived in Seattle: a diver had gone to the bottom of the harbor, brought up the handbag she had dropped during the ceremony (with her plane ticket, money and eyeglasses).

LIEUT. (J.G.) JOHN F. KENNEDY, 26-year-old son of the ex-Ambassador to Britain, was commanding a PT boat on night patrol north of New Georgia when a Jap destroyer sliced it in two. The aft portion went up in flames. Kennedy rescued two of his crewmen, clung to the bow with them and eight others for twelve hours, towed one of the men on a three-hour swim to a small island. There they lived on coconuts for three days, then swam to a larger island, where friendly natives found them the next day, carried back to the Navy base an S O S scratched on a coconut.

A. A. MILNE's 24-year-old son CHRISTOPHER ROBIN, hippety-hopping hero of *When We Were Very Young,* was one of the Britons fighting near Salerno.

Hollywood's SAMUEL GOLDWYN cleared up a point for a New York *Times* interviewer who asked him: "Do producers really make stars?" Confessed Producer Goldwyn: "As a matter of fact, they don't. God makes stars and the public recognizes His handiwork."

SPORT

JAN. 11 **WARTIME SKISCAPE:**

¶ All national and sectional championship ski events have been canceled for the duration.

¶ Most topflight tournament skiers are in the armed forces.

¶ All snow trains have been crunched by the Office of Defense Transportation.

¶ Manufacturers of skiing paraphernalia are working on war orders.

¶ Shortage of manpower, food and fuel have closed famed Sun Valley and other isolated winter-sport resorts.

Despite these bunkers on the U.S. skiscape, America's thousands of ski trails and slopes will not lie fallow this winter. The Government has urged winter-sport promoters to stress recreational skiing, particularly among teen-age tyros, as part of the national keep-fit program. But the snow-belt—from the White Mountains to the Sierras—will have a thumping headache: transportation.

JAN. 18 **BASEBALL RESOLVES:** To curtail rail travel, big-league baseball last week agreed to forego its southern training season—a practice that dates back to 1886 when fabulous Pop Anson took his Chicago White Stockings to Hot Springs, Ark. for a tonic. This year's unkinking must be done north of the Potomac and Ohio and east of the Mississippi (with the exception of St. Louis' two clubs, which may train anywhere in Missouri).

JAN. 25 **FADING HOOFBEATS:** Last Monday, for the first time in years, horse players were unable to place a bet anywhere in the U.S. Of some 15,000 thoroughbreds of racing age, not one was running. The 600 at Miami's Tropical Park were stalled when the track closed as a result of the Government's ban on pleasure driving.

Come what may, the Kentucky Derby will be the last to

disappear from the U.S. racing scene. "Unless the Government bans horse racing," declared the Derby's venerable impresario Matt Winn last week, "the Derby will be run on the scheduled date [May 1], even if only two horses go to the post and even if the crowd does not exceed a half-dozen persons."

RECORD FOR THE CENTURY: Of the 60 world's records that FEB. 8 swimmers strive for, only one has defied a generation of speedsters: the 51 sec. for 100 yards (free style), set by Johnny Weissmuller in 1927. Last week, in Yale's Payne Whitney pool, that mark too was washed away—by a 19-year-old Yale freshman named Alan Ford.

Ford, a slinky, five-foot-niner with a head as smart as his strokes are slick, is the fair-haired boy of Coach Bob Kiphuth's Yale team. He was given swimming lessons at the age of three and last year, as a student at Mercersburg Academy, caused a sensation by equaling Weissmuller's record—a feat accomplished by only three other U.S. swimmers (Peter Fick, Bill Prew, Howard Johnson). This year, under Coach Kiphuth, Ford set out to smash the classic 51. Last week, during a dual meet with Springfield College (which Yale won, 59-to-16), he did it—by three-tenths of a second.

THE GOOSE FLIES HIGH: The Harlem Globe Trotters, a barn- FEB. 22 storming colored basketball team, have produced many a freakish player. None has been more bizarre than their latest find: Reece ("The Goose") Tatum, a 22-year-old Arkansan who stands 6 ft. 3, has a reach (from left to right) of 7 ft. 3.

Tatum never meant to be a professional basketball player. But Abe Saperstein, the sapient impresario of the Globe Trotters, happened to see him playing first base with Cincinnati's Negro American League Ethiopian Clowns last summer. Last week Tatum's extensible equipment was helping the Globe Trotters to be one of the most successful professional basketball teams in the U.S.

Comedy has always been an added attraction of the Trotters. Tatum deliberately capers around the court in a rocking chimpanzee gait, his long arms swinging, his teeth bared. Going for the ball, he often flaps his arms gooselike; when he jumps, can reach eleven feet into the air to block opponents' shots. Sometimes he hides the ball under his shirt, perches it on top of a bewildered opponent's head. Despite such foolery, the Globe Trotters are measuring up to their standard. In 15 previous seasons, they won 2,163 games, lost only 162.

K-9S: At Manhattan's annual Westminster dog show last week, a brass band blared, the Dog Writers Association (just what it sounds like) stopped pecking at their typewriters, and 24 shepherds, Dalmatians and Doberman Pinschers paraded around the arena of Madison Square Garden. They were no prize pooches but hardworking war dogs recruited by Dogs for Defense, Inc., for whose benefit this year's Westminster show was staged.

Dogs for Defense was founded just after Pearl Harbor by a handful of dog fanciers who rounded up dogs suitable for training as messenger, sentry and pack dogs, offered them free to the U.S. Army. Today Dogs for Defense supplies the Army, Navy, Marines and Coast Guard with 800 to 1,200 rookies a month. The Army has four K-9 training camps with 1,000 dog trainers, and Army spokesmen agree that one sentry and one dog are worth from four to eight sentries. The U.S. K-9 Corps has a nickname ("Wags") as well as a marching song (the *K-9 Corps*) written by Dog Editor Arthur Roland of the New York *Sun:*

> *From the kennels of the country,*
> *From the homes and firesides too,*
> *We have joined the canine army,*
> *Our nation's work to do.*

To become a Wag, a dog must be a pure-bred or crossbred weighing at least 50 lb., between one and five years old, at least 20 inches tall at the shoulder, physically and temperamentally sound. For $1, a contributor's dog receives the rank of private or seaman, and so on upwards. Some Park Avenue generals or admirals ($100) may go so far as to have gold braid sewed on their strolling jackets, but officially each Home Guard K-9 of whatever rank receives the same insignia: a paw print on a celluloid collar-tag.

THE GAUDY TOUCH: Everybody loves a comeback. Last week APRIL 12
flat-faced little Henry Armstrong, who once held the feather-,
light- and welterweight championships of the world simultaneously, endeared himself to the ring fans with one of the
fightingest comebacks that ever lost the judges' decision.
His defeat was a great success.

Two years ago Armstrong staggered nearly blind out of
the ring. Tough little Fritzie Zivic had given him a cruel beating, cut him to pieces around the eyes. Armstrong quit the
ring and put his brain to work. He managed a couple of fighters, M.C.'d a band, wrote stories, verse, started a book (*My
Struggle for Three Crowns*).

Fortunately for fight fans (and readers) Henry has not
yet found a publisher for his book. One night a year ago,
while Henry watched a fight in California, a friend suggested
that he try fighting again. Armstrong, then a roly-poly 165
lb., scoffed: "Who would pay to see me fight again?" But
by last week he had staged an amazing upward climb: his
eyes were healed, he had slimmed to fighting weight (138),
won 16 of 18 comeback fights, defeated backsliding Fritzie
Zivic and gained a crack at the big money—a fight with Light-
weight Champion Beau Jack.

The Beau looked too young (22) and strong for elderly
Henry (30). But fight fans are notoriously gullible, and with
the help of sentimental sportswriters shrewd Henry and the
fight promoters put on a magnificently corny advance show.
Basis of its gaudy plot was that as a beginner in the ring
Beau Jack, the illiterate former Augusta Golf Club bootblack,
had once sparred with Armstrong. Master Armstrong proposed to give Pupil Jack another boxing lesson. When the
two fighters climbed into the Garden ring last week, Madison
Square Garden was jammed and the gate was nearly $105,-
000, more than Armstrong ever drew there when he was a
triple champion.

It was a good enough show to assure old Henry a 15-
round title fight with the champ this summer. But it was
not good enough for the judges. When they pronounced
Jack the winner, the crowd booed enthusiastically, less from
conviction than as a tribute to game Henry Armstrong and
his publicity staff. Henry won $25,000. The Beau, who
fights for fun and a fee from a syndicate of sportsmen who

handle his winnings, got two flashy new suits, a hat and a new pair of shoes.

APRIL 26 **THE COUNT OF STONER CREEK:** Cabman John D. Hertz once refused a cool million for a horse named Reigh Count. This year the Hertzes have their reward: a colt that is faster, smarter and shows promise of being greater than their 1928 Derby winner. He is Count Fleet, Reigh Count's three-year-old son.

All winter U.S. railbirds have been buzzing about fabulous Count Fleet. Those who saw him run in the Champagne Stakes last fall can never forget the sight of the Hertzes' yellow silks flying down the Belmont backstretch. That was the fastest mile (1:34 $^4/_5$) ever run by a two-year-old, and was only $^2/_5$ of a second away from the world's record set by the late great Equipoise when he was a four-year-old.

If Count Fleet goes on to win the Kentucky Derby next week he will make John Hertz one of the world's luckiest turfmen. A little over a year ago, Hertz was willing to sell him for $4,500. The colt's conformation was faulty: his weight and power had grown in front instead of behind, where experts insist it should be. And from his first workout, the staff at Stoner Creek, the Hertzes' Kentucky farm, had their hands full. Count Fleet was mischievous, willful. During a morning breeze he used to stop suddenly and paw the air. He walked sideways, jumped over his shadow, bucked his riders off. Stable boys nicknamed him Count Cuckoo. But this year the Count's behavior has improved. So far he has had no romantic notions—as he did in last fall's Belmont Futurity when he took a shine to a filly named Askmenow and refused to pass her in the stretch. But he still refuses to be bullied. He makes his own decisions during a race, diving into narrow openings that would stump a less self-possessed, less determined horse. Each race he takes in stride, even eats an enormous meal immediately afterward—a rarity for a high-strung thoroughbred.

MAY 10 **THE COUNT'S DERBY:** To the surprise of no one, Count Fleet won the Kentucky Derby last week. His time: 2:04, nearly three seconds slower than the record set by Whirlaway in 1941.

ARMY & NAVY NINES: MAY 17

¶ Private Joe Di Maggio is playing ball at Camp Santa Ana, Calif.

¶ Seaman Johnny Mize is minding first base for the Great Lakes Naval Training Station.

¶ At Nashville's Berry Field, Lieut. Johnny Beazley (Air Forces) is dishing out the pitching that made him the Cardinal hero of last year's World Series.

¶ The line-up at the Norfolk Naval Training Station includes Phil Rizzuto, Don Padgett, Dom Di Maggio.

¶ Trooper Pete Reiser is chasing flies for a Cavalry nine at Fort Riley, Kans.

¶ Ex-Dodgers Peewee Reese and Hugh Casey now play for the Norfolk Naval Air Station.

With stars like these, Army & Navy nines are not only serving the purpose for which they were originally intended (entertainment of trainees), but in some areas are drawing larger civilian crowds than big-league clubs. Five thousand civilians purchased nearly $100,000 in war bonds to see a recent exhibition game between the Norfolk Naval Training Station and the Norfolk Naval Air Station. And fortnight ago the Great Lakes "varsity," managed by Mickey Cochrane, drubbed the St. Louis Cardinals, 5-to-2.

FIREMAN ON THE TRACK: Eleven competitors lined up for the   JUNE 28
race, but the 17,000 foot-racing fans, sizzling in the stands at New York's Triborough Stadium, had eyes for only two. One was chunky, pony-gaited Gregory Rice, taking time off from his duties as chief petty officer at the U.S. Merchant Marine Academy at Kings Point, L.I. to defend the championship he had won for five successive years. The other: gaunt, gazelle-gaited Gunder Hägg (pronounced Hegg), the touted Swedish fireman who was making his U.S. debut in the national 5,000-meter run.

On form, things looked none too good for Greg Rice. "Gunder the Wunder," a self-coached runner, had smashed seven world's records ranging from 1,500 to 5,000 meters in 90 days last year. His time for 5,000 meters (3 miles, 188 yards, 2 inches) was 13 min. 58.2 sec. The fastest 5,000 Rice had ever run was 14:33.4.

Rice seldom sets the pace. Neither does Hägg. But after

the first lap of the big race, lean Gunder decided to take the lead. With effortless ease he glided over the cinders, his fringe of long hair flapping, his voluminous shorts billowing like a spinnaker. Now & again he turned his head to see how he was doing. Rice, pumping along with his peculiar heel-pounding gait, fell farther & farther back.

At the mile he was 6 yards behind. At two miles there were 60 yards between them. Gunder Hägg could not be caught. His time (14:48.5) was not exactly for the record books. But his racing stride was something never to be forgotten.

JULY 26   **MANPOWER'S MUSCLE:** Can you:

- Sprint 100 yards in 14.5 seconds?
- Run a mile in 7 minutes?
- Walk a mile in 10 minutes?
- Throw a baseball 150 feet?
- Broad-jump 13 feet?
- High-jump 3 feet, 6 inches?
- Put the 12-lb. shot 32 feet?
- Take five low hurdles in 19 seconds?

If you are over 35 and cannot do six out of eight, you are physically unfit. So says National Physical Fitness Director John B. Kelly [father of Actress Grace Kelly]. If you are under 35, you should be able to do better.

"Nearly 40% of our draftees," Kelly declares, "were rejected as unfit for military service, and a majority of those accepted did not possess skills necessary for self-protection. It is estimated that 50% of our armed forces, when inducted, cannot swim well enough to save their lives, and lack the strength, agility and endurance to jump ditches, scale walls, throw missiles and stand up under forced marches."

OCT. 18   **LANDIS' PROMISE:** Baseball is carrying on—just barely. This week the New York Yankees won the 39th (and probably worst) World Series, 4-to-1. The St. Louis Cardinals made ten errors. Millions cheered anyway.

For even bad baseball is baseball. Attendance for the year was off only 6 to 8%; soldiers still get as excited by short wave as they did before most heavy hitters and crack fielders were drafted. Last spring the game's utmost umpire,

Commissioner Kenesaw Mountain Landis, promised that baseball will go on while at least 18 men are left to play. This week's World Series proved that the promise is being kept.

MATHEMATICAL MILE: The four-minute mile is possible. So reported Dr. Alfred W. Francis, research chemist and amateur trackman, in *Science*. Using a plot of average speed in meters per second against the logarithm of the distance, he drew a graph of 17 record marks, from 200 meters to 10 miles. The point for one mile was well below Arne Andersson's present record: 4:02.6. Dr. Francis, whose own record for the mile is 4:38, figures it can be run in 3:58.7. [The 4-minute mile was first run in 1954 by Roger Bannister of Great Britain. In that same year, John Landy of Australia ran the distance in 3:57.9.] OCT. 25

MAN WITH AN ARM: On the first day of football practice at Columbia in 1938, photographers hauled out an old archery target. To get stunt pictures, they placed Quarterback Sid Luckman 25 yd. away and told him to toss passes. Six times in a row he hit the dead center of the four-inch bull's-eye. In seven years of college and pro football he proved that he was just as accurate under gridiron fire. NOV. 22

Count Fleet forgets his romantic notions and takes the Derby. Page 135.

Sid Luckman, Giant-killer, completes 23 out of 30, seven for touchdowns.

Last week burly Sid Luckman hit his marksmanship top. Before a record crowd of 56,696 in Manhattan's Polo Grounds, he showed himself the best passer of the year, perhaps the best in football history. As his Chicago Bears gave the New York Giants the worst drubbing ever, 56-to-7, Sidney Luckman:

¶ Threw 30 passes, completed 23 for a total gain of 453 yards.

¶ Passed seven times for touchdowns.

Both were alltime National Football League records. Said the New York *Times*'s William D. Richardson, astonished at this show of virtuosity: "The paper shortage doesn't permit a detailed recitation."

P.S.: The last pass in the season's strangest game was incomplete. The pistol shot sounded and the game was over. Score: 26-to-26. Ohio State and Illinois trotted toward their dressing rooms, and 36,331 spectators drifted from the stands. Twelve minutes later the teams lined up again in the almost emptied O.S.U. stadium. The linesman explained that Illinois had been offside, the final play had not counted, there were still two seconds left to play. Ohio State substitute John Sturgis dropped back, booted a field goal from the 21-yard line. Final score (official): Ohio State, 29; Illinois, 26.

DEC. 13 **NOT SINCE PEARL HARBOR:** Famed for wretched football teams before it dropped the sport in 1939, the University of Chicago is on its way to fresh athletic notoriety in basketball. Last week it lost its 41st straight game, to Fort Sheridan, 48-to-29. The last time Chicago won a basketball game was Dec. 6, 1941.

THE THEATER

"SOMETHING FOR THE BOYS" gives Broadway the musicomedy JAN. 18 it has been thirsting for. It reveals Songblitzer Ethel Merman at her absolute peak and Songwriter Cole Porter well above the timberline. It tells of three uninhibited cousins (Ethel Merman, Paula Laurence, Allen Jenkins) who inherit a Texas ranch next door to Kelly Field and set up a boardinghouse for soldiers' wives. In their spare time they also make defense gadgets out of carborundum. The hostelry turns into a scandal, and Actress Merman, by getting some carborundum in her teeth, turns into a radio receiving set. After that nothing even tries to make sense.

"OKLAHOMA!" (music by Richard Rodgers; book & lyrics by APRIL 12 Oscar Hammerstein II) pretty much deserves its exclamation point. A folk musical laid in the Indian territory just after the turn of the century, it is thoroughly refreshing without being oppressively rustic. Composer Rodgers has turned out

Cole Porter and Ethel Merman. In "Something for the Boys" she is at her peak and he is well above timberline.

one of his most attractive scores, and Choreographer Agnes de Mille has created some delightful dances. Even run-of-de-Mille dances have more style and imaginativeness than most Broadway routines, while the best are almost in a different world.

"Based on" Lynn Riggs's folk play, *Green Grow the Lilacs, Oklahoma!* chiefly concerns the struggle between a good cowboy (Alfred Drake) and an evil hired hand (Howard da Silva) over a fetching farm girl (Joan Roberts). There is warm romantic melody in such songs as *Oh, What a Beautiful Mornin'* and *People Will Say,* gay lilt in *The Surrey with the Fringe on Top,* humor in *Pore Jud* and *I Cain't Say No,* a roof-buster of an anthem in *Oklahoma!* If Oscar Hammerstein's lyrics lack polish, so after all did frontier Oklahoma.

SEPT. 20 **HOPE FOR HUMANITY:** For fighting men, this grimmest of wars is in one small way also the gayest. For never before have the folks who entertain the boys been so numerous or so notable; never have they worked so hard, traveled so far, risked so much. From the ranks of show business have sprung heroes and even martyrs (two USO performers were killed in a Lisbon plane crash), but so far only one legend.

That legend is Bob Hope. It sprang up swiftly, telepathically, among U.S. servicemen in Britain this summer, traveling faster than even whirlwind Hope himself, then flew ahead of him to North Africa and Sicily, growing larger as it went. Like most legends, it represents measurable qualities in a kind of mystical blend. Hope was funny, treating hordes of soldiers to roars of laughter. He was friendly—ate with servicemen, drank with them, listened to their songs. He was indefatigable, running himself ragged with five, six, seven shows a day. He was the straight link with home, the radio voice that for years had filled the living room and that in foreign parts called up its image.

Probably the first entertainer to work with the armed forces, Hope has also been the most frequent. Using trains, cars, trucks, tanks, Jeeps, Hope has played in virtually every U.S. camp, last fall hopped off with his USO team (Singer Frances Langford, Comic Jerry Colonna) to tour Alaska. Hope's gags got around so fast he had to keep chang-

Bob Hope with Dorothy Lamour. On the USO circuit he moves like a whirlwind; only his legend travels faster.

ing them. He ragged the Scots: "That blackout's wonderful; you should see the Scotchmen running around developing film." The real show, however, was for the Yanks, and he knew what they wanted: "Were the soldiers at the last camp happy to see me! They actually got down on their knees. What a spectacle! What a tribute! What a crap game!"

Sometimes head & heart worked together. When a wounded kid in a hospital busted out crying while Frances Langford was singing, Hope broke the agonized silence that followed by walking up & down between the beds saying: "Fellas, the folks at home are having a terrible time about eggs. They can't get any powdered eggs at all. They've got to use the old-fashioned kind you break open."

"CARMEN JONES" (music by Georges Bizet; book & lyrics by DEC. 13 Oscar Hammerstein II) turns the opera that Sir Thomas Beecham once called "the sturdiest oak in the operatic forest" into the most brilliant show on Broadway. Bizet's pulsing *Carmen* score remains intact—unswung, unsyncopated, unsentimentalized. *Carmen*'s vivid plot remains unchanged. So does the inner nature of its people. But the scene of the all-Negro *Carmen Jones* is a U.S. Southern town where hip-swaying, head-tossing Carmen works in a parachute factory.

The Don José who wins her, loves her, loses her and kills her is a harassed M.P. corporal. The triumphant bullfighter Escamillo, who steals Carmen from her soldier, is a towering prize fighter.

The new words for the *Toreador Song* make the only bull— they are no match for old associations. You can only smile when, instead of *Toreador, Toreador,* you hear:

> *Stan' up and fight until you hear de bell,*
> *Stan' toe to toe,*
> *Trade blow fer blow,*
> *Keep punchin' till you make yer punches tell,*
> *Show dat crowd whatcher know!*

DEC. 20 **"THE VOICE OF THE TURTLE"** (by John van Druten) offers the season's smallest cast and one of its gayest evenings. Playwright van Druten has not only written a winning light comedy around just three people, but has even managed to suggest that three's a crowd. Sergeant Bill, in Manhattan for a big weekend, is promptly ditched by his hot date (Audrey Christie), left high & dry in her friend Sally's flat. Bill and Sally get acquainted: Bill is decent, down to earth, off love since it scorched him a few years back. Sally is sweet, self-dramatizing, off love since it scorched her a week ago Tuesday. Because it is raining and he is tired and has no hotel room, Bill spends Friday night on the living-room couch. He stays Saturday night too. By Sunday morning the caterpillar of sex has become the butterfly of love.

The production matches the play. Thirty-two-year-old Actress Margaret Sullavan, back on Broadway after six years in Hollywood, plays Sally with skill, spirit and amazing youthfulness. Actor Elliott Nugent—beside whose naturalness a man in shirt sleeves with his feet on the desk seems posed—does a perfect job as Bill. And Actress Christie, as the trollop who gives Bill the go-by, gives the play just the right touch of tabasco.

MUSIC

CHANTEUSE: Manhattan's quietly swank Savoy-Plaza Caffé JAN. 4 Lounge was last week doing the biggest business in its history as a nightspot. The attraction was the face and the shyly sultry singing of a milk-chocolate-colored Brooklyn girl, Lena Horne. Unlike most Negro chanteuses, Lena Horne eschews the barrelhouse manner, claws no walls, conducts herself with the seductive reserve of a Hildegarde. But when Lena sings at dinner and supper, forks are halted in mid-career. She seethes her songs with the air of a bashful volcano, and, as she reaches the end of *Honeysuckle Rose* ("When I'm takin' sips from your tasty lips, seems the honey fairly drips"), her audience is gasping.

Daughter of a Negro actress named Edna Scotchron, 25-year-old Lena Horne was graduated from Brooklyn Girls' High School into a job as a chorus girl in an Ethel Waters show at Manhattan's Cotton Club. She was put in big time by a spell at Hollywood's Little Troc cabaret. Her first film appearance, a sequence in *Panama Hattie,* proved the high point of a dull show.

In Manhattan Lena lives obscurely in a small room in Harlem's Theresa Hotel. Every day her aging mother makes the trip from Brooklyn to the Theresa to see that Lena eats properly and wears her rubbers. Says Lena: "It frightens me a little I haven't got any voice. I don't know anything about music. I feel like the fellow who was dreaming: all he could say was 'Don't wake me up.' "

BASSO CANTANTE: A tall, brawny Italian kissed his wife good- JAN. 25 by in suburban Mamaroneck, swung behind the wheel of a Packard and drove to Manhattan's Metropolitan Opera House. There he encased himself in the beard and trappings of an ancient czar. Exactly one hour after his arrival, Ezio Pinza stubbed out the butt of a lighted cigaret and strode through the wings as Boris Godunoff.

Ezio was playing Moussorgsky's doom-shadowed hero for the 50th time but he made the part so live that his audience could almost smell the sweat of medieval Moscow. Next day critics tried hard to find a new way of saying that Ezio Pinza is the world's greatest operatic basso, the greatest singing actor of his generation.

Outside the opera house Basso Pinza looks like a prosperous retired bullfighter. He works over his roles as systematically as a strategist planning a campaign. To make his Boris Godunoff fall dead with proper dignity, he practiced hurling his 191 lb. on to the Metropolitan's floor boards for hours, until he was so badly bruised he could hardly walk.

Seventh child of a Roman carpenter, Basso Pinza happened to sing *O Sole Mio* in the shower after taking second place in a bicycle race. The man in the next shower told him he had a voice. Pinza was soon on his way, and, after voice lessons which were interrupted when he was mustered into World War I, Arturo Toscanini gave him a contract at Milan's famed La Scala opera house. There the late impresario Giulio Gatti-Casazza signed him for the Metropolitan. His fame as a singer he is still inclined to view as good luck rather than achievement. Says he: "I like to play parts. It is something you have or you have not. If you have, it's easy."

FEB. 1 **THE DUKE OF JAZZ:** For a score of years, while "kings" of jazz and swing have succeeded each other with Balkan rapidity, a "Duke" has exhibited most of the real majesty from beside the throne. So last week the U.S. music world helped the Duke celebrate his 20th year as a band leader. The American Federation of Musicians officially blessed a National Ellington Week in honor of famed Edward Kennedy ("Duke") Ellington, whose flamboyant band has played superb jazz longer than any other orchestra in the history of U.S. popular music.

It was well deserved. *Down-Beat's* poll had just rated Duke's band first in popularity, with Benny Goodman's and Harry James's trailing. Duke and his boys celebrated by giving a concert for Russian War Relief in Manhattan's hallowed Carnegie Hall. It was a spectacular sellout.

Dressed in grey coats, each with a jet black carnation in

his buttonhole, Ellington's 15 musicians played many such Ellington favorites as the *Black and Tan Fantasy, Mood Indigo, Rockin' in Rhythm.* His music, as usual, was incandescent, original jazz, sometimes ebullient, sometimes languid, the product of one of the few authentically creative minds in contemporary music. Today Duke lives in a small Harlem apartment where, on a small upright piano, he composes between orchestra dates. He reads the Bible, attends church regularly. "I always say," he declares, "that there are more churches in Harlem than cabarets."

ENTHUSIASTIC AMATEUR: One of the finest orchestral conduc- APRIL 5
tors alive, a sovereign interpreter of music old & new, is no solemn priest of tone but the ebullient son of Britain's most celebrated laxative manufacturer. This winter goateed, 63-year-old Sir Thomas Beecham has been one of the chief ornaments of the Metropolitan Opera's brilliant season. Between times he has galvanized the young, awkward Brooklyn Symphony into an ensemble which shamed the venerable New York Philharmonic Symphony across the river. During the past season he has also directed the symphony orchestras of Seattle, Salt Lake City, New Orleans and Montreal. A large section of the U.S. concertgoing public has thus heard Sir Thomas prove beyond question that the first requisite of a fine symphonic performance is not a great orchestra but a conductor of Sir Thomas' own shining ability.

His audiences have seen him jump about the podium like a college cheerleader, stand on one foot, kick up his heels, shake his fists, lunge with his arms, yell at the brass, lose his baton, nearly lose his balance. They have watched this catalogue of gestures bring from the orchestra a beautifully controlled flow of pliant, clearly articulated symphonic sound. No conductor has a more eloquent sign language for encouraging, warning, cajoling or just plain frightening orchestra musicians into giving him what he wants.

The wealthiest man who ever twitched a professional baton, Sir Thomas has lost more money conducting orchestras than any ten of his contemporaries have made. The money (a fortune estimated at $140,000,000) was amassed by his father, the amateur Lancashire horse doctor, Joseph Beecham, who invented Beecham's Pills. Joseph Beecham was one of the first British businessmen to grasp the power of modern advertising. He even circulated a hymn book edited with an eye to furthering his product. Most famous edited hymn:

> *Hark! the herald angels sing,*
> *Beecham's Pills are just the thing.*
> *Peace on earth and mercy mild,*
> *Two for man and one for child.*

MAY 10   **DOOLEY & DODO:** The composer and the plugger of the nation's biggest song hit met last fortnight for the first time. The song: *As Time Goes By* ("A kiss is still a kiss, a sigh is just a sigh, the fundamental things apply as time goes by"). The composer: massive white-haired Herman ("Dodo") Hupfeld, who wrote it in 1931. The plugger: a short, stocky Negro named (Arthur) Dooley Wilson. Dodo and Dooley met at Manhattan's Greenwich Village Inn, where the veteran Negro minstrel was doing a singing turn.

In 1931, *As Time Goes By* was sung in a broadway show called *Everybody's Welcome,* recorded by Rudy Vallee. Forty thousand disks were sold and then the tune dropped from U.S. memory. Composer Hupfeld, who in his time had turned out such Tin Pan Alley hits as *When Yuba Plays the*

Lena Horne. When she sings she is shy, sultry and seething. Page 144.   *Dooley Wilson. In "Casablanca" no one can sing it like Sam.*

Rumba on the Tuba, came to the conclusion that he was through. For ten years he seemed to be right.

Then, last year, Warner Bros., seeking a love theme for Ingrid Bergman and Humphrey Bogart in *Casablanca,* fished *As Time Goes By* out of the files. Instead of giving the tune to a conventional crooner, Warners picked Dooley Wilson. He is something special. He sings with a sense of mood worthy of a great lieder singer. Dooley gave *As Time Goes By* everything he had. And when Ingrid Bergman in the film says that no one can sing the song like Sam (Dooley), millions of moviegoers have agreed with her.

In 1942 President James Caesar Petrillo of the American Federation of Musicians had notified U.S. record companies that in order to insure maximum employment for members of his union he would no longer allow them to make recordings that could be played over and over again on juke boxes or over the radio. The ban was challenged by the U.S. Government but in 1943 it was still in effect. In 1944 U.S. record companies settled the dispute by agreeing to pay a fee to the musicians' federation for each individual record and transcription made with the assistance of union members.

PETRILLO PERPLEXED: Cracks were opening this week in A.F. JUNE 28 of M. Boss Petrillo's dam against phonograph recording. Decca records tried a new wrinkle. Decca's idea was to have vocal soloists accompanied not by the usual dance band, but by an all-vocal (hence non-union) ensemble. Decca issued two records by Vocalist Dick Haymes with singing support: *In My Arms; You'll Never Know* and *Wait For Me Mary.* Columbia, working on a similar plan, was about to release two orchestraless Sinatra recordings: *You'll Never Know* and *Close to You.*

Meanwhile one U.S. record manufacturer happily continued making records as though Boss Petrillo and his ban did not exist. Eli Oberstein, proprietor of Classic Records Co., has no truck with vocal ersatz. Many of his records are made in Mexico and shipped via air mail. Even well-known musicians, anxious to pick up some change, have brought him records they have made themselves. Canny, suave Eli Oberstein asks no embarrassing questions. His recordings bear such names as Johnny Jones, Willie Kelly. Oberstein's *Comin' in on a Wing and a Prayer* and *You'll Never Know* have rolled up sales of 200,000 disks.

JULY 12   **BACK, YE WAVES:** The lordly boss of the A.F. of M., James Caesar Petrillo, last week revealed himself as nothing less than the Canute of canned music. He blandly commanded the whole ocean of the U.S. transcription industry to dry up permanently. Said he: "I told the companies, 'We're not going to make transcriptions for you at all any more.' " Contending that this was the first time in history that a union had attempted to abolish an industry, seven transcription companies SOS'd the Department of Labor. This week the case was certified to the War Labor Board.

AUG. 9   **"FATS" WALLER:** Radio listeners who tuned in the Blue Network's Chamber Music Society of Lower Basin Street last Sunday night heard a mammoth left hand beating out the solidest bass in U.S. pianism, a right hand doing fine and jubilant things. The hands were those of the great Thomas Wright ("Fats") Waller. Even a tyro in such matters might easily guess what experts have known for years: that Fats Waller is the pay-off in the classic American jazz piano style —full chorded and hallelujah.

Of late the Waller hands have not been idle. In the motion picture *Stormy Weather,* they caused a battered piano to romp in rare fashion. For the Broadway musical *Early to Bed,* the Waller right hand picked out the tunes. Over the years, Waller has cooked up such numbers as *Ain't Misbehavin', I've Got a Feelin' I'm Fallin', Keepin' Out of Mischief Now.* Says a collaborator: "If we could keep Fats away from the bars, he could set the telephone book to music."

Keeping Tom Waller away from bars is a difficult feat. His capacity for both food & drink is vast. A Waller breakfast may include six pork chops. It is when he is seated at the piano that he most relishes a steady supply of gin. When his right-hand man, brother-in-law Louis Rutherford, enters with a tray of glasses, Tom will cry, "Ah, here's the man with the dream wagon! I want it to hit me around my edges and get to every pound."

That requires a lot of alcohol: Waller is 5 ft. 10 and weighs over 270 lb. That mass helps to account for the great strength of his basses, and makes his playing look as magisterial as it sounds. Whether he plays a stomping *Dinah* or lazy variations on *When My Baby Smiles at Me,* no other pianist gives quite his impression of commanding ease. Next to Lincoln and FDR, Fats considers Johann Sebastian Bach the greatest man in history.

ACT I: Arturo Toscanini, the most famous of all living Italians SEPT. 20 except Mussolini and the most famous living embodiment of the art of music, had for years been using the lever of his prestige to pry at the roots of Fascism. Toscanini's personal fight with Fascism began in 1922, when he first defied a request to play the Fascist hymn, *Giovinezza,* at Milan's La Scala Opera House. When the Fascists started to agitate for control of La Scala's policies in 1929, Toscanini resigned as director. Two years later, at a concert in Bologna, the peppery little maestro again refused to conduct *Giovinezza,* saying publicly that, in his opinion, it was not music at all. After the concert a Fascist mob beat him up, Fascist authorities temporarily confiscated his passport, and the Fascist Party surrounded his Milan home with *carabinieri.* He was under incessant attack in the Fascist press.

Last week in New York, the little white-haired 76-year-old master recorded a radio program to be short-waved to Italy. Toscanini conducted the NBC Symphony in the first movement of Beethoven's *Fifth* (V for Victory) *Symphony,* the overture to *William Tell, The Star-Spangled Banner,* and then broke into tears. Toscanini called his program "Victory, Act I." He was preparing two more acts.

BULL MARKET IN CORN: The dominant popular music of the OCT. 4 U.S. today is hillbilly. By last week the flood of camp-meetin' melody, which had been rising steadily in juke joints and on radio programs was swamping Tin Pan Alley. Big names in the drawling art of country and cowboy balladry like Gene Autry, the Carter Family, Roy Acuff and Al Dexter were selling on disks as never before. Top-flight songsters like Bing Crosby and Frank Sinatra were making their biggest smashes with hillbilly tunes. A homely earful of the purest Texas corn, Al Dexter's *Pistol Packin' Mama,* had edged its way to first place among the nation's juke-box favorites. Even many of Tin Pan Alley's bestsellers, such tunes as *Comin' in on a Wing and a Prayer, There's a Star-Spangled Banner Waving Somewhere,* were fragrant with hillbilly spirit. All over the country were the Appalachian accents of the geetar and the country fiddle. All this constituted the biggest revolution in U.S. popular musical taste since the "swing" craze began in the middle '30s.

NOV. 8 **JOHNNY'S DOLL:**

I'm goin' to buy a paper doll that I can call my own,
A doll that other fellows cannot steal,
And then the flirty, flirty guys with their flirty, flirty eyes
Will have to flirt with dollies that are real.

Last week, via the voices of Frank Sinatra and the Mills Brothers, this musical tickler was mooning out of every radio and juke box in the U.S. The top song hit of the month, *Paper Doll* was proving again that yesterday's flop may live to be today's smash, and recalling the story of a very woebegone resident of Tin Pan Alley.

Paper Doll was written 28 years ago, after an unhappy love affair, by an improvident Broadway dance-hall violinist named Johnny Black. The song did not even find a publisher. Black shelved it and went to work on another, the durable *Dardanella,* which became the rage of 1919 and has been under continuous revival ever since. But luckless Johnny Black sold *Dardanella* outright for $25, and, when he got around to suing Publisher Fred Fisher, who made a million out of it, he netted only $12,000. By the early '30s Johnny Black had given up music to run a roadhouse near Hamilton, Ohio. Outside this resort in 1936, in a brawl with a customer over 25¢, Johnny Black was knocked down. His head hit the pavement, and his assailant drove off. Three days later Johnny Black was dead.

DEC. 27 **JIMMIE:** The first man to pay public homage to the late, great jazz pianist, Thomas Wright ("Fats") Waller, who died last week in Kansas City of bronchopneumonia, was just the man to do it. He was Fats's great friend James Price Johnson. Genial, blue-black Jimmie worked out on a Steinway at one of Guitarist Eddie Condon's rousing jazz concerts in Manhattan's Town Hall, played a medley of Fats Waller's tunes including *Honeysuckle Rose, Clothesline Ballet, Ain't Misbehavin'*. He played them the way Fats would have wanted them played.

Jimmie Johnson should know how. It was he who became Fats's favorite mentor in Chicago in 1921, when Jimmie was 27 and Fats a big stripling of 17. No one has ever given a better description of what happened than Jimmie himself gave last week: "I taught him how to groove, how to make it sweet—the strong bass he had dates from that time. He stuck pretty well to my pattern—developed a lovely singing tone, a lyric, melodic expression, and then, too, him being the son of a preacher, he had fervor."

The son of a Harlem pastor, portly, powerful, 270-lb. Fats Waller once defined swing for a serious young woman: "Lady, if you got to ask, you ain't got it."

MILESTONES

DIED: Dr. George Washington Carver, most famed Negro scientist; in Tuskegee, Ala. His age was uncertain; he was born of slaves about 1864. Sad-eyed, fragile, he spent most of his life in his Tuskegee Institute laboratory exploiting the possibilities of the soybean, peanut, sweet potato and cotton. From the peanut he developed more than 300 synthetic products (including cheese, soap, flour, ink, medicinal oils), from the sweet potato more than 100 (including tapioca, shoe polish, imitation rubber). "When I get an inspiration," he once explained simply, "I go into the laboratory and God tells me what to do."

MISCELLANY

PROP: In Chicago, Mrs. Josephine Skrodenis won a divorce when she complained that her husband, a murder-story fan, took up most of her evenings making her lie on the floor as a "corpse" while he tried to reconstruct the crime.

PRIORITY: In Washington, Dr. L. C. Spencer, scheduled to make a speech in Louisville, lost his plane seat to a colonel with a higher priority, canceled his talk, learned that the colonel had flown on to Louisville just to hear him.

RAPPORT: In Johnson City, Tenn., police found an empty auto standing at a red light with its motor running. They ultimately learned the answer: the driver and his wife, he bound for work, she for a shopping trip, both in a hurry, had simultaneously dashed from the car by opposite doors, each sure the other had stayed to drive.

ARMY & NAVY

FEB. 1 **"DEAR RUTH . . .":** Private Al Schmid of the Marine Corps was facing life, and he was blind. In San Diego Naval Hospital he began his biggest readjustment.

"Dear Ruth . . . " he said. The Red Cross girl, Virginia Pfeiffer, wrote it down. She did not hesitate when he came to the part about breaking his engagement to Ruth "because I don't want to be a drag on anybody." She signed his name, "Al." The Jap bullet that blinded Al Schmid after his machine gun killed 200 Japs had struck far from Guadalcanal.

When she left the room Virginia reread the letter. Then she added a postscript asking Ruth to go on writing: "With his intelligence, personality and humor there is no reason why you can't build something pretty fine out of life."

Last week Al Schmid, Marine cap perched jauntily, stepped off a train on to the windswept Philadelphia station platform. His mother and father were there to meet him. So was Ruth Hartley. He could not see the tears in their eyes and he laughed when he felt the shape of Ruth's hat pressing against him. Said Ruth, bursting with wedding plans: "He'll never be a drag on anyone. Not that one!" Other welcome home news for Al Schmid was the doctors' verdict: that after more months of hospital care he possibly might regain partial vision in his one remaining eye.

FEB. 22 **YOUNG MAN IN A HURRY:** During the Louisiana maneuvers of September 1941, which saw the dawn of the present U.S. Army, Lieut. General Lesley J. McNair was talking about some necessary weeding out of generals gone to seed. The Army, he said confidently, could find the necessary younger officers to replace the spent militarists.

"Take this young fellow here," he said, nodding at Major Alfred Maximilian Gruenther. "He is capable of a much higher command."

Al and Ruth Schmid. He could not see the tears in her eyes. Page 153.   *General Gruenther. At 43 he is the Army's youngest two-star man.*

Made a lieutenant colonel during the maneuvers, the thin, slight artillery officer with a booming voice and a penchant for championship bridge was taken up by Colonel Dwight David Eisenhower, who made him Deputy Chief of Staff of the Third Army. Three weeks after Pearl Harbor, Al Gruenther became a colonel; last year he got his brigadier general's star, went to England with Eisenhower. Last week, when his chief reached a full general's rank, Gruenther became the youngest major general in the U.S. Army. He will be 44 next month. [In 1953 General Gruenther took over Eisenhower's former job as Supreme Commander of Allied Powers in Europe.]

HELL HATH NO FURY!: If soldiers in the Detroit area had MARCH 22 voted on it last week, they would doubtless have made it unanimous that Barbara Brown is vixen-of-the-year. Tall (6 ft. 1 in.), 22-year-old Barbara Brown got mad when a soldier failed to show up for a date—and took it out on the Army. A onetime telephone operator, Barbara marched to a telephone, called the police, represented herself successively as the operator at Fort Wayne, Selfridge Field and Wayne County Airport. Her message: all soldiers on pass in the area return to their stations at once. More than 2,000 did, leaving drinks, dates and shows and a trail of blue air.

Barbara was arrested, then released. Reason: there is no law against such japery. Said she: "If I couldn't have him, I was making sure no one else could."

APRIL 26 **IRONY OF WAR:** Lieut. General George Kenney, the Southwest Pacific's air commander, announced the loss of his fourth key airman in three months: Major Kenneth McCullar, partner with the late Major William Benn in developing low-level skip-bombing. Major Benn and Brigadier Generals Kenneth Walker and Howard Ramey were lost in action, but Major McCullar's death was due to a freak accident. A pesky wallaby (small kangaroo) ran in front of his Flying Fortress as it took off, broke a hydraulic line on the landing gear. Flames from the exhaust fired the fluid. In a few seconds, the fire set off the bomb load and all on board were killed.

MAY 17 **LOOK AGAIN:** At a base in the Army's Desert Training Center (Calif.), Captain Francis E. Rogan made an inspection, finally commented: "The camouflage is only fair. They'd better work on it." Then he drove his staff car smack into the outfit's camouflaged staff headquarters.

ADVICE TO THE HOMESICK: *Roundup,* U.S. soldiers' newspaper in Delhi, India, spoke earthy words against homesickness:

"All you jerks want to return to the States because of some woman. This type of thinking, gents, is a snare and a delusion. Now she's probably driving a six-by-six truck. When you get back that nice smooth back will have so many muscles that she will look like the rear view of a General Grant tank. You'll tell her about fighting the battle of China or India and she'll say, 'Yes, yes, angel, but have you heard of our new union—the Amalgamated Order of War-Working Sweater Girls?' "

JUNE 21 **BEHIND THE WIRE:** For the 40,000 Axis prisoners now quartered in wire-ringed camps scattered through the U.S. hinterland, the war is over but not the duration. One of the most notable camps, because it houses the most explosive elements (German and Italian officers), is Camp Crossville, Tenn. Within the wire, the POWs wait through their days:

sullen, unreconstructed Nazis, cheerful Italians. Among the guests: several Italian generals.

Planned as an officer camp, Crossville houses some 1,000 of these privileged prisoners, together with 400-odd enlisted POWs who serve as valets, waiters and cooks, according to the terms of the Geneva Convention. They are still soldiers, maintain their own military discipline, salute only their captors of superior rank. They live like soldiers—but in a cage—and they gripe like soldiers. Higher Italian officers want to buy more phonographs. One German officer demanded a canary.

Germans and Italians are quartered separately—another Geneva rule. Food is regulation U.S. Army field rations, but national tastes are considered. Germans get more potatoes, fewer of the vegetables (such as carrots) which they dislike. Italians get more spaghetti, more flour for the solid Italian bread they bake for themselves.

The Germans sing a lot, especially with their beer. Marching to the soccer field, they thunder out *"Heute gehört uns Deutschland, Morgen die ganze Welt"* ("Today we have Germany, tomorrow the world"). Marching back, they sing their sad, old soldier favorite, *"Ich hatt' einen Kameraden"* ("I had a comrade"). Italians seem to like to listen rather than sing, are always buying more records (mainly operatic) for their phonographs. Officer POWs are not required to work, keep themselves amused with their hobbies and the elaborate pebble work common to all prison camps. One barracks at Crossville boasts an iron cross featly executed in gravel.

TOO YOUNG: As turret-gunner in a Martin Marauder, stubby, JUNE 28 husky Staff Sergeant Clifford R. Wherley of Elmwood, Ill. has made 21 sorties against the enemy, won the Air Medal with three oak-leaf clusters, been an all-round good fighting man. But in North Africa last week his career was ended. Before his group adjutant stood Sergeant Wherley to hear an unwelcome order: he was being sent home, would be discharged on arrival in the States. Reason: after more than a year of service, Gunner Wherley was still only 16 years old.

At San Diego Jimmy Baker, who enlisted in the Marine Corps a year ago, has been a private first class for seven months, was also honorably discharged. His age: 12.

JULY 26 **SERGEANT SNUFFY:** You would never think, to look at him, that solemn-faced Staff Sergeant Maynard H. Smith is a dashing soldier, an intrepid airman. He is a calm, unimpressive man who stands five feet four. In civilian life he worked variously as an income-tax field agent and an assistant receiver for the Michigan State Banking Commission. In the Air Force his diminutive stature made him a natural for gunner in the cramped ball turret suspended from the belly of a B-17 Flying Fortress. His nickname was "Snuffy."

On May 1, during a raid on the Nazi U-boat pens at St.-Nazaire, his bomber, Fortress 649, was badly hit and burst into flame. The fire sweeping the fuselage drove the radio operator and both waist gunners to bail out. Emerging from his turret, Snuffy cast aside his own parachute, tackled the fire with extinguishers and water bottles. When he had used them up, he beat out the last flames with his hands. Meantime, he had contrived to man both waist guns in turn, helped to beat off harrying Focke-Wulfs and had given first aid to the wounded tail gunner.

Last week Sergeant Snuffy carefully peeled the last potato of a stretch on K.P., then climbed into his best uniform, went out to the windswept airdrome, stood at deadpan attention while War Secretary Henry L. Stimson read the citation and pinned around his neck the blue ribbon and golden star of the Congressional Medal of Honor. Sergeant Snuffy was the second soldier in the European Theater of Operations to receive the nation's highest award (the first, a flyer, has not been announced), the first live man to wear it.

SEPT. 6 **THE COST:** The announced cost to the U.S. of 21 months of World War II:

Dead	18,112
Wounded	22,781
Missing	30,857
Prisoners of War	22,341
Total U.S. Casualties	94,091

OCT. 4 **BAMs:** When the Marines began recruiting women reservists seven months ago, the Corps decided that its uniformed women would carry no telescoped name like WACs, WAVES or SPARS; they would be Marines. But "women Marines"

is a lip-twisting phrase. "She-Marines" was frowned on, too. But the eventual development of some unofficial nickname was certain. Last week the Corps had it: BAMs. In leatherneck lingo that stands (approximately) for Broad-Axle Marines.

DISSENTERS: A Boston Lowell last week headlined the tight- OCT. 25
ening and toughening of Selective Service. The Back Bayer was a young (26) poet, Robert Traill Spence Lowell Jr., son of a retired naval commander, scion of a famed family with members in every war since the Revolution. No ordinary conscientious objector, Lowell twice tried to enlist, later reversed his views because he decided the bombings of total war are unethical. So he refused to serve "as a matter of principle." He was sentenced to a year and a day in Federal prison. [In 1965 Poet Lowell made news by giving the presence of U.S. troops in Vietnam and the Dominican Republic as his reason for turning down an invitation from President Lyndon Johnson to participate in a White House festival of the arts.]

GENERALS ALSO DIE: The U.S. armed services totted up their losses among high-rankers last week, found that World War II, with its emphasis on air fighting, is no respecter of generals, admirals.

In the 22 months since Pearl Harbor the U.S. Army has lost 30 general officers—killed, captured or missing in action. Three Navy admirals have been killed in action, an admiral and a commodore killed in air crashes; two admirals have died at sea.

LOOSE LIPS: When a certain troop transport left Seattle re- NOV. 8
cently, three of the crew were caught after they had slipped ashore to make forbidden last-minute telephone calls. Checking up, military intelligence officers called the same numbers, to find out what information had been spilled. They found plenty. Posing as cigaret-company representatives, they said they wanted to send each man a carton as a gift. A wife, a mother, and a girl friend quickly supplied the information that their men had just sailed on a transport. One woman cheerily volunteered its destination.

NOV. 15 **OLD SOLDIER:** It was Dec. 7, 1941. That afternoon General John J. Pershing, 81, went driving in Rock Creek Park. For 23 years his country had done its best to forget that it had a military tradition. It had reduced its Army to impotency, had neglected its training. Twenty-three years before, his nation had refused to heed his warning: "The complete victory can only be obtained by continuing the war until we force unconditional surrender." Now it was Pearl Harbor and the day of reckoning.

Robert Lowell. The young poet decides bombing is unethical.

General Pershing. There is no fire in his fireplace, no one at his desk.

That evening the aging General of the Armies returned to Walter Reed Hospital where he had been cared for since 1941. He read the newspapers. Every two or three weeks he was pleased to receive U.S. Chief of Staff General George C. Marshall. Marshall could talk freely and respectfully with his old chief, and the old man, who had seen greatness in the youngsters in 1917, had no suggestions to make. But he was angry when he was neglected. He was piqued when Ike Eisenhower went off to Europe without taking leave of him. He glared and snapped: "I don't even know the man." Every day he rose at 8, draped a bathrobe over his pajamas and watched his breakfast roll in—grapefruit, cereal, soft-boiled egg, toast, coffee. There were few things an old man could enjoy, but he damn well did like and insist on grapefruit, and for lunch a chop and spinach. He liked spinach. No cigars. Gave up cigars 35 years ago on the advice of his doctor. A touch of whiskey now and then.

In the State Department building is an office with a door marked in gold letters, "General of the Armies." A beribboned colonel sits inside the door. General Pershing's own room is beyond. The room is blue-carpeted; on its walls hang four portraits of America's dead and buried Generals: Washington, Grant, Sherman, Sheridan. There is a fireplace, but there is no fire in it. There is a large desk but no one sits there. The long mirror hanging over the cold fireplace reflects no living presence. The office of the General of the Armies is empty. [The only U.S. officer to hold that title—Eisenhower and MacArthur were five-star Generals of the Army—Pershing died in 1948.]

HELPMATE: He said he was a family man. To his draft board in Poinsett County, Ark. he presented a letter:

"Dear United States Army: My husband asked me to write a recommend that he supports his family. He cannot read, so don't tell him. Just take him. He ain't no good to me. He ain't done nothing but raise hell and drink lemon essence since I married him eight years ago, and I got to feed seven kids of his. Maybe you can get him to carry a gun. He's good on squirrels and eating. Take him and welcome. I need the grub and his bed for the kids. Don't tell him this, but just take him."

PATTON'S SLAP: The U.S. was shocked by the first scandal in NOV. 29 the U.S. Army High Command in World War II. It centered on a hero: gaudy, profane Lieut. General George Smith Patton Jr., Commander of the U.S. Seventh Army. The very serious charge against "Old Blood & Guts" was that he had committed one of the unforgiveable military sins: he had struck, vilified and degraded an enlisted soldier. Worse than that, the soldier was a casualty of battle. The story:

During the action in Sicily, General Patton visited an evacuation hospital. He was conducted to the receiving tent, where 15 casualties had just come in from the front. The General went down the line, asking each patient where he had been hurt. On the edge of the fourth bed sat a soldier with no visible wounds. He had been sent back by his divisional medical officer, tentatively diagnosed as a severe case of psychoneurosis. He was still in battle dress.

The General asked him the routine question. The soldier answered: "It's my nerves. I can hear the shells come over but I can't hear them burst."

Patton turned to the medical officer and asked, "What's this man talking about? What's wrong with him—if anything?" Patton began to shout at the man. His high voice rose to a scream, in such language as: "You dirty no-good — — — —! You cowardly —! You're a disgrace to the Army and you're going right back to the front to fight." Patton reached for his white-handled single-action Colt. The man sat quivering on his cot. Patton slapped him sharply across the face, turned to the commanding medical officer who had come in when he heard Patton's high-pitched imprecations. "I want you to get that man out of here right away. I won't have these other brave boys seeing such a bastard babied."

Patton started to leave the tent, wheeled when he heard the man sobbing, ran back and hit him again. Patton went to another tent and asked more questions of wounded men. Then he broke into a sob: "I can't help it, but it breaks me down to see you brave boys."

As he left the hospital, General Patton spoke again to the medical officer: "I meant what I said about getting that coward out of here."

The soldier whom swashbuckling Georgie Patton struck was a volunteer; he had been in the Army for four years. He had enlisted when he was 18, had served in both the Tunisian and Sicilian campaigns. The preliminary diagnosis turned out to be incomplete. He was also suffering from malaria, had a high fever. On his record he was no malingerer. Before the General appeared, he had asked the receiving officer to let him go back as soon as possible.

A U.S. correspondent wrote a full report, sent it to General Eisenhower. General "Ike" acted immediately. He sent a general officer to Sicily in a special plane the day he received the report. When the investigating officer confirmed the report, Eisenhower wrote Patton a slashing rebuke. Patton was ordered to apologize publicly to the patients concerned, to the staff of the hospital, and to make a clean breast of the affair to the staff officers of each division of his command. He was told bluntly that he was on probation.

PEEWEE: Peewee Maloney is a little trick with a turned-up nose, brown hair and wide smile—neat and cute as a .22 bullet. Back home in Rochester, N.Y., she had been cashier in a cafeteria, until she persuaded the Army to make an exception to its 5-ft. rule and let her in the WAC, all 4 ft. 11 in. of her. As Private Margaret H. Maloney she was soon stationed in North Africa.

One morning Peewee was acting as supply sergeant for her company when Private Kenny Jacobs came into the WAC's kitchen. Helpfully he poured some gasoline into the stove to prime it, splashed some on his clothes, set himself afire and collapsed in a mass of flames. Peewee threw herself on him, smothered the fire with her body, beat it out with her bare hands.

Private Jacobs was carried off to the hospital, lucky to be alive; Peewee was carried off with him, for treatment of burns on her face and legs.

Last week while an Army band played, a color guard and three platoons of WACs stood at attention, a trembling Peewee did a front and center, stood alone. The adjutant read a citation from General Dwight Eisenhower. On her O.D. blouse Major General E. S. Hughes pinned the first Soldier's medal awarded a WAC. Then, though the regulations do not prescribe it, towering General Hughes unbent in the middle, leaned down and planted a kiss on the glowing cheek of Private Maloney.

SEAGOING JEEP: From grinning Navy men the U.S. Army finally found what had happened to a missing Jeep. It had been parked on a dock in a West Coast port hard by a submarine. Next day both submarine and Jeep had gone. To newspaper ads asking for information leading to recovery of the little car, the Army got no reply. The reason: the submarine's crew had dismantled the Jeep, stored it in various nooks and crannies below. It was handy to have around. When the sub hit port the pieces were lugged ashore, the Jeep was assembled, the crew had free transportation.

DEC. 6   **ANOTHER SLAP:** The first tendency of the nation was to regard the Patton affair as a shocking but isolated incident in an officer's career. It was not. The isolated incident quickly became two. Bellicose General Patton had degraded another enlisted man. Private Charles Herman Kuhl had written home to Indiana: "General Patton slapped my face yesterday and kicked me in the pants and cussed me." Kuhl, like the unnamed artilleryman whose slapping precipitated the Patton case, had also been hospitalized for psychoncurosis.

There were other stories of unsoldierly conduct by West Pointer Patton. On one occasion he had pounced on a group of antiaircraft men who had just beaten off an enemy attack, with casualties. Those who could stand were lined up and dressed down by Patton for not wearing their leggings. In Sicily, a Patton outburst was touched off by a mule cart which blocked a bridge. Patton ordered the cart tipped over, then ordered the mule shot.

DEC. 27   **CHRISTMAS DINNER:** The Army, which got Thanksgiving turkey even in front-line foxholes, announced its Christmas dinner menu—subject to no change except for the most extreme fortunes of battle.

Creamed Celery Soup with Croutons
Roast Turkey, Sage Dressing, Giblet Gravy
Cranberry-Orange Relish
Snowflake Potatoes
Head Lettuce with Russian Dressing
Hot Rolls, Butter
Mince Pie   Chocolate Nut Cake
Assorted Fruits   Candy Nuts
Coffee   Cigarets Tobacco

SCIENCE

FOR THE HUMAN RACE: Death came in Manhattan last fort- JAN. 4
night to Columbia's Professor Franz Boas, who more than
30 years ago scientifically demolished "this Nordic nonsense"
in *The Mind of Primitive Man,* a book which has since been
called the Magna Charta of self-respect for the so-called
lower races. For 59 years he measured, compared, talked
facts about humanity, trained most of the outstanding U.S.
anthropologists of today.

Boas wrote, in a letter to TIME in 1936: "The assumption
of the biological homogeneity of any race is a fiction. Every
race contains many family strains which are biologically dis-
tinct. Personality cannot be assumed to be determined by
the so-called racial groups but is a matter that must be determined individually."

After his retirement in 1936 Boas became an active cru-
sader. Said he: "Hitler taught me that it is not only necessary
to discover truths about man; it is necessary to spread them
in the world. Science alone was not enough to check the
wide acceptance of the race nonsense of Naziism."

He also said: "If we were to select the most intelligent,
imaginative, energetic and emotionally stable third of mankind, all races would be represented."

When death came to Franz Boas, 84, he had earned the
title of a great humanitarian.

THE BLIND CAN FIGHT: The blind are finding increasing op- JAN. 11
portunities in the war effort:

❡ Blind, 23-year-old Byron H. Webb of Chicago was graduated from De Paul University last month, wanted to fight
the Axis somehow. He was told of various relatively nonessential jobs he could do. Dissatisfied, he thought hard,
sold himself to the Signal Corps. His job: teaching Signal
Corps men to make emergency radio repairs in the dark.

❡ Toledo Scale Co. has a new instrument, invented by blind

Evelyn Watson of Buffalo, which permits blind people to weigh by ear such things as powder for fuses, mica for radio installations, buttons, screws. The machine is set to indicate a certain weight, signals *dit-dah* when the needle is under the mark, *dah-dit* when it is over, *buzzzzzzz* when it is "on the beam."

NOV. 22   **6423 = A ROSE:** There is some great smelling going on in Cambridge, Mass. It has to do, among other things, with spices. A natural spice is an extremely subtle blend of many ingredients, and the absence of even a trace of a key ingredient may make a big difference in odor and taste. Therefore, attempts to find out how to synthesize spices by chemical analysis have not been successful. But an inventive Cambridge chemist named Ernest Charlton Crocker has just produced three synthetic spices very close to the real thing— nutmeg, cinnamon and white pepper. In so doing, he has used only his remarkable nose and taste buds.

Chemist Crocker, who is pioneering a new science of the senses, works in the top-flight Arthur D. Little industrial laboratory. (The Little laboratory, just to show it could be done, once made a "silk" purse out of a sow's ear.) In classifying his vapory perceptions, he reduces all odors to four basic ones: fragrant (*e.g.,* animal musk), acid (vinegar), burnt (roasted coffee), caprylic (goaty or sweaty). Each is further classified in eight degrees of strength. These basic smells in various combinations make up thousands of different odors, most of which Crocker can recognize at one sniff. In analyzing smells, Crocker sniffs for each basic component, like an orchestra conductor listening for specific instruments, then describes the total effect by numbers. Thus, the Crocker description of a rose is 6423, representing the relative strength of its fragrant, acid, burnt and caprylic components, respectively.

To synthesize nutmeg, Crocker analyzed the natural spice with his tongue and nose, then tried hundreds of chemical combinations to get the right shades of odor and flavor. The result was a compound of more than 40 different ingredients, including several varieties each of phenols, alcohols, esters and aldehydes. All these were mixed in a meal ground to nutmeg's consistency.

RED RESEARCH: A thousand U.S. scientists in Manhattan last week saw dead animals brought back to life. It was the first public U.S. showing of a film picturing an experiment by Soviet biologists. They drained the blood from a dog. Fifteen minutes after its heart had stopped beating, they pumped the blood back into its lifeless body with a machine called an autojector, serving as artificial heart and lungs. Soon the dog stirred, began to breathe; its heart began to beat. In twelve hours it was on its feet, wagging its tail, barking, fully recovered.

This picture was shown to a Congress of American-Soviet Friendship and explained the work of a group of Russian scientists at the U.S.S.R. Institute of Experimental Physiology and Therapy at Moscow. The scientific audience thought this work might move many supposed biological impossibilities into the realm of the possible.

The autojector, a relatively simple machine, has a vessel (the "lung") in which blood is supplied with oxygen, a pump that circulates the oxygenated blood through the arteries, another pump that takes blood from the veins back to the "lung" for more oxygen. It can keep a dog's heart beating outside its body, has kept a decapitated dog's head alive for hours—the head cocked its ears at a noise and licked its chops when citric acid was smeared on them. But the machine is incapable of reviving a whole dog more than about 15 minutes after its blood is drained—body cells then begin to disintegrate.

In chemistry the Russians have pioneered in the preparation and use of blood plasma, in synthetic rubber, photochemistry, explosives, helium, winter lubricants for tanks and planes. Soviet scientists have also found ways to extract iodine cheaply from the foul waters of oilfields, sugar from watermelons, vitamin C from pine-tree needles for hungry Leningrad. Important contributions have been made to molecular physics, optics, electronics.

RADIO

JAN. 25 **BLACKOUT:** It could not be so—yet it was. After 15 years and some 4,000 airings, Amos 'n' Andy were scheduled to leave the air next month. Campbell Soup Co., its domestic output halved by the tin shortage, no longer was willing to spend $1,800,000 yearly to sponsor the pair five nights a week. Millions of loyal radio fans will miss them. So will Henry Ford, who writes fan letters, J. Edgar Hoover, James Thurber, Vincent Astor, and countless others whose addiction approaches that of the late Hearst editor, Arthur Brisbane, who sometimes telephoned breathlessly after the broadcast to find out what would happen in the next episode.

Since March 1928, when Freeman F. Gosden, onetime egg-bearer for Thurston the Magician, became the long-suffering Amos, and Charles J. Correll, onetime Peoria bricklayer, became turgid, blustering Andy, they have had but one vacation —eight weeks in 1934. No radio performers have made more broadcasts. They were radio's first great national program. They were the chief instigators of the habit of listening to a fixed program night after night.

FEB. 1 **FIRST WAR YEAR:** Although 1942 was U.S. radio's first year of war, there was no great change in public listening habits. The year's greatest audiences were drawn by Franklin Roosevelt. The greatest audience gains were made by news broadcasts. These were the conclusions of the Cooperative Analysis of Broadcasting (Crossley) report for 1942. Some other C.A.B. findings:

¶ The year's most popular program was *Fibber McGee & Molly,* followed in order by Jack Benny, the *Chase & Sanborn* program (Charlie McCarthy), Bob Hope, *The Aldrich Family, Lux Radio Theatre, Maxwell House, Kraft Music Hall* (Bing Crosby), Walter Winchell, Kate Smith. Only newcomers to the first ten were *Kraft Music Hall* and Walter Winchell.

¶ President Roosevelt's first two broadcasts after Pearl Harbor hit an alltime high of 83% of set owners.

WIT'S END: To author Edna Ferber, he was a "New Jersey FEB. 1 Nero who mistook his pinafore for a toga." Critic Percy Hammond found him "a mountainous jelly of hips, jowls and torso, but with brains sinewy and athletic." Caustic Wit Dorothy Parker thought that he did "more kindness" than anyone she had ever known.

These descriptions became part of the carefully nurtured legend of Alexander Woollcott. The legend was no more varied than the man. Despite his activities as dramacritic, radio raconteur, cinemactor, women's club lecturer, magazine contributor, author *(While Rome Burns,* etc.), playwright, Broadway actor, he achieved his greatest success in the tireless, diverse role of Alexander Woollcott—a complex of childish petulance, fierce, blind loyalties, sentimental sophistication, and a cannibalistic curiosity about people and things.

He conferred himself upon the New York *Times* in 1909, fresh out of Hamilton College, where his fraternity mates were said to have used him to frighten away unwanted prospects. His writing style, which in terms of liquors was a decidedly pink drink, bubbled up in the *Times*'s drama department, where he acquired an unsmiling assistant named George S. Kaufman. When Kaufman eventually satirized him as the waspish subject of *The Man Who Came to Dinner,* Woollcott declared: "The thing's a terrible insult and I've decided to swallow it."

In a couple of decades Woollcott made himself a notorious wiseacre occupying a Manhattan apartment ("Wit's End") where he struck extravagant attitudes, greeted friends ("Hello, repulsive"), dismissed bores ("I find you are beginning to disgust me, puss. How about getting the hell out of here?"). As radio's *Town Crier* he got a big audience for his twelve-cylinder whimsies and became a cultural campaigner of such influence as had not been known since the palmy days of William Lyon Phelps. He was a national phenomenon.

Alexander Woollcott was ailing last week when he sat beside the microphone in CBS's Manhattan studios with two authors and two college presidents. Their broadcast subject on the *People's Platform* was "Is Germany Incurable?" Woollcott answered: "It's a fallacy to think that Hitler was the cause of the world's present woes. Germany was the cause of Hitler." They were among his last known words. A few minutes later, without the audience knowing it, Alexander Woollcott, 56, suffered a heart attack, and later that evening he died.

MARCH 8   **SCRATCH ONE BOXTOP:** The best in radio—and a lot of it—goes to U.S. forces at the fighting fronts. They have received over 1,000 special programs which U.S. radio fans would give plenty to hear. *Command Performance* gives the boys a variety show of anything they ask for (from Bing Crosby to Ann Sheridan frying a steak).

Comedian Bob Hope closed one *Command Performance* broadcast with the remark that if the boys wanted Songstress Ginny Simms to purr another number, "just tear off the top of a Zero and send it in." The boys sent a big hunk of wing with the Rising Sun on it.

JUNE 21   **NEW YORK HICK:** A score of U.S. celebrities have gone as guests to *Duffy's Tavern* and come away thoroughly buffooned. The buffoon is Barkeep Archie, a likable mug, strictly from Brooklyn, who shares the great American love of irreverent ribbing. In real life, Archie is a lean, mischievous, battered six-footer named Ed Gardner, whose indignities are delivered with a kazoo-voiced good nature which keeps everybody happy, including his victims. The result is grade-A American foolery.

In two years *Duffy's* has acquired about 7,000,000 steady listeners. Prisoners at San Quentin (their warden's name is Duffy), like the show so much that they call their jail Duffy's Tavern.

The program contains some of radio's oddest characters. Duffy, proprietor of a Third Avenue saloon where "the elite meet to eat," never shows up, is merely a stubborn Irish character on the telephone. Man-crazy Miss Duffy, the boss's daughter and pure Tenth Avenue, is Gardner's pretty, redheaded ex-wife, Actress Shirley Booth (*My Sister Eileen, Tomorrow the World*).

Frank Sinatra. "Frankie," the girls all scream, "you're killing me!" *Raffles with Ed Gardner of "Duffy's Tavern." He or she is a sensation.*

THAT OLD SWEET SONG: At Manhattan's Paramount Theater, JULY 5 and at the *Lucky Strike Hit Parade,* hundreds of little long-haired, round-faced girls in bobby socks sat transfixed. They were worshipers of one Francis Albert Sinatra, crooner extraordinary. Their idol, a gaunt young man (25), looked as if he could stand a square meal and considerable mothering. As Sinatra intoned *Night-And-Day-You-Are-The-One,* the juvenile assemblage squealed "Ohhhhhhh!" He aimed his light blue eyes and careless locks at a front row devotee. It was too much; she shrieked: "Frankie, you're killing me!" Cocking his head, hunching his shoulders, caressing the microphone, Sinatra slid into *She's Funny That Way,* purring the words: "I'm not much to look at, nothin' to see." "Oh, Frankie, yes you are!" wailed the audience. The song over, Sinatra started to leave the stage. "Don't go!" whimpered the little girls. He gave them an encore, mooned: "The mate that fate had me created for." Thereupon a delegation of them rose, whinnying: "Frankie, look at me!" The band had to play the *Star-Spangled Banner* to get him off the stage.

In various manifestations, this sort of thing has been going on all over America the last few months. Not since the days of Rudolph Valentino has American womanhood made such unabashed public love to an entertainer.

NOV. 1   **A BIRD:** Hollywood has found a sensational new comic of peerless proportions and undiscovered sex. He or she (nobody can tell) is a black-bodied, yellow-legged, orange-beaked Mynah bird named Raffles which has a positive genius for saying the wrong thing at the right time in an Oxford accent.

On *Duffy's Tavern* last week the bird laughed, whistled, sneezed and sang the *Star-Spangled Banner.* It brought down the house. On Fred Allen's program last spring Raffles, who is crowsize, flew away with the show by the simple expedient of soaring up to the balcony, banking gracefully back toward the stage and coming in on the orchestra leader's head.

In Hollywood, Raffles has met Walt Disney, Charlie McCarthy, David Selznick, many other bigwigs. Elsa Maxwell gave a party for the bird. Paramount signed Raffles up for eight weeks at $3,500 to play opposite Dorothy Lamour in a forthcoming movie. On the lot Raffles' dressing room, complete with nameplate, is next to Dorothy's.

Probably the highest-paid bird in the world ($500 a radio performance), Raffles belongs to the explorer-lecturers, Mr. & Mrs. Carveth Wells. Mrs. Wells adopted Raffles in Malaya four years ago after its mother was killed by a snake. Mrs. Wells worked hard on the bird's diction, avoiding profanity, and taught Raffles to speak only on cue (a process involving bribery with the bird's favorite food—grapes). The bird now has its own personal maid, whom it summons either by name or by making a noise like a buzzer.

DEC. 13   **STRAIGHT MAN:** George Burns, the most famous straight man in U.S. radio, observed his 40th anniversary in show business this week with a straight man's true imperturbability. As "the brain" and foil of the comedy team of Burns & Allen, he was thankful that his old vaudeville routines, neatly brought up to modern times, were worth $10,000 a week as a package show to his sponsor (Swan Soap), and he was delighted with the show's 15,000,000-odd listeners.

Now 47, dry, petulant, hawk-voiced George Burns had an early training in antics. Born Nat Birnbaum into a family of twelve children on Manhattan's crowded Pitt Street, he began his theatrical career of necessity at the age of seven, after his father died. George organized the Pee-Wee

Quartet, featuring himself and a six-year-old basso. The four took turns passing the hat in saloons and backyards.

At an early age George quit public school and joined a roller-skating act. Then he formed a ballroom-dancing act with a 16-year-old girl whom he named Hermosa José, after a five-cent cigar. In 1922, one of George's friends brought Gracie Allen, daughter of a song & dance man, to see Burns's act at Union Hill, N.J. Hunger had persuaded Gracie to abandon her own vaudeville career for secretarial school. Burns promised to feed her if she would join him. When he found that as the straight member of the act she was getting all the laughs, he forgot his comedian's pride and took the straight role himself.

The vaudeville mood is still their mainstay, despite the elaborate plot of the script and the guest stars. Last week this was apparent in the opening dialogue introducing Charles Boyer. Going home from a Boyer movie, George said: "Gracie, could you walk a little faster?"

Gracie (in a daze): "Hmmm?"

George: "I said, could you walk a little faster?"

Gracie: "If you wish, Charles."

George: "Gracie, I'm George Burns, your husband. Remember? I'm not Charles Boyer!"

Gracie: "Oh, well, that's life."

MILESTONES

DIVORCED: Thomas Franklyn ("Tommy") Manville Jr., 48, asbestos-wealthy Manhattan playboy; by Billy Boze Manville, 20, his sixth; four months after marriage; in Reno. Her explanation of why she married him: "It was like a new job that somebody tells you nobody can hold. I thought I could do it where they couldn't."

MISCELLANY

NEVER MIND: In Boise, Idaho, Police Chief R. G. Haskin caught up with a motorist, whipped out his pencil and book, asked him his name, learned it was Aloises Zachary Abernathy Mefgenthenwallerberry, let him off with a lecture.

FUELISHNESS: In Philadelphia, the fuel rationing office for the North Side had to shut up shop, having neglected to ration itself some fuel.

THE CURRENT SCENE: In San Francisco, Mrs. Lucille Riquard testified that her husband had punctured 55 cans of her rationed fruit and vegetables. She won a divorce. In Kansas City, Walter Solt, who had had trouble with the maid service at his hotel, was fined $1 for taking his jampacked wastebasket down to the lobby and dumping it out on the clerk's desk. In Manhattan, department stores offered a new preparation for sale—a liquid to take the shine off the seat of the pants.

RELIGION

FEB. 8 **DISHTA OF PONDICHERRY:** In southern India, New York *Times* Correspondent Herbert L. Matthews last week stumbled on a daughter of Woodrow Wilson. The spit and image of her father, she lives in Pondicherry as a *sadhak* (follower) of an Indian religious teacher, Sri Aurobindo. Said she: "I never felt more at home anywhere."

Margaret Woodrow Wilson, now 56, and a spinster, broke with her family's Scotch-Irish Presbyterian traditions years ago when she stalked from church during Communion service. Now, at Aurobindo's *ashram* (a retreat for disciples) Margaret Wilson responds to the name Dishta, meaning in Sanskrit the discovery of the divine self. Her religion, not concerned with mortifying the flesh, permits her to wear American clothes, read magazines and newspapers, puff an after-dinner cigaret. When she first arrived in India some three years ago she tried to be a vegetarian, but she lost so much weight that she was put back on meat. She spends most of her time trying to acquire "a state of serenity." She finds it "extremely hard."

FEB. 22 **BELL'S BROADSIDE:** "I do not know if men will understand, I am persuaded that God understands, and that He is telling me to go ahead." Thus Bernard Iddings Bell, gadfly of the Episcopal Church, introduces his latest book, *The Church in Disrepute.* Bell is a modern Episcopal Jeremiah who, speaking in cultivated accents, excoriates the thing he loves—the Church—and has attracted his own, modern version of the prophet's unpopularity.

Bell absolves man from blame for the world's dilemmas. After all, he is "a small and unreliable creature . . . erratic, frequently fooled by his five inaccurate senses, largely irrational, unduly emotional, seldom sane." The blame, he holds, lies on the Church, which has grown soft, functions as "a minor decorative art," carries on its work like any big busi-

Margaret Woodrow Wilson. Serenity *The Rev. Bernard I. Bell. He finds*
eludes her in India. Page 173. *man "small, erratic, seldom sane."*

ness corporation, supports ministers who warble "minor plat-
itudes like twittering birds almost alone in unawareness of
the hurricane."

The Church's purpose, says he, should be the same as it
was nineteen hundred years ago: to proclaim "the nature of
God, the nature of man, the right relationship between the
two, as these are revealed in the person and teaching of
Jesus called the Christ." The result of such proclamations,
Bell is sure, would be trouble. But if the Church would get
out in the world and make trouble, people would respect it.

Short, chubby, beetle-browed Bernard Iddings Bell, 56,
was a chaplain at the Great Lakes Naval Station in the last
war. Then for 14 years he headed St. Stephen's College, An-
nandale-on-Hudson, N.Y. With the help of the late vaudeville
impresario Edward Albee, Bell raised about a million dollars
to revolutionize the St. Stephen's faculty and methods. But
the depression spoiled his plans and Columbia University
took over the college, renamed it Bard. Today Bell lectures
in the leading universities, broods about a civilization "cor-
rupted through and through with malignancy."

LATEST EASTER: This year Easter falls on its latest possible APRIL 5
date, April 25. Only once in the past 100 years—in 1886—
has it been so late. It will not happen again in this century.

(The earliest possible date, March 22, last occurred in 1818, also will not recur in this century.) The timing of Easter, a confusing system mixing astronomy and ecclesiasticism, was worked out by the early Christian Church at the Council of Nicea in 325 A.D. and has never been changed. The Council provided that:

¶ Easter must closely follow the spring equinox, in accord with the pagan tradition of spring festivals. For convenience, the Council arbitrarily set the equinox on March 21.

¶ Easter must closely follow a full moon in order to light the way for pilgrims' travel to the festivals.

¶ Easter must follow the Jewish Passover (which always falls on the 14th day of the paschal month) to avoid conflict between the two holy days.

¶ Easter must be on a Sunday.

IN TROUBLOUS TIMES: On a raft in the Pacific with Eddie Rickenbacker's shipwrecked airmen, Lieut. James C. Whittaker saw the stirrings of a national movement. "We all saw Johnny Bartek reading his Bible, his freckled face solemn as an owl's and the sun glinting on his red hair," Whittaker wrote in his new book *We Thought We Heard the Angels Sing.* "No one kidded him."

What Pvt. Bartek and many another soldier was doing, civilians back home were doing, too. Under the stress of war, people were turning to religion. One sign was a definite rise during the past year in the sale of religious books.

Some facts & figures:

¶ The Bible, still the world's best-seller, is going stronger than ever. Typical figure comes from Harper's: sales up more than 25% since Pearl Harbor.

¶ Mary Tileston's *Daily Strength for Daily Needs* (prayers and meditations) has doubled its peacetime sale, passed the 500,000 mark.

People have turned to inspirational reading more quickly, and in far greater numbers, than they did in World War I. The current national best-seller list includes two novels with religious themes. Jewish refugee Franz Werfel's *Song of Bernadette* (a story of Our Lady of Lourdes) has sold over 500,-000 copies. Protestant Minister Lloyd C. Douglas' *The Robe* (a story of Christ's passion) has sold 240,000 copies.

TESTAMENTS FOR CASTAWAYS: For the first time in its exis- MAY 24
tence, the American Bible Society is sending out New
Testaments it prays will never be read. Reason: the pocket-
size books go in standard equipment on all U.S. lifeboats
and rafts for use of castaways at sea. After Captain Eddie
Rickenbacker's saga of planewreck in the South Pacific had
publicized Scripture as a comfort for castaways, the Bible Society offered to furnish them to all rafts and lifeboats. The
Army and Navy gladly accepted. By last week 21,000 New
Testaments had been installed. Ten thousand more were
awaiting assignment.

ELECTION OF A LEADER: To one of U.S. Protestantism's most JUNE 7
celebrated ministers last week came an honor long past due.
Affable, handsome, internationally known Dr. Henry Sloane
Coffin, 66, president of New York's Union Theological Seminary, was elected Moderator of the Presbyterian Church in
the U.S. Son of a wealthy Manhattan family (merchants
and philanthropists), Coffin went to Yale, studied further in
Europe. Back in the U.S. he went to Union, was ordained a
Presbyterian minister in 1900. His first parish was a room
over a Bronx fish market. There he preached "damnation
with the Cross in it," displayed such zeal that his congrega-
tion vowed the odor of sanctity overcame the odor of fish.

Five years later, he went to take over run-down midtown
Madison Avenue Church. The rich came to the church, the
poor East Siders went to the chapel which the church supported. Coffin abolished the chapel, brought the two congre-
gations together. In 1926 Coffin became Union's president.
The onetime Presbyterian seminary (it became interdenom-
inational 51 years ago) appealed to him as a place "to turn
out men of adventurous spirit, unfettered by tradition." Students who refused to register for the draft drew his rebuke,
also the warning that Union would not become "a haven
for draft dodgers." [In 1968, the Rev. William Sloane Coffin Jr., 43, chaplain of Yale University and a nephew of Dr.
Coffin, was indicted on charges of advising students to vi-
olate draft laws in connection with the war in Vietnam.]

SECOND THOUGHT: New York's Roman Catholic Archbishop NOV. 29
Spellman got back to the U.S. last August from a 46,000-

mile visit to 34 countries in Europe, Africa, Asia, South America, thousands of U.S. fighting men, Pope Pius XII, practically every top-flight Allied statesman and military leader, and Generalissimo Franco, and promptly published the highlights of his trip in *Collier's*.

As soon as installment No. 1 appeared the Archbishop found himself raked fore & aft by the U.S. Protestant, liberal and leftish press for his praise of Franco. Wrote Archbishop Spellman in *Collier's:* "My impressions of him are in accordance with his reputation as a very sincere, serious and intelligent man. Whatever general criticism has been made of General Franco (and it has been considerable), I cannot doubt that he is a man loyal to his God, devoted to his country's welfare, and definitely willing to sacrifice himself in any capacity and to any extent for Spain."

This week the Archbishop's articles appeared in book form (*Action This Day*). His former opinions of Franco have been somewhat edited, are now attributed to hearsay: "I had been told by some who had known him all through his life that the Generalissimo was a God-fearing, serious and intelligent man, striving to do what he thought best for Spain."

MILESTONES

BORN: To King Farouk, 23, and Queen Farida ("The Only One"), 22; their third princess, third non-heir to the throne; in Cairo.

DIED: Stephen Vincent Benét, 44, Pulitzer Prize-winning poet (*John Brown's Body*); of a heart attack; in Manhattan. He published his first volumes of verse when he was 17, wrote *John Brown's Body* as a Guggenheim Fellow in 1926-27. This 100,000-word verse narrative sold over 180,000 copies.

MISCELLANY

NUDGE: In Brazil's Amazon Valley, rubber gatherers got priorities on a new supply of 1,500,000 fish hooks, result of their telegram to U.S. Ambassador Jefferson Caffery: "No fish hooks, no fish; no fish, no eat; no eat, no rubber."

TO HALVE & HALVE NOT: A young woman in Chicago, who complained in court that her boy friend had put off paying his share of their Dutch treats for four years and then married somebody else, won a $179.89 judgment against him for half of 250 purchases, including a package of pistachio nuts, a bag of potato chips and an ice-cream cone.

MANNERS: In San Francisco, a harried bus driver, cracking under the wartime rush of trade, refused to let his passengers off till they said, "Please." Inflated with success, he then tried to make them say, "Pretty please." They called a policeman.

MEDICINE

PENICILLIN: The wonder drug of 1943 may prove to be pen- FEB 8
icillin, obscured since its discovery in Britain in 1929, only
now getting its thorough sickroom trial. It is made from a
mold by a slow, laborious process. All the penicillin in the
U.S. at any one time has never been more than about
enough to treat 30 cases.

Experiments have already shown that penicillin attacks certain bacteria more successfully than sulfa drugs do. Unlike
sulfa drugs, penicillin's effects are not inhibited by pus and
other materials formed in infected wounds. Used in low con-
centrations in the blood stream, penicillin prevents bacteria
from multiplying and renders them easy prey for white
blood corpuscles. Several doctors are now making small-
scale penicillin trials, but their work is a military secret. No
secret is the drug's use on casualties of last November's Co-
coanut Grove fire. Each patient got sulfadiazine to prevent
streptococcus infection on burned surfaces and then, if he
still had a temperature six days later, intramuscular injections
of 5,000 units of penicillin every four hours to prevent
staphylococcus infection. It is notable that no patient so treated died of staphylococcus blood poisoning.

GENEROUS VEINS: If there were a champion U.S. blood do- MARCH 8
nor, a Pittsburgh truck driver, Russell O. Armour, would appear to be it. Last week he gave his 41st pint in 42 months.
Sometimes he has had to use fictitious names, since the Red
Cross will not knowingly take blood from anyone oftener
than once every two months. Armour has altogether been
drained of about three times as much blood as he has in his
body at any one time. His weight has stayed the same:
around 216 lb.

CASTORIA TAKES ITS MEDICINE: After 75 years disturbed only MAY 17
by babies crying for it, Fletcher's Castoria (soothing, laxative)

was last week in the biggest dither in the drug trade. A mysterious emetic had cropped up in some of the medicine and nauseated a few takers. The preparation's makers, the Centaur Co., a division of Sterling Drug, Inc., temporarily withdrew Castoria from the market.

First warning came when two North Carolina doctors told the Food & Drug Administration that tried & true Castoria had made their little patients ill. Centaur Vice President Joseph Bohan at once ordered up a bottle, tasted it, got sick. Four assistants tried it. They got sick too.

Centaur's board of directors met immediately. Though less than 50 complaints had come in, they decided to 1) shut down the Rahway plant from which the bad medicine came, 2) send telegrams to 5,000 wholesalers offering money back for all Castoria on hand, 3) put advertisements in 2,000 newspapers telling consumers to get their money back through retailers.

Both Centaur and the Food & Drug Administration were stumped to find the guilty emetic. Company chemists analyzed a sample of Castoria, found only what was to be expected in a compound of alcohol, senna extract, bicarbonate of soda, peppermint, anise and flavoring. But when the chemists confidently took a swig, they upchucked too. [After withdrawing the medicine for study, the company announced that a change in formula had been necessitated by a wartime cut in sugar. The formula was then fixed, and the medicine was put back on the market.]

JULY 26 **HEALTH IN THE ARMY:** White-haired, hale & healthy Major General Norman T. Kirk, head of the Army's huge (90,000 officers, 450,000 enlisted men) Medical Corps, last fortnight told Manhattan newspapermen that the U.S. Army is haler & healthier than any army has ever been in any war. Some of his specific points on Medical Corps problems, solved and unsolved:

¶ Malaria is still the No. 1 worry. Italy, the General pointed out, is heavily infected with malaria.

¶ A number of U.S. war casualties are psychiatric (Army's released figure: 30%). In General Kirk's own medical experience about 85% of the psychiatric casualties had a history of instability in civil life. The Army, he said, would be spared much trouble and expense if draft boards would get a man's full record before shipping him off to an induction center. Said he: "The idea that the Army is making the boys crazy is not so. It's just finding out those that are."

¶ A new type of wound is causing many amputations: land mines damage legs and feet of men afoot or riding in trucks or Jeeps. The Navy has many similar wounds among men standing on deck just above a torpedo burst—the effect of the deck concussion is the same as though a man landed on his feet from a 40-ft. fall.

BROOKLYN SYNDROME: Sometimes a recruit being examined DEC. 27 by psychiatrists is truculent, has a chip-on-the-shoulder attitude. Navy psychiatrists have learned by experience that such a recruit is not necessarily a psychiatric personality unfit for service; he may be a perfectly normal guy from Brooklyn. Says the *New York State Journal of Medicine,* the Navy doctors have christened this "harmless social pattern" the "Brooklyn syndrome."

MILESTONES

DIED: Beatrice Potter Webb, 85, researcher, author, collaborator and wife of Socialist Sidney Webb (first Baron Passfield); in Liphook, Hants, England. Famed for their 1909 "Minority Report" on British poor laws and for their subsequent crusade (backed by Winston Churchill) to prevent public destitution, the gradualist Webbs spent their lives investigating and reporting. Bernard Shaw called them "walking encyclopedias."

MISCELLANY

TREE PLAN: In West Plains, Mo., the walnut tree which C. A. Widener planted in 1893 went to its planned reward. His coffin was made from it.

ROLL OUT THE BARREL: Near Helena, Mont., Carl Oase's truck, full of beer, stalled on a mountain grade, rolled backward, right into a picnic, overturned and tossed out Oase, who stayed for the fun.

HAZARDOUS: Near Camp Edwards, Mass., Private John J. Czeike pitched his tent at night, woke the next morning to discover that he had slept with a skunk in a bed of poison ivy.

MEATLESS: In Washington, the War Food Administration made out its usual paychecks to Employes Mary Bean, George Fruit, Maybert Corn, Samuel C. Salmon, Esther Olive, William Meal and Fairfax Oyster. Mr. Oyster is an expert on peanuts.

ANOTHER COLOR: In Detroit, a city-bred horse named Davie, long accustomed to auto traffic, ran away and wrecked his buggy when he met a frightening sight: another horse.

BUSINESS & FINANCE

JAN. 4 **TOUGHER NEW YEAR:** In the year just ended the most important —and least publicized—fact about the alleged plight of the little businessman was that he did *not* go out of business. In the coming year it is a fairly safe prediction that the going for the small businessman is going to be a lot tougher.

Business deaths in general stood at the lowest figure since 1933. Perhaps the most outstanding survivor was the auto dealer, whose ingenuity in turning his business inside out to cope with the complete loss of his normal stock in trade was a 1942 miracle.

This survival of the small businessman had two explanations. First, many a small firm converted to war work and is now doing a bang-up production job at subcontracting. But, a much more important factor was the huge boom in the production of goods and services which, despite war, stood above the 1929 level. It is because this boom cannot continue in 1943 if the U.S. is to produce a maximum amount of war goods that the problem of the small businessman is so acute.

JAN. 11 **ALLIGATORS BY ROEBLING:** Hulking, 300-lb. multimillionaire, twice-divorced Donald Roebling never set out to to be a munitions inventor. Grandson of Brooklyn Bridge Builder Washington A. Roebling, he could have raced fancy cars, captained yachts, cavorted on his Clearwater, Fla. show-place estate for a lifetime. But last week amphibious tractors, invented by 34-year-old Donald, were rolling off the production lines of four big U.S. manufacturers, were the pride & joy of the U.S. Navy, were one of the reasons for U.S. successes at Guadalcanal.

It all started back in 1935 when a disastrous hurricane screamed through the Florida Everglades, left young Donald convinced that an amphibious vehicle could have saved many lives. So he built an expensive, well-equipped machine shop on his estate, hired experienced workers, on the fourth try put a lumbering boxlike four-ton monster through its paces. With a terrible roar it clambered through mangrove swamps, crunched eight-inch trees, splashed over bayous. Donald promptly named his new machine Alligator, went to work on bigger & better models.

He did so well that in February 1941 the Navy ordered Alligators worth over $3,000,000 to haul men, munitions and supplies from battleships and transports on to enemy shores, thus speed and simplify dangerous invasion jobs. However vital to the war effort, Donald Roebling is not making a penny from his Alligators. He turned the whole invention over to the Government, waved aside all commissions. To Donald this is his contribution to the war.

MEAT MYSTERY: Who ate up all the meat in the U.S.? Last MARCH 15 week consumers heard that beginning March 29 the meat ration will be 28 oz. a person a week—and will be pieced out by an undetermined amount of cheese. The announcement shocked most U.S. steak eaters. The plan would reduce the U.S. almost to the low British level of meat consumption. The British are allowed 16 oz. of meat and 4 oz. of bacon and ham, plus 4 oz. of cheese a week.

But a report by Lend-Lease Administrator Edward R. Stettinius punctured the theory that the U.S. was short of meat on Britain's account. Meat exports by Lend-Lease last year amounted to only 5% of the total supply. Nor are the armed forces getting most of the meat. In a scholarly study two Cornell professors pointed out that even if eight million armed men eat up to 20% more that they did as civilians, as eating mouths they would be equivalent only to a mere 1% added to the U.S. population.

The only apparent explanation for the meat shortage was that the U.S. people themselves were eating more meat. The citizenry, always regarded as underfed by economists, now had the biggest income ever, was shielded from high prices by a benevolent OPA, was spared higher taxes by a pussyfooting Congress. Result: a national orgy of carnivory. For seldom in its history had the U.S. been all at work at one time. The country was getting suddenly rich—everywhere, all at once.

MARCH 22 **A TYCOON PASSES:** J. P. Morgan stepped into No. 23 Wall Street, the building known on every bourse in the world as "The Corner," on Feb. 23. Driving in from his great Matinicock estate at Glen Cove, Long Island, he had come into the bank as usual at about 10:30 a.m. That evening he was on a Florida special, southbound for a rest. Early on the morning of the 25th he suffered a slight heart attack, walked from the train to a cottage at Bocagrande, a tiny hamlet on a Florida key.

Seventy-five-year-old John Pierpont Morgan died at 3:15 in the morning of March 13. This week J. P. Morgan was buried at Middle Village, Queens, New York. With him the U.S. laid away not so much an era as a great misinterpretation of an era.

The U.S., for two decades, had largely believed in a fairy story of Marxist origin—the legend that international bankers sucked the nation into a war [World War I] which was none of its business, that U.S. participation in that war had been a mistake, which must never be repeated. The defaulted war debts, the failure of the League of Nations, the legend of the "Merchants of Death" all made for disillusionment, and out of that came the national attitude of cynicism toward the world, expressed as isolationism.

A great part of that legend was associated with the position of the House of Morgan. The legend began with the elder Morgan, John Pierpont (Maximus), a Hartford boy who went down to New York to integrate U.S. industry through the power of finance. The J. P. Morgan who died last week was not of that breed. A tycoon by inheritance, he was not a buccaneer by nature.

When the 1929 crash came the younger Morgan joined with other bankers to stem the tide. A $240,000,000 pool was formed to bolster the market—a gesture which failed. The market crashed on down. In 1933 came the New Deal, and with it the campaign against "princes of privilege" and "economic royalists." The Pecora banking investigation was a series of field days. When someone used the word "circus," a pressagent had an idea that made photographic history— planting a midget on dignified Banker Morgan's lap, while flash bulbs flared.

Morgan stressed always that if the private banker had

power, it was because of his reputation for integrity. But the Pecora investigation spelled the end of the Morgan power in the old sense. Came the Banking Act of 1933, splitting apart the business of deposit and investment banking. Result: Morgan's son Harry and two other partners formed the separate investment firm of Morgan, Stanley & Co., Inc. Son Junius Morgan stuck with the bank, which now became merely the 18th largest bank of deposit in the U.S. By 1940 the firm's net worth, which had stood at $118,600,000 in 1929, was down to $39,156,000. At that point Morgan took a final step. The partnership of J. P. Morgan & Co. was dissolved in the formation of a stock corporation, J. P. Morgan & Co., Inc. The era of "personal" banking, and with it the great Morgan tradition, was over.

BOWLING ALLEYS & CUSPIDORS: The world's biggest hotel put MARCH 29 on the world's biggest auction sale last week in Chicago. Everything movable (and some choice stationary items) in the 3,000-room Stevens Hotel went on the block. The Stevens, now the home of some 9,000 U.S. Army Air Forces students, cost its builders $28,000,000 in 1927, was sold to the Army for only $5,559,000 last December. Proceeds of the auction of its furnishings, which were last valued at $2,200,000, will apply against the Army's purchase price. To prospective buyers who flocked into auction headquarters, the items listed in the 995-page inventory were mouthwatering reminders of the days before rationing and stop-production orders:

¶ 10,000 dozen knives, forks and spoons, 200,000 dishes, 150,-000 glasses and goblets, 1,000 18-carat gold-plated banquet plates (all just a headache to soldiers on K.P. duty who had been put to polishing them for the sale).

¶ Enough beds and innerspring mattresses to sleep 8,000 people.

¶ Five completely equipped bowling alleys, one 60-foot oak bar, 15 portable bars, 25 buffets.

¶ All the flotsam & jetsam of a huge hotel: used umbrellas, 750 pairs of doormen's gloves, 742 cuspidors, the flags of all nations, an elephant tusk.

BIG-TOP BUSINESS: George W. Smith could tell most war pro- APRIL 26 ducers a thing or two about a businessman's problems in wartime. As general manager of Ringling Bros. and Barnum & Bailey Circus, he has to feed, house, transport, costume and otherwise provide for "the greatest show on earth"— without benefit of any priorities whatsoever. But last week as the Big Show boomed into its second jampacked week at Manhattan's Madison Square Garden, George Smith was calm & collected in the midst of his bedlam.

The first problem facing the Big Show this year was whether the Office of Defense Transportation would let it go on at all. Its pressmen, trained in superlative promotion, flooded the country with quotes on the morale value of circuses ranging all the way back to Greek literature. ODT crumpled, said the Big Top could use the railroads if there were any locomotives available. Excess baggage went overboard: the whole show now fits into 70 cars, moves in three trains (*v.* 90 in four trains last year).

The 1943 circus economics are well in hand. The clowns (who buy their own make-up) use hundreds of pounds of scarce zinc oxide and glycerine, but they had hoarded enough for the season, too. There is a real shortage of silk tights and stockings—but a barelegged circus girl does no lasting damage at the box office. And one thing that pleases the managers is that Thelma Williams, the 350-lb. side-show fat girl, owes her box-office appeal more to her glands than to her appetite. As for the animals, they have no ration books, but starvation is stoutly staved off and so far the meat-eating bears, lions and tigers have had the 1,150 lb. a day it takes to keep them happy. Reason: they all love horse meat, not yet under OPA control.

JUNE 7   **DEATH OF A SON:** On Detroit's tree-shaded Grand Boulevard stands Henry Ford's own hospital, famed for its skillful surgeons, its spacious research laboratories. But when ailing Edsel Bryant Ford stepped through its doors seven weeks ago with his quick, springy stride, nothing could be done for him. So, at 49, Edsel Ford returned to his sprawling grey stone house beside grey Lake St. Clair to await death. Last week it came. [The cause was cancer.]

Whalebone tough as he is, Henry Ford, 79, had never expected (until recently) to outlive his only son. All his life Edsel was the pupil, his father the teacher, empire management the subject. As a baby, Edsel watched his father tinker with his first horseless carriage, rode proudly on a special little seat when it first sputtered along Detroit's dusty Bagley Avenue in May 1896.

So rapidly did this mechanical wonder beget thousands of other mechanical wonders sputtering over the land that young Edsel had no time for college. He pulled on greasy overalls, went into the shop at 19. It was not until the years of World War I that Edsel first learned what it was going to mean to live within the Ford legend. Deeply opposed to war, Henry insisted that Edsel be deferred from the draft as one of the company's key men. Edsel was condemned as a "slacker" and "coward." The next williwaw came in 1919, when Henry Ford rowed bitterly with Ford stockholders, finally bought them out for $75,000,000 ($70,000,000 of which was borrowed from hated Wall Street) and installed Edsel as president. Henry Ford had learned that Edsel's great value was in soothing the rows his father raised.

In later years Edsel's job was to keep the company up to date. It was Edsel who finally persuaded Henry to junk the obsolete Model T and bring out the gearshift Model A. It was Edsel who argued for snappier designs, brighter colors, a complete line of low-priced cars. And when it became plain that the U.S. might be drawn into World War II, it

Edsel (left) and Henry Ford. The father outlives the son and once again firmly grasps the reins he never entirely dropped.

was Edsel who counteracted his father's bone-deep hatred of war. But when Henry Ford confidently stated that he could build 1,000 planes a day, it was up to Edsel to prove that the company could at least build 500 planes a month at Willow Run (he lived to see the goal in sight).

At no time during the long years when Edsel sat in the presidency did his father permit him to rule alone. As Henry explained: "He knows some things better than I do and I know some things better than he does."

One thing which Henry Ford knows better than anyone— while he lives, no one but Henry Ford, who has now renamed himself President, will continue to run the Ford empire.

JUNE 14 **UP THE LADDER:** Two years ago sober, scholarly William McChesney Martin left his $48,000-a-year job as president of the New York Stock Exchange, entered the Army at $21 a month. Private Bill Martin learned that a man who had worked 18 hours a day in civilian life (as he had) could climb fast in the Army. Painstakingly he learned to shoot a rifle, even tried to pay the Government for extra practice ammunition. In his tent at nights, he studied military histories, textbooks on strategy.

Bill Martin was promoted as rapidly as regulations allowed: to 1st lieutenant, to captain, and, last Feb. 12, to major. Given special duty in Washington, he was transferred to the executive staff of the Munitions Assignments Board (Harry Hopkins), later moved to Lend-Lease. When Joseph E. Davies made his second mission to Moscow, Major Martin accompanied him. Last week, when Major Martin returned, he beamingly let it be known that at the state banquet, Premier Joseph Stalin had raised a glass, toasted the former chief of Wall Street. [In 1951, after serving in various financial posts, Martin began a long term as Chairman of the U.S. Federal Reserve Board.]

JUNE 28 **HAUNTED HOUSE:** Last week the U.S. Army Air Forces, which bought the huge Stevens Hotel (world's largest) in Chicago only six months ago, now reversed itself and put it up for sale. Chicago innkeepers forthwith went into a deep dither over the "economic disaster" they would suffer if the Stevens came back into competition. Plain citizens went into a dither over what seemed to be Army stupidity, grade A.

The Army, waving aside all advice, had stubbornly insisted on buying the Stevens for $5,559,000. Then, in a fabulous five-day sale, the Army had auctioned off almost all the internal fixings of the Stevens with a replacement value of over $2,000,000 and realized only $440,000 from the sale. The auction came just 90 days before the Army decided to sell the Stevens. Yet for only $3,000 a month in storage charges the Army could have held on to all the furnishings. The Army Air Forces now face the fact that an unfurnished hotel in wartime is just about as valuable as an airplane without an engine and the Stevens began to look like the biggest haunted house in the U.S.

SICILIAN SIDELIGHT: When Lieut. General George S. Patton JULY 26 Jr.'s U.S. Seventh Army splashed up the beaches of Sicily last week, the innards of much of Patton's motor equipment were protected from the sea with a thick, gummy substance that was the result of a near-miracle of production back home. Last week Standard Oil Co. (New Jersey) proudly let the miracle out of the bag.

Late one Friday, Army Ordnance telephoned Jersey Standard in Manhattan. Said Ordnance: General Dwight D. Eisenhower had cabled, asking for immediate delivery of 45,-000 lb. of a special water-repellent compound never before made in the U.S. Eisenhower had just heard of the new compound from the British, who had used it with great success. The goo was sketchily described. By Monday enough machinery had been thrown together to fill the order; materials had been rushed by police-escorted Army trucks to Standard's Baltimore plant.

Then the fun began. First off, a sample of the real goo (flown in from North Africa) turned out to be different from the Army's original description, and more hard-to-get materials had to be commandeered. The goo was also so unusual and heavy that Standard's grease equipment had to be jacked up with Rube Goldbergian extra belts, pulleys and paddles. But by the following Sunday the order was done, four hours before the promised delivery time. By that time the plant was half-wrecked, as equipment collapsed under the strain. Then the Army asked for another 200,000 lb. by the following weekend. At that point Standard threw in its big Pittsburgh grease plant, while more Army trucks dashed all over western Pennsylvania gathering up extra drums and materials.

The Pittsburgh plant, as well as the limping Baltimore factory, worked night & day, while supervisory staffs took cat naps on the floor. Army bombers took the last 22,000 lb. of production to the seaboard. By 11:45 a.m. on Friday, June 11, just two weeks after the first Army phone call and only seven hours after it left Standard's Pittsburgh plant, the final vat was stowed away and bound for North Africa.

The whole thing happened so fast that no one even thought to talk about contracts and cost. But by last week, with the new invasion an amphibious success, the cost of Standard's Sicilian sidelight seemed academic.

Chicago's Hotel Stevens. Under a barrage of criticism, the U.S. Army buys it, sells it, and enjoys the last laugh.

SEPT. 13 **THE ARMY LAUGHS LAST**: When the U.S. Army suddenly decided to sell Chicago's huge Stevens Hotel which it purchased for $5,559,000 last June, the joke was on the Army. Some people even talked about turning it into an office building or a free home for soldiers' wives. But this week the Army had the last laugh. From five bids for the Stevens it chose to take $5,251,000 cash on the barrelhead from Arnold Kirkaby, who already owns Chicago's Drake and Blackstone Hotels. Thus, after selling off the furnishings for $440,000, the Army made a small profit of $132,000 on its white elephant.

ALBINA'S AL: In the shadow of giant Henry Kaiser's three Co- SEPT. 27 lumbia River shipyards, the small Albina Engine & Machine Works of Portland has turned out 38 sub-chasers, won three "E" pennants, chopped down absenteeism, kept its 4,-500 workers happy. Its secret: slick showmanship in employe relations. Samples:

¶ "Vow Girls," 350 female employes in the yard, have signed a "No Work, No Woo" pledge not to date any Albina man unless he has perfect job attendance for the week.

¶ When workers ran short of alarm clocks and washing machines, Albina bought up 800 old clocks, sent as far as St. Louis for a broken-down washing machine, fixed them up and sold them at cost. Absenteeism among workers who claim they need haircuts was cut by persuading nearby barbers to sloganize "An Albina Man Is Always Next." Result: absenteeism at Albina has dropped to almost nothing.

NEW FORD PROJECT: Last week Henry Ford was busy on a OCT. 11 new long-range project. He was grooming his tall, handsome grandson, Henry Ford II, 26, to fill his own quick-moving shoes—some day. When Edsel Ford died, Henry II was rounding out his second year in the Navy as a lieutenant. Mindful of the some $4,000,000,000 in war contracts held by the Ford Co.—and of the 80 years of its president—the Navy released Henry II from active duty so he could resume his job of learning how to run the empire. Six days a week he gets up at 6 a.m., is at the Rouge plant by 8. There, under the wing of Ford's right-hand man, bantam-sized Harry Bennett, young Henry is learning his job. He gets other frequent lessons from Ford's production boss, white-crested Charles E. Sorensen.

Henry II puts in a ten-to twelve-hour day, finds little time for golf (he shoots in the nineties). There is only one plan for him now—to get production know-how. That was what built the Ford empire, and canny old Henry is dead sure it will keep it together.

NOV. 22 **THE PASSIONATE ENGINEER:** Donald Wills Douglas is a tall, good-looking, brown-eyed, brown-haired, brown-tweedy sort of man, who acts as if he doesn't really believe in the future of aviation. He dislikes flying, and flies as rarely as possible. Prophets of "the coming Air Age" bore him.

Douglas himself, at 51 president of the biggest aircraft company in the world, thinks this way partly because he is a hardheaded manufacturer, with no room in his head for nonsense—or for dreams. He is primarily an engineer, with a passion for airplanes as things embodying engineering designs, and a passion for precision. Last year Douglas made one-sixth (by weight) of all the airplanes made in the U.S.

As a youth, Douglas had gone from his birthplace in Brooklyn to the U.S. Naval Academy at Annapolis where he spent all possible time building model planes. After three years he switched to Massachusetts Institute of Technology where he helped design one of the first airplane wind tunnels in the U.S.—and on the strength of this got a job with the up-&-coming Glenn L. Martin Aircraft Co. By the time he was 28 he was 1) a vice president and chief engineer, and 2) unhappy. He wanted to make his own planes. With $600 in his pocket, he quit, went to California, set up office over a Los Angeles barbershop. His backlog: one plane.

Soon after, a Douglas-designed torpedo plane turned out so well that the Navy gave him a $120,000 order. He later bagged an Army order. It was for only four planes, but they shot him to the top of the aviation world. For those planes were the famed DWCs, which were the first to fly round the world (1924). Then in 1932 Transcontinental & Western Airlines came to Douglas with a proposition: they needed a new two-motored passenger plane that would outfly, outcarry and "outeverything" every plane in the commercial air. In a week the designs were whipped out. The plane turned the aviation world upside down, with Douglas on top. The plane was the DC-1, the first of the famed broad-winged DCs that eventually carried 95% of all U.S. air traffic, and are now as familiar in the U.S. sky as sparrows.

Today Donald Douglas' company operates: A $36,000,000 plant in Tulsa, employing 16,000; a $45,000,000 plant in Oklahoma City, employing 20,000; a $33,000,000 plant in Chicago, employing 11,000; a $30,000,000 plant in Long

Beach, employing 40,300; a $30,000,000 plant in Santa Monica, employing 44,000; a $20,000,000 plant in El Segundo, employing 21,000, and more than 100 other small plants and repair stations tucked away in worldwide spots from Persia to China. In this galaxy of plants, the company turns out:

¶ The slim-bodied, two-motored, over 300-mile-an-hour Douglas A-20 light bomber.

¶ Four-motored Flying Fortresses and Liberators, under lease from Boeing and Consolidated.

¶ The transport version of the DC-3, the Army's C-47.

¶ The four-motored C-54, transport and cargo plane that hauls a freight car load through the skies.

¶ The Navy's single-motored SBD dive-bomber, which is generally credited with sinking more combatant enemy tonnage in the Pacific than any other weapon in the U.S. war kit.

MILESTONES

DIVORCED: Cinemactor Mickey Rooney, 22; by Ava Gardner Rooney, 20; after 16 months of marriage, two reconciliations; in Los Angeles.

DIED: Benjamin Anzelevitz, 52, "Ben Bernie, the O-O-Old Maestro," genial, plush-voiced veteran of stage, radio, screen; of a lung infection with heart complications; in Beverly Hills. In the early '20s he formed one of the country's leading dance bands (for a while his pianist was Oscar Levant). On the radio he became famous for the sign-off he gave Jan. 15 for the last time: "Au revoir, a fond cheerio, a bit of toodle-oo, God bless you, and pleas--ant dreams."

MISCELLANY

EXPEDITER: In Oklahoma, Harry Scherer explained why he had laid some ties across a railroad track and stopped a passenger train: he wanted to get on.

PRIVATE LIVES: In Wilmington, Del., Mrs. Olive Robertson complained to a judge that she had caught her husband kissing the blonde who had been sleeping in the Robertsons' bed with them because of the housing shortage. She won $16 a week support.

NUISANCE: In Washington, D.C., the Treasury Department informed the public that there was a shortage of $10,000 bills.

THE WAY IT IS: In Los Angeles, a café proprietor finally had his front window permanently lettered in gold leaf: "Monterey Café—Waitress Wanted."

EXCELSIOR: In Chicago's new subway, first aid was administered to an old lady who had finally stopped trying to get up a downgoing escalator, had coasted to the bottom and collapsed.

CINEMA

JAN. 18 **"SHADOW OF A DOUBT"**—Alfred Hitchcock directed it; Thornton Wilder and Sally Benson helped write it; two of Hollywood's best young actors—Teresa Wright and Joseph Cotten—play in it. The result: a superb film.

This Hitchcock masterpiece has the same general theme as his 1941 film, *Suspicion*—the slow, terrible growth of fear of a loved one—in this case the fear of a moon-struck girl (Miss Wright) that her tall, handsome uncle (Mr. Cotten) wants to murder her. But, unlike *Suspicion, Shadow* hits few false notes, maintains suspense to the end. And good as Director Hitchcock and Actor Cotten are, the show is really Miss Wright's.

FEB. 22 **HUGHES'S WESTERN:** All advance signs indicated that *The Outlaw* would be either the best or the worst picture of the year. Its making cost $2,500,000. Its two young stars, full-breasted Jane Russell and slim Jack Buetel, had been ballyhooed to magazine cover fame for two years—and yet the U.S. had never seen them on the screen. Howard Hughes, the eccentric designer-aviator-producer, personally directed the picture and surrounded it with such provoking secrecy that not even the actors in it were allowed to see the finished product. Last fortnight *The Outlaw* had its première. What Hughes apparently had for his pains: a strong candidate for the flopperoo of all time.

In 1940 Hughes and his friend, Director Howard Hawks, decided to collaborate in producing a Ben Hecht script-biography of Billy the Kid. For the chief roles Hughes insisted on new faces, specified the girl must be "primarily sexy." The Hughes lightning struck Californian Jane Russell, 19, a dentist's receptionist.

Hawks, no niggardly director, moved 250 actors and technicians to location in the Arizona desert, began to shoot, speeding rushes to Hughes in Los Angeles by Hughes's pri-

Jane Russell in "The Outlaw." Her femininity is flaring, her ballyhoo extensive, her picture a strong candidate for flopperoo of all time.

vate plane. Deeply moved by these first samples, Hughes demanded that Hawks spend more lavishly. By second week's end Hawks had become so appalled at Hughes's extravagance that he resigned. Hughes took over. An incredible perfectionist, solemnly eccentric Director Hughes exasperated his actors, once made veterans Thomas Mitchell and Walter Huston go through the same scene 26 times, after which Mitchell took off his hat, jumped on it and stalked away. On the set, where shooting took place mostly at night (to allow Hughes to design planes for Henry J. Kaiser by day), he was usually unshaven, always unpredictable.

To keep his two novice stars in the public eye during the picture's long delay, Hughes hired Press Agent Russell Birdwell. Birdwell's solution: high-pressure exploitation of Miss Russell's flaring femininity. Result: some 60 magazine articles, innumerable news pictures. The Hays office helped by censoring one or two shots from *The Outlaw.* When the Hays office objected to a Beutel line, "You borrowed from me; now I borrowed your gal," Hughes changed the line to "Tit for tat." Hastily the Hays censor agreed the first version was O.K.

"THE HARD WAY" is the old Hollywood story about a harpy MARCH 1 who claws her way up the ladder to fame, riches and disaster. The plot, a corny tale of heartbreak and backstabbing in show business, has almost no surprises. But thanks to the adept treatment of this routine material, *The Hard Way* is a fine film, one of the best thus far in 1943. Jack Carson's job as a simpleminded, big-hearted hoofer is masterly. But top acting honors go to Ida Lupino, who plays the most hateful jade since Bette Davis in *The Little Foxes.*

APRIL 26 **"MY FRIEND FLICKA"** is a sun-drenched, innocent film as wholesome as graham crackers. It is mainly 89 minutes of handsome Technicolor shots of Utah landscape animated with horses. Both scenery and animals are so lustrous that they overshadow the picture's slight, demi-idyllic story about Schoolboy Ken McLaughlin (Roddy McDowall) and his nervous sorrel filly, Flicka. Young Ken trains the horse, nurses and loves her. He learns through these tasks and emotions much about the equipment he will need in adult life.

MAY 31 **"DU BARRY WAS A LADY"** is the Hollywood version of Songwriter Cole Porter's tuneful Broadway dream about the Court of Louis XV. The Broadway dream was lively enough to wake anybody up and offered the team of Bert Lahr, Ethel Merman and Betty Grable, with a good grade of gents'-room humor.

The Hollywood dream is all too easy to sleep through and substitutes Red Skelton, Lucille Ball, and Virginia O'Brien, with vulgarity from the lesser lavatories.

AUG. 2 **FOR WHOM?:** In a human omelet which included Dorothy Lamour and Myrna Loy, an audience of 2,089 packed into Manhattan's Rivoli Theater to witness the most important screen première since *Gone With the Wind*—the first showing of *For Whom the Bell Tolls.* For months, for years, the build-up had been developing. The impatient audience knew Paramount had in Ernest Hemingway's novel the possibilities of one of the best pictures, greatest popular entertainments and most colossal money-makers ever produced. It wanted to see precisely for whom, in Paramount's fabulously invested opinion, *The Bell* did, or did not, toll.

As it turned out, the tremendous *Bell,* upon whose casting Paramount had spent three years and nearly three million dollars, tolled for nobody in particular, and tolled off key at that.

There was fine stuff in it, in great ill-digested, nervous chunks. But *For Whom the Bell Tolls* was not, by the kindest stretching of critical standards, a good picture.

The screen version of Ernest Hemingway's novel is still a story of love and violence in the Spanish Civil War. Gary Cooper is Robert Jordan, Hemingway's young Montana schoolteacher who has come to Spain to fight for democracy everywhere. Cooper has become, for millions, a sort of Abraham Lincoln of American sex. And he plays modestly, sometimes beautifully.

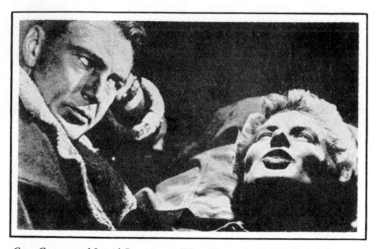

Gary Cooper and Ingrid Bergman in "For Whom the Bell Tolls." Others may have muffled the clapper, but she hits the bell a valiant clang.

As the guerrilla leader, Pablo, Hemingway's terrible symbol of a man devastated by the fear of death, Akim Tamiroff has some magnificent moments. As Pilar, Hemingway's salty symbol of Spain's people, Greek Actress Katina Paxinou would walk away with any less leaden show. But those are the surprises. The rest of the time these actors go corky on their lines, overact operatically or sit and talk. Above all they talk.

When all is said & done, the fact remains that whoever else may have fumbled at the rope or muffled the clapper, the 27-year-old Swedish actress, Ingrid Bergman, as Maria, hit the *Bell* such a valiant and far-sounding clang that there has been nothing like it since her great compatriot Greta Garbo enchanted half the world.

DEC. 13 **"THE HEAT'S ON"** restores Mae West to cinema after three years of meditation and literary activity. In her great days, Mae West was a one-woman saturnalia. In this film she plays a musicomedy star who, sick & tired of William Gaxton (a producer), switches to Alan Dinehart (a producer). Then all three get complicatedly busy trying to corner the money that dim-witted Victor Moore has embezzled.

Cinemactress West is still one of the most entertaining and original personalities in pictures. She can still make something unmailable out of the twitch of a feather or a polysyllable. But Mae and her playmates no longer seem certain of their style. As a result, much of *The Heat's On* has the weary, if good-humored halfheartedness of "Stop me if you've heard this one."

MILESTONES

MARRIED: Orson Welles, 28, showman; and Rita Hayworth, 24, cinemalulu: each for the second time; three months after Rita announced that she would marry Coast Guardsman Victor Mature after the war. Sleight-of-handed Welles, who at the ceremony could not get the ring out of its box, had featured his bride in his Hollywood magic show. Said Mature: "Apparently the way to a girl's heart is to saw her in half."

MISCELLANY

HOT STUFF: In Salt Lake City, the Utah Building & Construction Congress decided that the city's two worst fire hazards were the central fire station and the public safety building.

PERSONNEL RELATIONS: Mrs. William Burns of Newark advertised desperately for a maid, offered her the use of a mink coat on her days off, got a maid—after receiving 600 phone calls in two days.

RATIONAL: In Elberton, Ga., Judge C. B. Thornton asked a groom what bride's name he should write on the marriage license. Said the groom: "Leave that blank. I heard that licenses were going to be rationed. I'm courting two women and I don't know which one I'll get."

SUITCASEFUL: In Philadelphia, the thief who stole Gladys Ferber's suitcase may or may not have been happy about the swag in it: two strip-tease dresses, a string of beads, three feathers, a sarong, a new brassière, a rhinestone G-string, and a purple Cellophane shirt.

HANDLE: In Portland, Me., Andrew Tokio finally gave up, went to court to have it changed.

EDUCATION

MR. LOWELL: In his mansion in Boston's Back Bay last week JAN. 18 died Abbott Lawrence Lowell, 86. "Harvard College, as it stands today, is to a large extent his handiwork," said his successor, Dr. James Bryant Conant. Abbott Lawrence Lowell, for 24 years Harvard's president, himself largely represented what both admirers and detractors meant when they spoke of Harvard, Boston, and the New England cultural tradition.

Lowell—who preferred being called "Mr." rather than "President"—reined in the elective system so that students had to concentrate in one field after introductory courses, and he pioneered Harvard's individual tutorial system, which has been widely copied. But he was never satisfied. "No wonder there is so much knowledge in colleges," he grumbled. "The freshmen always bring in a little, and the seniors never take any away." Said he of I.Q. tests: "No good, no good—like trying to measure Tremont Street with a codfish."

RUSSELL TUSSLE: Bertrand Russell last week found himself in FEB. 1 a clamorous scrap for the second time in less than three years. In 1940 the philosopher's appointment to the College of the City of New York was revoked after outraged parents called attention to such old Russell saws as, "I am sure that university life would be better, both intellectually and morally, if most university students had temporary childless marriages." Russell's more recent boot was delivered by Philadelphia's Dr. Albert C. Barnes, whose foul temper is as famed as his gallery of Cézannes, Matisses, Renoirs and Picassos.

Barnes, the South Philadelphia boy who invented Argyrol, made millions, and settled down to insult Philadelphia society and accumulate paintings, hired Bertrand Russell to lecture for the Barnes Foundation, an art school connected with the gallery. Barnes gave Russell a five-year contract ($8,-000 yearly) with "no restrictions." Barnes chose a house for

Bertrand Russell. He is no cozy com-   *Lady Russell. She needs no advice on*
panion for the Argyrol king.   *the care of five-year-olds.*

Russell and his third wife, arranged its furnishings and offered free advice on the care of their five-year-old son. This decisive hospitality grated on Mrs. Russell's British sense of privacy. She wrote Barnes a polite note inviting him to mind his own business, selected a less expensive house 25 miles from the Foundation.

Barnes soon discovered that Russell, who regularly changes his unlisted telephone number, did not intend to become a cozy companion. Russell also preferred not to lecture in the Foundation's main gallery, where the glowing nudes distracted him, and moved his lectures to less fleshly quarters on the second floor.

Though Russell, a British earl, dislikes his title, his wife called herself Lady Russell when telephoning the Foundation. This infuriated Barnes, who carried anti-snobbery to a point of fanatic snobbism. One day Lady Russell worked on her knitting at the Foundation during her husband's lecture. She soon got a letter from the Foundation's Board of Trustees (Mrs. Barnes and three of Barnes's employees) saying that her knitting was "harmful to the Foundation's interests."

Mrs. Russell then pinned back the Barnes ears. She wrote: "When I consulted my husband, he remarked that I had disturbed no one by my knitting at far more difficult and technical lectures at the Universities of Oxford, Chicago,

California and Harvard and that, therefore, I might assume that I would be giving no offense. I marvel that anyone should wish in a world so full of mountains of hostility to magnify so grandiloquently so petty a molehill."

On Jan. 7 Russell did not show up for his regular lecture. It was the chance Barnes had been waiting for. His trustees immediately announced that "Mr. Bertrand Russell has discontinued his lectures" and that the contract was broken. Russell last week sued Barnes for the $24,000 the philosopher was to receive through 1945. [Russell received $20,000 in settlement of the case.]

HUTCHINS AT THE BRIDGE: "Victory cannot save civilization. MARCH 1 It can merely prevent its destruction by one spectacular method. Since civilization was well on its way to destruction before the war began, success in war will not automatically preserve it."

So says President Robert Maynard Hutchins of the University of Chicago in a new little book, *Education for Freedom*. He considers that prevailing U.S. ideals—above all, as reflected in U.S. education—must take a good part of the blame for the disintegration of civilization.

"At the root of the present troubles of the world we must find a pervasive materialism, a devastating desire for material goods. We know now that mechanical and technical progress is not identical with civilization. We must conclude, in fact, that our faith that technology will take the place of justice has been naïve. We look upon our neighbor either as a customer or a competitor or an instrument of production. . . . We must reconstruct education, directing it to virtue and intelligence. To formulate, to clarify, to vitalize the ideals which should animate mankind—this is the incredibly heavy burden which rests, even in total war, upon the universities. If they cannot carry it, nobody else will; for nobody else can. If it cannot be carried, civilization cannot be saved. The task is stupendous."

DR. BUTLER AND THE RABBITS: Columbia's 80-year-old Nich- MARCH 15 olas Murray Butler called progressive education a nasty name: "the rabbit system of education." Said President Butler in his 41st annual report:

"A chief reason why there is in the U.S. a widespread outbreak of crime and disorder on the part of American youth is that the fundamental place of discipline in education seems to have been quite forgotten. The rabbit is at liberty to run about the garden where his life is passed, and feed upon such plants, weeds and flowers as may attract him. To call any such process education is in the highest degree absurd."

The Public Education Association of New York straightway stood aghast. Cried they: "We stand aghast!" And would the good Doctor pray explain, if that was the way he felt about progressive education, why Columbia maintained its progressive Bard College and Horace Mann-Lincoln School of Teachers College?

JUNE 7 **DEAR OLD USAFI:** In spare moments between the hottest fighting on Guadalcanal, about 40 U.S. servicemen swatted mosquitoes, sweated over correspondence-school lessons. When they had done their homework, they mailed it to the University of Hawaii, a branch of Usafi (U.S. Armed Forces Institute). Last week the number of fighting men taking correspondence courses from Usafi was not far from 30,000, more than half of them overseas.

Some students on the rolls last week:

¶ Sergeant Albert Joseph Erickson, on duty with a South Pacific mobile reconnaissance squadron. His third test paper on the duties of a railroad rate clerk was held up: "A little of the real McCoy popping over here."

¶ Corporal Luther Leroy Roberts, fuse-setter with an overseas antiaircraft battery, after taking a premedical course at Washington, D.C.'s Howard (predominantly Negro) University. He was late with his trigonometry test papers; some "have been destroyed by tropical insects."

¶ Seaman First-Class Marvin R. Eienbass of Michigan, studying on the high seas to be an automobile mechanic. In six lessons he has had no grade lower than 88.

Usafi offers 64 courses to men of all services at $2 each. Courses include English and social studies, mathematics and sciences, business, mechanical, electrical and engineering trades. In addition, Usafi splits with servicemen the higher cost of any of 700 correspondence courses given by 80 U.S.

universities. Successful Usafi students get certificates, and many colleges will give them credits.

BROWN STUDIES: Unusual lessons are being taught to first- JUNE 21 graders in Chicago's public schools. One is a story called *Billy's Ride,* which ends as follows:

"A Policeman held up his hand and the cars stopped. Although Billy was usually polite, he stared and stared! He had never seen a colored policeman. 'Mother,' Billy called, 'look at the brown policeman.' 'Yes,' said Mother, 'there are many brown policemen. In our country we have many kinds of helpers.' Just then the policeman waves his hand for the cars to move on. Then Billy and Jack did have an exciting time. They were looking for more brown policemen."

While first-graders learn about Negro policemen, other primary pupils (white and colored) are being told of Negro contributions to civilization, U.S. history, the war effort. Examples of Negro subject matter woven into the general class material:

¶ 2nd grade: George Washington Carver, who made many things "from funny little peanuts."

¶ 3rd grade: Life in West Africa's Dahomey as an example of the ancestors of U.S. Negroes.

¶ 4th grade: The careers of Negro notables such as Contralto Marian Anderson, Bass-Baritone Paul Robeson.

¶ 5th grade: "Chicago's first settler, Negro Jean Baptiste Point de Sable."

¶ 6th grade: Negro Captain Alonzo Pietro of Columbus' good ship *Nina.*

¶ 7th grade: U.S. slavery and its abolition.

¶ 8th grade: Negro military heroes, contemporary Chicago Negroes.

The person who originated this program and got Chicago's Board of Education to okay it is a handsome, 36-year-old Negro teacher, Madeline Robinson Morgan. As a girl Mrs. Morgan knew days and nights of terror during Chicago's 1919 race riots. She got a year and a half's leave to do research, work out a curriculum, integrate it with the school program as a whole. She says she had her "fingers crossed all the time but most teachers are enthusiastic about the material and children take it as a matter of course."

AUG. 9 **COOKING WITH WATER:** Princeton, N.J. has one school whose teachers do not count on teaching their students a single solitary fact. It is the ten-year-old Institute for Advanced Study. Its faculty of 16 includes Albert Einstein. Its 28 students do post-postgraduate research, are so expert in their fields that they are presumably aware of all the known facts involved. All that the Institute's teachers hope to do is to broaden and deepen their students' points of view toward their subjects by joint approaches from new angles. The students hear few formal lectures, take no examinations, get no degrees.

Last week, however, many were hard at work in the kind of abstruse study which used to be a European specialty. Albert Einstein himself was busy trying to unify certain theories of gravitational and electrical forces in order to solve some complex mathematico-physical problems for the U.S. Navy. His aureole of white hair droops in summer's heat, a string upholds his cheap blue denim pants. Says he: "Here we cook with water." Interpreted a colleague: "We perform no miracles." A current item of Einsteiniana titillating the Institute: on one of his blackboards bearing a brain-taxing mathematical equation, the charwoman found the word "Erase." On another blackboard, marked "Do not erase," was blazoned the formula "$2+2=4$."

AUG. 30 **YALE'S PHELPS:**

> *"I strove with none. I always hated strife.*
> *Nature I loved, and God and Man and Art:*
> *I warmed both hands before the fire of life:*
> *It sinks, yet I'm not ready to depart."*

When William Lyon Phelps wrote these words, warping the famed quatrain of Walter Savage Landor, he still had four years in which to get ready. Last week, Professor Phelps finally departed, after a transitory rally from a stroke. He died where he was born and spent most of his 78 busy, happy years: in New Haven. Said University President Charles Seymour: "All Yale mourns the death of her Billy Phelps." Nor would the mourning be limited to Yalemen.

This breezy, tweedy, pun-loving admirer of Turgenev, Tolstoy, Hardy, James, Howells and Meredith was a great teacher, because his enthusiasm was infectious. Student Sinclair Lewis, '07, called him the one college teacher of his generation able to "inoculate students with his own passion for the secret joys of good literature," a man who changed the university into a "friendly concourse of human beings interested in learning."

For years his T. & B. course (Tennyson & Browning) met in four sections of 150 students each—including athletes who knew Phelps would not readily flunk a contributor to Yale's glory. An estimated ten million read his syndicated newspaper column, *A Daily Thought*. On the air for Swift's hams and the Heinz 57 varieties, he was the literate housewife's delight. To his equal glow for the great and the trivial in books ("As I grow older I find Shakespeare more thrilling, more enchanting; yet I relish a good detective story"), Phelps added a stock of anecdotes about literary greats he had known (Galsworthy, Barrie, Maeterlinck, Conrad, Shaw, *et al*.), and the seductions of wit: Phelps's own citation of Hollywood's Walt Disney for an honorary Yale degree: "He labored like a mountain and brought forth a mouse."

MILESTONES

MARRIED: Betty Grable, 26, pin-up girl; and trumpeting Harry Haag James, 32; each for the second time; in Las Vegas, Nev. Her first husband was onetime cinema juvenile Jackie Coogan.

MISCELLANY

FELLOW CREATURE: In Petrusberg, South Africa, churchgoers voted not to get rid of a friend—a cobra who lived in the ceiling, always came out to listen when the organist played the organ's flute stops, fled back to its hole when the preaching started.

HERO: In Washington, a patent was awarded to the inventor of a handbag with a translucent bottom, which makes it possible for a woman to discover what is in the bag by holding it up to the light, instead of disemboweling it on a restaurant table.

HIS OWN LIGHTS: In Chicago, Mrs. Alice Mischal, 23, got a divorce after testifying that her husband made her burn candles because he hated the electric company, cook with kerosene because he hated the gas company.

WORKS PROGRESS: The mayor of Asheville, N.C. got a letter announcing that because WPA was being liquidated the agency could not build the Asheville Auditorium—completed in 1940.

THE PRESS

MARCH 8 **LOST:** Sunday is the traditional big day for newspaper classified advertisements. But last week the Baltimore *Sun* found a silver lining in the rationing cloud—on a Wednesday it carried 203 classified ads from people who had lost ration books.

APRIL 5 **CARTOONIST SOLDIER:** David Breger is a round-faced, snub-nosed, chunky man who is cramming two successful careers into his nearly 35 years. As a cartoonist, he has a profitable contract with King Features Syndicate, Inc.; his drawings appear in some 50 U.S. and Canadian papers. As a soldier, Dave Breger was drafted as a buck private in 1941, by last week had become a second lieutenant. Sent to Camp Livingston, La., to nurse a fleet of trucks, Private Breger continued to draw at nights, squatting in a truck with netting over his head to keep bugs at bay.

When the Army awakened to Breger's talent, he was transferred to the Special Services Division and sent to serve as photographer-artist for the Army's weekly, *Yank.* Dave Breger's best-known creation is his daily panel called *Private Breger.*

"Private Breger" is a wide-eyed, overspectacled, freckled little soldier, clumsy, meek, confused but undismayed. Cartoonist Breger likes to think of "Private Breger" as typical of all the nation's millions of little men, to whom soldiering is alien, but who cheerfully acquiesced when war came. Through *Private Breger,* Cartoonist Breger translates Army life into civilian terms. One cartoon showed a squad of soldiers being stopped by a game warden, who demanded to see their hunting licenses.

MAY 10 **HEARST IS 80:** William Randolph Hearst, monarch of a communications dynasty (16 newspapers, eight magazines, four radio stations, one news service, one feature syndicate, one photo service), art collector, exponent of yellow journalism, worshiper at circulation's shrine, reporter, reformer, politico, columnist and multimillionaire, was 80 last week. For a man of his means and mightiness he celebrated modestly.

At the lavish Santa Monica, Calif. beach house of ex-Film Star Marion Davies he read congratulatory messages, played his daily hour of tennis. No one ever keeps score in a Hearst tennis match; he covers the court only to arm's length each way and it is taken for granted that the ball must be hit within his reach. Birthday dinner guests were Marion Davies, four Hearst sons and their wives, Movie Columnist Louella Parsons, Film Actor Arthur *(Dagwood Bumstead)* Lake, several others. They nibbled a red and white cake (16 candles).

Grey, jowled like a coon dog, no longer nimble, Tycoon Hearst still stands impressively erect to his full 6 ft. 2, is remarkably healthy. He still bubbles with new ideas for his publications, over which he maintains the vigilance of a whimsical despot. His newspapers are still wild-eyed, red-inked, impulsive, dogmatic, often inaccurate and lettered with grade A, boob-catching circulation features. Currently Hearst papers are promoting "Total Warfare Against Japan . . . NOW."

Commented Hearst's Los Angeles competitor, the *Times,* in a birthday editorial: "Even those who have not always agreed with him can wish him well at this milestone in a career which will be long remembered."

HOMESPUN REPORTER: Ernest Taylor Pyle, better known to MAY 31 millions as Ernie, is an inconspicuous, frail, 110-lb. man of 42, homely and quiet-mannered. He looks exactly as if he came smack off an Indiana farm—which he did, some two decades ago. This week this pixyish little man, America's most widely read war correspondent, won a National Headliners Club's award for "best foreign feature" reporting.

For the past six months Ernie Pyle has padded around North Africa, talking with infantrymen, artillerymen, pilots, truck drivers, nurses, doctors, and writing a uniquely refreshing column in the identical manner in which he had written about the U.S. for many years. In his smooth, homespun style, he has told his readers what the American soldier eats, how he dresses, whether his socks are warm enough, how & when & where he sleeps, what he feels in battle, what he thinks when he is not fighting, how he lives and how he dies. To do this, he has lived with the troops. Examples of his stuff:

¶ "You become eminently practical in wartime. A chaplain who recently went through the pockets of ten Americans killed in battle said the dominant thing he found was toilet paper."

¶ "The men are walking. They are 50 feet apart, for dispersal. Their walk is slow, for they are dead weary. It is the terrible deliberation of each step that spells out their tiredness. Their faces are black and unshaven. They are young men, but the grime and whiskers and exhaustion make them look middle-aged. In their eyes as they pass is not hatred, not excitement, not despair, not the tonic of their victory—there is just the simple expression of being here as though they had been here doing this forever."

JUNE 14   **MACARTHUR'S MUSCLES:** The last word in Army etiquette came last week from Australia. General Douglas MacArthur, 63, played Emily Post. His confused pupil was Lee Van Atta, 24, I.N.S. bureau head and ex-Hollywood juvenile *(Captains Courageous,* etc.). Teacher and pupil reached the

Ernie Pyle. He knows what the troops think; he lives with them.

Lee Van Atta. One shove, one whack make him expert on MacArthur.

lobby floor of Melbourne's Hotel Menzies in the same elevator. The door opened. Van Atta retreated to let the General out first. The General insisted that the reporter go first. They argued politely. MacArthur finally broke it up by projecting Van Atta into the lobby with a muscular shove.

After this introduction to Four-Star etiquette, Van Atta got another lesson in Lieut. General George Kenney's headquarters in Port Moresby. The reporter was sitting on the floor talking to Kenney when MacArthur entered. Van Atta started to get to his feet. MacArthur told him to stay put. Politely, Van Atta still strove to rise. The General hollered "Sit down," and enforced the order with a whack on the shoulder that crumpled the correspondent to the floor.

Says Van Atta: "I'm probably the greatest living authority now on MacArthur's physical strength and am able to assert most solemnly that it's still terrific."

MORALE AND MORALITY: Ever since it was cited by the U.S. OCT. 11 Post Office last month for naughtiness (mostly because of its lithe, leggy, lightly clad "Varga Girl" drawings), the magazine *Esquire* has been crusading zealously in its own behalf. In a series of advertisements in newspapers and trade magazines it had been preparing for a hearing at which postal examiners will determine *Esquire's* right to continue to use second-class mail by back-patting itself as a soldier-sailor morale builder.

The first ads were calmly logical, only slightly pouty. One mentioned "the galaxy of pin-ups and other divertissements demanded by the armed forces." Another was eloquent about "the boys" who want "pleasant things to think of, and to look at. They want to think of girls and gaiety and good times. They want to be reminded of all the pretty, pleasant, soft and gentle aspects of the life they've left behind."

Last week, apparently playing its ace, *Esquire* enlisted the clergy's aid. With elaborate piety the latest *Esquire* ad features a picture of a Guadalcanal chaplain, the Cross of Christ on his collar, rays of holy light slanting across his fighting face. Its title ("If Holy Joe can go out there, who are we to be holding back?") seemed to be addressed to the U.S. Post Office itself. Said the ad's text: "Chaplains have acquired a new breadth of both understanding and tolerance from their daily contacts with men in the armed forces. That's what we have sensed from the letters we have had from chaplains telling us of the tremendous morale-value of copies of *Esquire.*"

NOV. 1   **THE EXPERTS FAILED TO BLUSH:** *Esquire* is the kind of magazine in which a mother says, "Have a good time at the party and be a good girl," and her daughter replies: "Make up your mind." In Washington last week the Post Office Department began a hearing to determine: 1) whether *Esquire*'s jokes and its "Varga Girl" drawings are obscene; 2) whether second-class mail privileges should be denied to the widely read (circ. 695,285), 50¢ smoking-room slick.

For four days, balding, humorless Post Office Attorney Calvin Hassell, a pious man and a Boy Scout worker, led witnesses on a sexy jaunt through a collection of ribald material culled from eleven *Esquires.* Spectators had the most fun. Harvard Psychiatrist Kenneth Tillotson gazed soberly at samples of Artist Alberto Varga's skimpily clad babes, then testified "as a doctor who has examined hundreds of women." Said he: Varga girls are "inspiring" and not abnormally hippy, though sometimes their feet are too big. He was shown an *Esquire* joke about a corporal who found two luscious blondes in his Pullman berth and said, "One of you girls will have to leave." Dr. Tillotson's reaction: "That I call funny."

At week's end more witnesses were to come. Because defeat would be expensive (loss of second-class, cheaper-rate mailing rights would cost some $400,000 a year), *Esquire* was ready to appeal to the Supreme Court if it lost.

NOV. 15   **THE EXPERTS BLUSHED:** For two weeks witnesses had been testifying that *Esquire* is a clean-living, right-minded magazine. Now the Post Office Department had its inning. To the witness chair in Washington trooped a psychiatrist, clergymen, an educator, a clubwoman, all Washingtonians. Gum-chewing P.O. Attorney William C. O'Brien put them through their paces. But *Esquire*'s attorney, quick-witted Bruce Bromley, thoughtfully tripped them.

Psychiatrist Benjamin Karpman studied a magazine illustration (of a nude) handed him by Attorney Bromley, found it "sexually stimulating." Bromley promptly turned the magazine's cover, showed that the picture was in the *Ladies' Home Journal.* The Rev. John K. Cartwright, a Catholic priest, contended that *Esquire* has a tendency to encourage low ideas of women. When Attorney Bromley brought out the fact that the *Catholic Digest* has carried reprints from *Esquire* and that Father Flanagan, of Boys' Town fame, has contributed articles to *Esquire,* Witness Cartwright countered: "Bad judgment."

To Rabbi Solomon Metz, Bromley read a series of borderline gags. One involved two London charwomen discussing the inconveniences of a blackout. Said one: "It's a necessary evil, else we're likely to be blasted into maternity." Replied the other: " 'Tis so. But the worst of it is we'd never know who done it."

Another had to do with a hostess saying to a guest: "I won't offer you a cocktail, Mr. Brown, since you are the head of the Temperance League." "No," replied Mr. Brown, "I am president of the Anti-Vice League." "Oh," said the hostess. "Well, I knew there was something I shouldn't offer you."

Rabbi Metz called these gags objectionable. Attorney Bromley revealed they had all been culled from *Reader's Digest.* At week's end, testimony ended, the Post Office's three-man Board of Judges retired to draft their recommendation. [In 1944 the U.S. Postmaster General ordered that second class mailing privileges for *Esquire* magazine be withdrawn. In 1945 the order was revoked by a U.S. Court of Appeals.]

MISCELLANY

WAR EFFORT: In Snipe, Tex., the State Prison Farm manager told his charges that soldiers needed knives, set up a box for donations, with "no questions asked." The take: 40 knives.

FOR THE RECORD: In Seattle, Chief Petty Officer T. Kelly, home at last from the South Pacific, leaned a ladder against a monument to the war dead, climbed to his own name, with a paint brush set the record straight.

ANSWER: In Los Angeles, Mrs. Janet A. Michel complained that her husband forbade her to listen to radio quizzes because "he said he knew all the answers and I didn't need to know them," won a divorce.

BOOKS

JAN. 11 **"ALL NIGHT LONG"**—Erskine Caldwell. Sergei Korokov and his wife, Natasha, lived in a Russian village that was overrun by the Nazi Army. Sergei got orders to join the local force of Russian guerrillas. Escaping from his village, he killed a Nazi sentry, "felt the blade sink downward easily." To reach the guerrillas he had to shoot one German ("his body rolled silently"), then another ("his body crumpled").

Among the guerrillas Sergei met Fyodor, whose pregnant wife had been bayoneted to death by Nazis, his child daughter raped. Fyodor and Sergei were sent to dynamite a Nazi radio station. Fyodor dispatched a Nazi sentry with "a brief flash of his knife blade." The Germans were "perfect targets." Sergei's and Fyodor's bullets "tore into their bodies."

Coming from the author of *Tobacco Road,* Caldwell's 19th book is also the most prominent war casualty of recent U.S. writing.

JAN. 18 **"GENERATION OF VIPERS"** by Philip Wylie is a raging and sometimes very funny set of lay sermons about the human predicament as examined in terms of "you—your home and kiddies, mom and the loved ones, the Brooklyn Dodgers and the *Star-Spangled Banner*—in short, the American scene." Novelist Wylie's high desire is to save the human race from its own worst enemy—itself. Whether he will succeed where such distinguished predecessors as Christ and Dostoevski have so far failed is open to question.

His prose ranges between brilliant neo-Menckenism and embarrassing vulgarity. A good example of Wylie in action is his discussion of the American figments he calls mom and Cinderella. Says he: "I cannot think, offhand, of any civilization except ours in which an entire division of living men has been used, during wartime, or at any time, to spell out the word 'mom' on a drill field." Mom is the inevitable result—and creator—of Cinderella. When Cinderella finds that her husband is not much of a Prince after all, the Prince spends the rest of his life trying to make it up to her, and Cinderella, "turning from a butterfly into a caterpillar," becomes "the puerile, rusting, raging creature we know as mom, a noisy neuter by natural default or a scientific gelding sustained by science, all tongue and teat and razzmatazz. She is a middle-aged puffin with an eye like a hawk that has just seen a rabbit twitch far below. In a thousand of her there is not enough sex appeal to budge a hermit ten paces off a rock ledge."

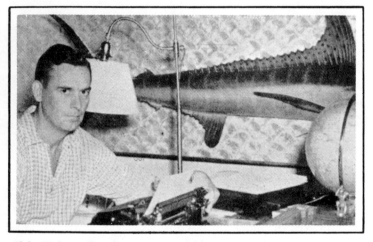

Philip Wylie, author of "Generation of Vipers." Like certain distinguished predecessors, he strives to save the human race from its worst enemy: itself.

That is a fair sample of Author Wylie's prose and of his powers of observation. It is a fair sample, too, of one of the liabilities of this kind of high temper. For whatever Mr. Wylie clamps his talons on—mom; the "pompous male sluts" whom we elect to govern us; or even sexy advertising— he yanks at it as if, for the moment, he was sure it was the root of all evil.

"GUADALCANAL DIARY" by Richard Tregaskis is thorough reporting on one of the most dramatic battles of 1942. Six-foot-seven-inch, bespectacled Correspondent Tregaskis, 26, landed with the first Marine contingents to hit the Solomons. For

JAN. 25

seven weeks he lived with the Marines, became as tough and wiry as any. Jap snipers shot at him. Jap pilots strafed and bombed him. On his way out of the islands by bomber he started to write about it. In Honolulu he finished his book.

Thirteen dollars' worth of airmail stamps took the manuscript to New York. Within seven days it had been accepted for publication and picked as a Book-of-the-Month Club selection. Shortly thereafter it had been sold to 20th-Century-Fox. The book's secret is the simple secret of all good reporting—fidelity and detail. Excerpts:

¶ "Everywhere one turned there were piles of bodies; here one with a backbone visible from the front, and the rest of the flesh and bone peeled up over the man's head, like the leaf of an artichoke; there a charred head, hairless but still equipped with blackened eyeballs; pink, blue, yellow entrails drooping; a man with a red bullet hole through his eye; a dead Jap private, wearing dark, tortoise-shell glasses, his buck teeth bared in a humorless grin. There is no horror to these things. The first one you see is the only shock. The rest are simple repetition."

¶ "Down the beach one of the Japs had jumped up and was running for the jungle. 'There he goes!' was the shout. 'Riddle the son of a bitch!' And riddled he was."

MARCH 1 **"THE HUMAN COMEDY"**—William Saroyan. A lot of people have wondered whether William Saroyan had it in him to write a whole novel. *The Human Comedy,* though it inevitably leaves its grandiloquent title looking like a half-inflated blimp, is a very nice novel indeed. It is, unfortunately, too nice to be as good as it might have been if Saroyan were capable not only of goodness but of a concern with evil.

The Human Comedy is the story of a happy family in a small town in wartime. It is William Saroyan saying that life is not only worth living, fighting and dying for, but can be an almost unmitigated pleasure. As Mrs. Macauley tells her son Homer, if the world seems to a man "richly sad and full of beauty, it's the man himself so, and not the things around him. And so it is, if it's bad, or ugly, or pathetic —it is always the man himself, and each man *is* the world."

Saroyan shapes such moments in words of almost primer lucidity. Among his still-pursuing faults are glints of facetiousness, excessive sentiment. His essential limitation—which is also his cardinal virtue—is perhaps incurable. That is his chronic ecstasy, his almost Franciscan loving kindness and optimism. It clearly transfigures the world for him and, for a time, is bound to transfigure any sympathetic reader.

FASTEST-SELLING BOOK: Wendell Willkie's *One World* got off APRIL 26 last week to the fastest start of any book in the memory of U.S. booksellers. It easily outstripped *Gone With the Wind, How to Win Friends and Influence People* and *Your Income Tax.* Within eight days, there were half a million copies in print, breaking all records.

"FOUR QUARTETS"—T. S. Eliot. T. S. Eliot has never been an JUNE 7 artist likely to please the bulk of the great general reading audience. Simply as a rather solemn American-turned-Englishman, he is personally unsympathetic to many. His work requires a patience of ear and of intellect which many readers lack; patience not merely in one reading but in many. But in a little short of 900 lines, these subtle, magnificent religious poems contain more beauty and sense than any book within recent memory. They are capable of charming, and teaching, many thousands among the great general reading audience.

Readers familiar with the great "last quartets" of Beethoven will suspect that Eliot derived from them his title, much of his form, elements of his tone and content. They will almost certainly be right, for both Beethoven and Eliot are working with the most difficult and quintessential of all materials for art: the substance of mystical experience. Throughout the poems, in constant undertone and, more often than not, by indirection, Eliot writes of the time-bound society he lives in, and of the war:

> *The dove descending breaks the air*
> *With flame of incandescent terror*
> *Of which the tongues declare*
> *The one discharge from sin and error.*
> *The only hope, or else despair*
> *Lies in the choice of pyre or pyre—*
> *To be redeemed from fire by fire.*

SEPT. 6 **"A TREE GROWS IN BROOKLYN"**—Betty Smith. A Brooklyn girl named Betty Smith has pleasantly seasoned her first novel —an old-fashioned family pudding of well-baked corn— with two simple and staple condiments: authentic recollections of childhood and a well-communicated respect for the endless valor of the poor. The story is that of Francie Nolan from her twelfth to her seventeenth year in the Williamsburg section of Brooklyn before and during World War I. The book has most of the time-tested character types and situations in fiction: Katie, the hard-working, self-sacrificing mother; Johnny, the lovably alcoholic, singing-waiter father; Francie, the good, book-loving slum child who yearns to be a writer; Neeley, her little brother; and an assortment of incredible relatives, including a peasant grandmother who speaks with the wisdom of Confucius and the force of the King James Version.

William Saroyan. "The Human Comedy" is too nice to be good.

Betty Smith. She has written a pudding of well-baked corn.

There are authentic scenes: Francie and her brother collecting junk in the Brooklyn slums; purchases of five-cent soup bones, stale bread and smashed pies; the traditional childhood customs and mores of the Brooklyn streets. Example: storekeepers on Christmas Eve tossed their unsold trees at children; if the children stood upright under the impact of a tree, they could have it free.

"TAPS FOR PRIVATE TUSSIE"—Jesse Stuart. When they buried DEC. 13
Uncle Kim the coffin was covered with a flag. "I had been
to one or two funerals before, but I had never seen one like
this funeral. . . . The grass felt soft and warm to my bare
feet and the little puddles of sand were hot enough to burn
my toes. . . . 'Trouble, trouble, trouble,' Grandpa whispered.
. . . 'Man born of woman is full of trouble.' "

Six of Uncle Kim's first cousins lifted the big black coffin
to their shoulders. "My kinfolks . . . walked in the procession behind with their arms around their girls' backs. . . .
It was the greatest bit of excitement that I had ever seen,
just to walk in the great procession and hear the people
laugh and talk. . . . Before we had gone far up on the mountain, Brother Baggs said: 'Brothers and sisters, let us sing
Beulah Land! ' If you don't think it's hard to climb a mountain and sing, you try it one of these days. Try it when the
July sun comes down upon your back with blisterin heat
and the lizards are scurryin over the dead leaves a-huntin a
wisp of shade on the backbone of a mountain that is steam-
in in the swelterin heat like a pan of bread in an oven.

"They lowered Uncle Kim down into the mountain earth
to the bottom of his shallow grave. . . . Now the great procession of people moved down the mountain faster than
they had climbed it. . . . I walked beside of Grandpa a-
holdin to his hand. Many sang songs as we walked down
the mountain, a mountain so steep that it made the knees
creak to hold us back."

The main story of *Taps for Private Tussie* is about the
surviving Tussies (known as the Relief Tussies to distinguish
them from the Tussies who remained Republican) in their
swift squandering of Uncle Kim's $10,000 insurance. It is
thus a *Tobacco Road* of the hill people, more shocking because it deals with the death of a soldier, painful and
raucous in many of its details of low life among the people
for whom he died, but enlivened all the way through by
Jesse Stuart's magnificent use of his native idiom and his
love for the country where it flourishes.

Numerals set in italics indicate an illustration of subject mentioned.

PICTURE CREDITS

X

PRODUCTION STAFF FOR TIME INCORPORATED
John L. Hallenbeck (Vice President and Director of Production),
Robert E. Foy and Caroline Ferri
Text photocomposed under the direction of Albert J. Dunn and Arthur J. Dunn

QUOTES OF THE YEAR

Senator Kenneth Wherry

> *(on President Franklin Roosevelt—p. 13):* "No man who has such personal charm should serve more than two terms. We've got to safeguard the American people."

Stripteaser Gypsy Rose Lee

> *(on her chances of running for Vice President of the U.S.—p. 51):* "I'd like to, but I haven't kissed a baby in years."

Author Philip Wylie

> *(criticizing the American "Mom" in his book "Generation of Vipers"—p. 212):* "In a thousand of her there is not enough sex appeal to budge a hermit ten paces off a rock ledge."

The Boise City (Okla.) "News"

> *(after the town was accidentally bombed by U.S. planes on a training mission—p. 26):* "What this place needs are some searchlights and antiaircraft guns."

A wounded G.I.

> *(returning home on a U.S. hospital train—p. 27):* "Even the dump piles look swell."

ANSWERS TO PICTURE QUIZ—1: Soviet Premier Joseph Stalin; 2: Madame Chiang Kai-shek, wife of China's Generalissimo; 3: U.S. Senator Harry S. Truman; 4: Conductor Sir Thomas Beecham; 5: President Franklin D. Roosevelt; 6: General George S. Patton Jr.; 7: Comedian Bob Hope; 8: General Mark Clark; 9: New York Governor Thomas E. Dewey; 10: Ingrid Bergman, star of "For Whom the Bell Tolls"; 11: General Claire Chennault; 12: Adviser to Presidents Bernard M. Baruch; 13: General Dwight D. Eisenhower; 14: Economic Czar James F. Byrnes; 15: Secretary of the Treasury Henry Morgenthau Jr.; 16: Italian Premier Benito Mussolini.